GLEN TANAR

VALLEY OF ECHOES AND HIDDEN TREASURES

ABOUT THE AUTHOR

Born in Torphins in 1928, Pierre Fouin grew up on Glen Tanar estate on Royal Deeside where his father was butler/valet to the Lords Glentanar from 1914 to 1956. He was educated at the wee Glentanar School, Aboyne Higher Grade Public School, then Aberdeen Grammar before graduating in Medicine from Aberdeen University in 1954. He spent his National Service with the Black Watch.

He returned to hospital practice until 1958 when he entered General Practice in Lower Deeside. As a committed moderniser and educationalist, he was instrumental in the provision of the Health Centre in Peterculter and the Medical Centre in Cults. A founder lecturer in the Aberdeen University Department of General Practice, he was a frequent contributor to medical publications.

Pierre's first book, *Glen Tanar Exile*, has been enthusiastically received in the North-East as an example of a lifestyle long gone.

A keen angler, shooter, golfer, gardener, hill walker and a collector of fine art, he believes that at eighty, he is still capable of climbing Lochnagar.

GLEN TANAR
VALLEY OF ECHOES AND HIDDEN TREASURES

PHOTOGRAPH BY ALAN FINDLAY

Etnach

First Published in 2009 by Fouin Books

A catalogue record for this book is available from the British Library

ISBN 978-0-9534534-4-3

Design and typesetting by Leopard magazine
www.leopardmag.co.uk

Printed and bound in Scotland by Bell & Bain

Published by Leopard Press
Auld Logie, Pitcaple, Inverurie, Aberdeenshire AB51 5EE

GLEN TANAR

VALLEY OF ECHOES
AND HIDDEN TREASURES

FRANÇOIS LOUIS PIERRE FOUIN

PRESS

DEDICATION

To my two children Peter and Nikki.
Sharing this love for Glen Tanar has been a bond
between us throughout our lives.

Also in loving memory of my five Labradors,
Chocolate, yellow and three black, all of whom were
superb companions and whose unbounding enthusiasm
for the wide open spaces will live with me forever.

Acknowledgements

Writing the history of a district involves much research with different institutions and contacting innumerable people. Whether in the libraries, museums, among the experts, or just talking to the country folk, I have been heartened by their ready interest and thank them all most sincerely.

Eileen Bailey, archivist at the Birse Community Trust, has been ever helpful and provides a service that other larger communities should copy. Archaeologists S. Duthie, D. Harding and H. MacFarlane also have my thanks and I wish them success in unearthing the past in the Glen.

At Braeloine the Ranger Service has given valuable assistance, with Mike Martin and especially head ranger Eric Baird keeping me right on the present day set-up. Recently-retired head gamekeeper Eoin Smith has been a fund of knowledge and has facilitated my way around the estate, while Colin Espie has drawn my attention to many features. It is also fitting to pay homage to Jimmy Oswald, late head keeper, whose part in the book will soon be revealed. The stimulus for this book came from realising how much he knew and would be lost on his passing and I trust he will look down from above and maybe say grudgingly, "It's nae bad".

Ean and Alan Mann, brought up in the Tower of Ess, responded to my request for help and have added greatly to the memories. Douglas Harper, with his vast knowledge of his great-grandfather's business, has guided me through fencing and bridge-building, adding information that would have been completely lost. Douglas Young, the factor's son and friend, has added memories, while the ready input from the farmers along the Dee valley has also been much appreciated.

Alan Findlay's photography appeared on Google and finding so many Glen Tanar pictures I contacted him; he has been a tower of strength in improving and providing a number of illustrations throughout the book. Anne Burgess, Hans Kruuk and Colin Smith have also kindly allowed use of their photographs.

Michael and Claire Bruce, carrying forward the Coats' tradition, have been very supportive and without their ready assistance the Coats' chapters would have been absent. Thanks to Jane and her Glentanar Ballroom team for their cheerful presence; Liz Peck in Glentanar House has made access there a real pleasure.

Graham Hunter and Prof. Alex Adam have kept me right about the academic Francis C. Diack and also Surgeon Major Colin M. M. Miller, while Alfie Dawson, Jim Cheyne and George Shirriffs have been my main support. Alfie cleaned, recorded and photographed most of the artefacts, Jim has been a constant companion and source of never-ending information, while George has vetted the content.

Finally, my grateful thanks to my publishers Lindy Cheyne and Ian Hamilton at *Leopard* for their interest and involvement in making this project such a fulfilling and interesting experience.

CONTENTS

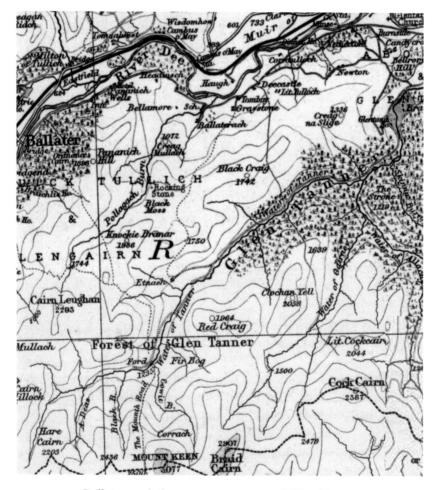

Ballater and the western aspects of Glen Tanar.
Bartholomew Survey Atlas of Scotland 1912 *(Balmoral)*

PROLOGUE

The thought of Bronze Age men burying possessions and their dead on top of the Knockie Hill gives one an odd feeling regarding our own life span in a world millions of years old. Standing there quietly at the foot of the Knockie with the sound of the Tanar burbling past, it is odd to remember that all we would recognise from those Bronze Age days would be the hill and river. No Knockie bridge, no proper road, no lake with its quaint boat-house, no man-made maze of policies with Wander Walks – so difficult now to think of it as a wilderness. So can my reader detect any echoes from that far back?

Only two centuries ago harsh voices urged weary beasts ever onwards as the drovers made their gentle way around the Knockie, out along the Firmounth track to Tarfside and the cattle markets of the south. Today we can almost feel their presence and hear those voices. At Coirevrauch, in the drover's inn, the stillness of the night is broken with the noise of hearty laughter as we peer through the darkened windows at the dim interior. Here, rough hardy men relax in bare surroundings before driving their kye up and over the shoulder of Mount Keen in the morning mist. And in that morning half-light we hear the high-pitched screech of the peregrine falcon as man and beast come just too close to his nest high up on the nearby quartz cliff.

Echoes are all around us in this, our own modern wilderness.

The distant happy sound of children at play stops me at the Black Ship and I look across the river Tanar to the long-gone clachan with its dozens of woodcutters' wooden houses nestling there in 1810. That linden tree, standing so powerful and mature, was but a sapling then, yet will survive long after I have departed this life.

Now the accents change and the sound of refined English voices are heard as the ladies and gentlemen sit around the base of the eagle's eyrie at the Porphyry bridge, partaking of cold grouse washed down with a fine claret. I can hear those voices so clearly from my own past and sense the confident superiority of class, while their servants sit quietly in the background awaiting their bidding.

Heading homewards in the twilight, three hundred yards beyond the Black Ship, I pause by my most memorable inscribed stone. Set among heather and insignificant in relation to Sir William Cunliffe Brooks' other artefacts, it echoes my past. Nostalgically, I hear again the steady tap tap of my mother's stick as she passes on her daily walk, as she did hundreds of times in thirty years of life in this, her solitary glen.

The Pine is King of Scottish Woods,
And the Queen – Ah who is she?
The fairest form the forest kens,
The Bonnie Birken Tree.

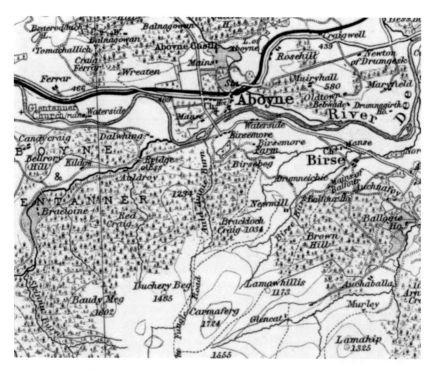

Aboyne and the eastern aspects of Glen Tanar.
Bartholomew Survey Atlas of Scotland 1912 *(Aberdeen)*
REPRODUCED BY PERMISSION OF NATIONAL LIBRARY OF SCOTLAND

1

Setting the Scene

Walkers and visitors to the lovely valley of Glen Tanar are enthralled with the scenery and the ambience of their surroundings. Yet many remain ignorant of its heritage and are unaware of the treasures left behind from previous ages. This publication tries in some small way to enlighten readers on Glen Tanar's history, going back to the Bronze Age. Sir William Cunliffe Brooks' ownership of the Glen in the latter half of the 19th century and the Coats involvement from then onwards are also intimately considered.

Situated on Royal Deeside in Aberdeenshire, Glen Tanar is just four-and-a-half miles to the south-west of the prosperous village of Aboyne, With Ballater nine miles to the west and Balmoral Castle a further eight miles away, this is a part of the world that through the centuries has become used to tourism and celebrity.

Glen Tanar as a separate sporting estate dates back only to the mid-19th century when it was developed to attract the wealthy to savour the sports of fishing, stalking and shooting grouse. Belonging to the Marquis of Huntly's lands it incorporated not only the valley of the river Tanar, but ground to the north bordering the south bank of the river Dee between Aboyne and Ballater. That this land lying outwith the valley is termed Glen Tanar is confusing, but was obviously necessary so that the valuable Dee salmon fishing could be included in the estate.

In our youth we accept things as they are, but in our more senior years we look back and appreciate so much that we took for granted. Inscribed stones and wells belonged to our every day lives. No one looked at the roof of Glentanar School and remarked on its oast-house outline. The Tower of Ess never dawned on us as being anything special and all those carvings on the stone pillars at the gateway to the estate were scarcely noticed. Only through writing *Glen Tanar Exile* did I begin to appreciate the significance of that wonderful upbringing.

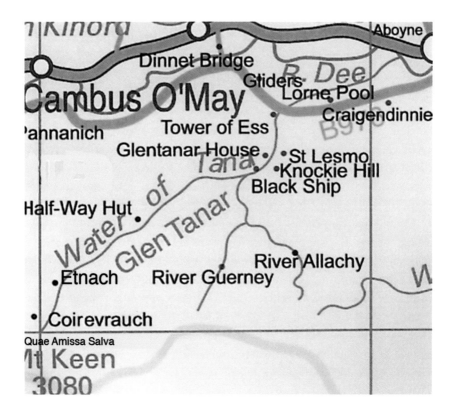

The Glen Tanar of my youth is no more. The fortune of Manchester banker Sir William Cunliffe Brooks in the late 1800s, followed by the Coats' linen thread millions in the early 1900s ensured a valley to be described, with some derision, as an "English rural vernacular". World War II saw the replacement of linen by more advanced fibres and the gradual demise of the Coats' empire. Now the estate has to stand on its own feet and despite valiant efforts by the present owners, Michael and Claire Bruce of the old Coats dynasty, the relative trivia of yesteryear are inconsequential in the battle to maintain continuity.

Lord Thomas Glentanar died in 1971 and his only child, the Hon. Mrs Jean Bruce, inherited the estate. With a shrewd perception that the estate could no longer prosper in its present form, she instigated The Glen Tanar Charitable Trust to look after the Chapel of St Lesmo and provide the Braeloine Visitor Centre while setting up the Ranger Service. In 1979 she agreed to the creation of the Glen Tanar National Nature Reserve, a large area of woodland along the banks of the Allachy.

The Hon. Mrs Bruce died in 2007 and this brought to an end the era of a millionaire's playground dating from Cunliffe Brooks to her grandfather, father and finally herself. Hopefully, however, her planning will have guaranteed the estate for the foreseeable future so that it can continue to bring enjoyment to those who spend so many leisure hours in its tranquil surroundings.

The Nature Reserve Agreement (NRA) was implemented and involved an understanding between the landowner and Scottish Natural Heritage (SNH) regarding policies on habitat, wildlife, grazing management and access. Now the National Nature Reserve is managed by SNH which has gained national recognition, especially for its interest in the preservation of the capercaille and reforestation. Funding of the Ranger Service is supplemented by grant aid via Cairngorms National Park Authority with the main funding coming through The Glen Tanar Charitable Trust. In 2007 SNH had a budget of just over £2 million to fund over three hundred staff, so there is no pot of gold for the individual estates; such funding can vary in the light of economic circumstances or political priorities from the Scottish Executive or Government. Individuals as well as local public bodies have therefore a part to play, as only those closely involved with their district's needs can be relied on in an ever-changing world.

Based at the Visitor Centre at Braeloine Bridge, rangers Eric Baird and Mike Martin are on hand to explain life, past and present, on the estate. Eric Baird as head ranger organises outings and walks for groups, opening their eyes to the wonderful world around them. Resources are limited and he at times has volunteers uncovering and cleaning wells and troughs – a never-ending, rather thankless job with nature constantly intervening.

The preservation of the estate is a massive task, as is obvious to the perceptive observer, though not perhaps to the casual walker tramping the well worn paths. The unique Glentanar School alone requires repairs costing many thousands of pounds, showing the impossible burden for the estate or any one single national agency. Farm buildings of great distinction are gradually deteriorating. Not only are the financial demands of restoration crippling, but the artisans who built them are long gone and our era of mass production has little time for such intricate and costly skills. Some treasures, such as the Menawee Stones at the back of the Knockie, are in danger of toppling over in the future and need restoration now, but that would be an extremely costly exercise.

We must remember the estate is private property and also a working entity. Hordes of visitors seeking out the old memorabilia while walking through the forests and over the hills could become too intrusive. Where disharmony could also arise is illustrated by such as Robert Smith's excellent little book, *25 Walks – Deeside*, which was produced without the apparent knowledge of those on the ground. Such a publication could upset those feeling responsible for the safety of visitors to the area, possibly souring relationships so that the unwary walker, lost in the hills clutching the *25 Walks*, may find only a modicum of sympathy.

I am very aware that there is a balance between drawing attention to all the treasures of Glen Tanar and stimulating others to see that they are preserved, while also being mindful that the proprietors have rights. We the public, having such ease of access to this lovely glen, should be sensitive to the privilege and make certain we do not abuse it.

The Deeside Heritage Society based in Aboyne has become involved in attempting to keep nature at bay, which is very heartening. Some wells and horse troughs, set in little arbours with stone seating incorporated must have been hugely impressive, especially those set in a semicircle. If the society encouraged members to restore and keep even one of these it would, in my opinion be a real bonus.

As to the book itself, it started off as a recording of the Brooks' era of the late 1800s, detailing all his inscribed artefacts from that period. Wells, horse troughs, bridges and buildings such as the Tower of Ess gave it a very wide approach, highlighting Cunliffe Brooks' own diverse interests. His often quaint and at times puzzling inscriptions we can ponder as we go along.

Alfie Dawson, my childhood next door neighbour and friend, has shared with me the work of seeking out, photographing and cleaning these stones and wells. Our discoveries, after over a hundred years, cannot be complete, however, as we know from such stalwarts as the late head keeper at Glen Tanar, Jimmy Oswald.

Jimmy had the temerity to die on us in 2006, just when we were due to uncover the last of his memories. By that time he had already supplied us with so much information tucked away in his impressive brain. It was always a pleasure to sit and listen to him, even into the sma' oors when the whisky bottle was in grave danger of running dry, as his mind ran riot. Going out on the hill with him was a total education, for not only was he knowledgeable about everything related to his job, but he had such an inquisitive mind, always putting forward thoughts for discussion. Then stooping down he would discourse about the flora and the signs of prehistoric man. Not always popular with his strongly held views, he was a real character who would regularly show up my ignorance with the remark, "You University folk are a' the same – ken naething".

Eoin Smith, following in Jimmy's footsteps as head keeper, also with a great knowledge and love of the estate, has been ever helpful to us as we seek the outlying treasures. Our greatest triumph, however, goes to stalker Colin Espie for unearthing the Mount Keen well, something we and Jimmy Oswald had sought for over two years.

Francis C. Diack's sixteen volumes of *The Glen Tanar Estate Papers* have provided me with a mine of information. The three chapters on the Coats' dynasty come from previously private papers and give a wonderful insight into many lives. I have been hugely privileged by being allowed access to these records through the kindness of Michael and Claire Bruce. Their open-handedness has been one of the most heartening features of my whole investigation.

I have also scanned as many records and publications as I can uncover in order to draw them all into one interesting publication for the Glen Tanar brotherhood to browse through. Other than the Coats' papers there will be little that is outstandingly original in the following chapters, as someone somewhere has already provided the essential details. Writers of the calibre of Cuthbert Graham, George M. Fraser, the Rev. J. G. Michie, Alex I. McConachie, Fenton Wyness and Robert Smith, to mention but a few, have all contributed hugely to the body of knowledge about our district. Their expertise is massive and I do not see my purpose as competing with them. My main object is to provide a framework so that others wishing to delve more deeply into particular areas can turn to these experts for the greater detail. With this in mind I have therefore appended references as to possible sources of further information.

Throughout my research various spellings have occurred for places and people. For example Glen Tanar is spelt in at least four different ways, as are a host of other words. I have not always attempted to standardise spelling throughout the text, but simply recorded the words as they turned up in the research. This may give a more authentic feel through the centuries, but I believe Cunliffe Brooks would have heartily disagreed with my modern spelling of his beloved estate as he detested the 'r' on the end of Tanar. Lord Thomas Glentanar invariably spelt Etnach as Atnach while others, including Robert Smith in *Land of the Lost*, spell it Eitnach.

Another spelling that has dogged me throughout the book is Coirevrauch near Etnach, the site of the old drover's inn. Spelt Corrievrauch, Coiryruach and even the more original Coirebhruach it has left me in a quandary as to which one to adopt. Turning to my friend Donald MacAulay, the distinguished Gaelic poet and academic, I find an intriguing insight into the word 'vrauch'. Without hesitation he related it to the distilling of whisky without even knowing the context. In a later chapter there is reference to the sparse lands here being used to grow barley for the illicit whisky trade in the late 1700s, making for an intriguing association.

Coirebhruach, which seems to be the earlier Gaelic name for the area of Coirevrauch, appears to relate to a corrie on the hillside, so perhaps Coirevrauch was invented by those associated with the distilling of whisky. My friend, however, pours cold water on my enthusiasm by pointing out that the letter 'b' in Gaelic changes, in certain circumstances, to 'bh' which sounds like 'v', so that Coirevrauch could simply be down to some local worthy in the past getting the spelling wrong.

All supposition, but I shall stick to Coirevrauch as it breathes a really romantic association while allowing the uninitiated to pronounce it adequately. Even the experts often differ in their attempts to translate the Gaelic words into English and I do apologise if I seem to prefer some versions.

In describing objects on the estate as well as recording the inhabitants' lives and works through the ages, it seems to me imperative that the reader is conversant with just enough national history to get the perspective of estate life and where it all fits in. For instance, those of us of a certain age have had our lives influenced by two world wars wherever we have lived. Similarly I feel so has every laird, farmer or servant through the ages, whether in Reformation or Jacobite times for instance. I have, therefore, spent some time in setting in place the historical framework on which to hang facts, figures and illustrations, so that they are fully understood.

To make historical facts less tedious, wherever possible I have attempted to lighten the research with my more personal remarks and reminiscences. After all, this is not supposed to be a dusty history book, nor yet a tourist manual, but a labour of love by someone whose early life was formed among the valley and hills of this intriguing countryside.

The echoes from the past from the book's title require little explanation from me. Just to stand in the silence of the Glen is enough to imagine the sounds coming down from the generations. Some may question what I consider to be hidden treasures. Day after day walkers pass inscribed stones in ignorance without a backward glance, as we stop to clean them. Oddly enough it is often the very young who will come over and ask what we are doing and the significance of the wording. Yes, stones, wells, horse troughs, arbours, vague ruins, ancient field walls, bridges and buildings are all little pieces of often hidden treasure.

Treasure is also to be found in records held in various libraries. Volumes such as the *Glen Tanar Estate Papers*, the *Aboyne Papers* and especially those in the custody of the Coats / Bruce family at Glen Tanar are hugely important. Many records appear to have been lost over the years, including the recollections of Murdo M'Farlane, first schoolmaster in Glen Tanar. It is imperative that the present records are cared for, so that future generations can appreciate their significance.

Sadly, a treasure totally lost to us and never to be retrieved is that of personal memory. Handed down from generation to generation in story and song, all this is lost to our modern youth. Tight communities have fragmented with the march of education, opportunity and travel so that we have been left with nothing of folk memory but the odd fragment tucked away in some elderly mind. This saga is almost bereft of such memories but when I have uncovered one, it has shone out like a sparkling jewel so making this whole venture so much more satisfying.

2

THE PERSONAL PERSPECTIVE

I was born in 1928 and for fifteen years of my life was brought up on Glen Tanar estate. I left for the Aberdeen Grammar School in 1944, but as my father only retired in 1956 aged seventy-five, my close relationship with the estate spanned a full twenty-eight years. Since then I have continued my interest in the area and both my children have been imbued with a love of the Glen, having worked there as grouse beaters during their student days.

For the past few years, as a family, we have taken the holiday cottage West Lodge, for a week in July and now our UK grandchildren have come to treasure the valley as well. Glen Tanar is even part of our world family tradition in that the Australian grandchildren have been introduced to the joys of its environment and insist on holidays there on their regular visits back to the old country. Recently, staying for a few days in the Butler's Lodge, a beautifully appointed holiday house, brought home to all the grandchildren what it was like to live and even sleep in their grandfather's childhood bedroom of yesteryear.

Butler's Lodge in 1937 – Mother enjoying the flowers

That such family commitment should result in a second book with Glen Tanar as its central theme is therefore no passing whim. In my previous book, *Glen Tanar Exile*, I gave an insight into life here some eighty years ago from a very personal view point. When having the original manuscript of that book vetted, I gave it to that well respected author and intrepid rambler Robert Smith for his evaluation. He literally rubbished my book, as anything so nostalgic was anathema to Bob. However he did add that Glen Tanar was just waiting for someone to write a proper history, but my effort was not that answer. If Bob were still alive he would probably be equally sceptical about my latest effort, but I am not deterred; this latest addition is but another stone in the wall and may yet stimulate someone in future to complete the edifice.

My father had started his career with the Coats family back in 1914. Turned down by both the French and British armies as physically unfit for war service, he was engaged by the then George Coats as his valet/courier. George Coats, having bought the estate in 1905 from the family of Sir William Cunliffe Brooks, was knighted in 1916 so becoming First Baron Glentanar, only to die two years later. His son Thomas, returning from World War I, inherited my father along with an estate of 29,000 acres and a noble title. Both lairds travelled widely around the world as well as maintaining residences near Ayr at Belleisle, and 11 Hill Street, London, along with large yachts, giving my father an absorbing life. Hill Street, however, held a diversion for my father in the form of a young lady a few doors away. So it was that in 1926 my mother agreed not only to get married, but to banish herself from the bright lights to come to Aberdeenshire and end up in the Tanar valley.

My upbringing was idyllic, as life on a millionaire's estate missed out on all the hardships of the world of that time. As wild boys roaming wherever we pleased we came to know all the old artefacts left from the Cunliffe Brooks' era. Now in my senior years it has struck me that we are in grave danger of losing many of these relics as they get lost in undergrowth, disintegrate with age, or are simply discarded as changes occur on the estate. As no one is totally committed to their preservation, my friend Alfie Dawson and I have been alerted to take more positive action. Documents do exist with the estate Ranger Service and in private hands, but this does not fully reassure us as we have found omissions on both lists. The descriptions and locations are vague, and in our opinion, a publication for future generations is justified.

Glen Tanar 1938: Lake, Mansion House, Round Field and Chapel of St Lesmo far right

It has been suggested that recording all the particulars on the internet would be equally valuable, but I remain unconvinced that this media will prove as easily accessible as the old-fashioned written word. Something tangible to browse through, or carry on days of exploration seems so much more satisfactory than surfing the net.

Walking the two miles across the hills to Glentanar School as infants, we became aware of two particular inscribed stones. Climbing up northwards from the Visitor Centre you pass through gates flanked by two impressive granite pillars at Belrorie and then descend gently into the valley of the Dee. At the top of the Firmounth is a large stone telling of the invasion by Edward I, 'the Hammer of the Scots', as he used this route in the years 1296 and 1303, while lower down on the stone there is a record of the army of Montrose taking this route in 1645. It meant nothing to us at the time, but a little further down the road is the long flat stone of the Snake's Well. The inscription, *The worm of the still is the deadliest snake on the hill* had us watching our feet whenever we approached that boggy area with its stone seating all around. No one ever wondered what it really meant and a worm of a still making whisky never dawned on us. Deadliest snakes to us meant adders and that is always how I think of it even today.

Running down the Firmy Brae to Glentanar School had us pass the

Looking down on the Home Farm and some of the Norwegian Fjord horses PHOTO: ALAN FINDLAY

imposing Queen Victoria Diamond Jubilee fountain – something we barely looked at except for trying to drown each other with water on our way home. Then trooping into the Victorian setting of the school we were surrounded by all those adages carved into the wooden panels between the two schoolrooms and around the fireplaces. *Spare the rod and spoil the child* still makes me smile and causes disbelief on the faces of my grandchildren. Yet perhaps *A stitch in time saves nine* has left its imprint on many of our minds to make us into diligent citizens. You can almost sense the grim-faced dominie in those far-off days of 1900 sternly teaching the basics of reading, writing and arithmetic with the black tawse lying handily on his desk.

In the 1930s the horse and cart were still prominent, both on the farm and in estate work. Horse troughs were still very much part of our environment, whereas now they are as out of date as the penny-farthing. It was one of Cunliffe Brooks' great projects to adorn and inscribe these troughs, and no one would have dared to remove the copper cups that went with most of them. Of all the wells and troughs we have uncovered only two now have cups attached. Probably many have become collectors' pieces for enthusiasts, but is still very disappointing.

Heart of Glen Tanar: the Stable Yard, Estate Office and Recreation Hall in full view.

Through the years I have returned to the estate and viewed its gradual deterioration with sadness. Taking my young children to see my old school in the 1970s we found it shut down and partially derelict. Yet in the teacher's little side room all the papers and registers still lay around from the years gone by. My nostalgia was heightened by finding the attendance register back to the 1930s with my name regularly ticked off as being present. Then to my astonishment, there in the margin where my name appeared for the last time was written in a characteristic hand, "Graduated MB ChB Aberdeen University 1954".

Having scanned the internet for references to Glen Tanar I see there are 28,500 hits involving these two words, yet having pored over a large proportion not one makes any detailed reference to the objects left behind from the Brooks' era. In fact there is little evidence of any sort of history of the district which is very surprising. A number of our best known local authors through the ages have made passing references, but not one has made any attempt to pull all the facts together into one publication. Bob Smith was correct that the Glen Tanar story was just waiting to be told but who would tell it? As probably one of only a handful of people still alive from those past glory years, it seems reasonable that I should at least make a stab at it.

I am aware that I am no impersonal bystander in this saga. Brought up as part of this environment I am interwoven into its fabric. That this could lead to prejudice is always a danger. Although I detest our present day class structure I recognize that in the past the way of life and standards of behaviour were quite different.

Finally, I have frequently been asked why I would wish, at my time of life, to take on such an onerous thankless task as recording the history of a relatively insignificant backwater like Glen Tanar. Is it to sell books, give publicity to a glen that is struggling to survive in the harsh reality of modern living, or is there something else much less obvious?

Certainly there is no sense of commerce in this project. In fact if I were asked whether I wished to sell a thousand books, or just have the volume held in libraries for reference in the future, this second reason would be far and away my priority. The fact that my first book was seen by some in the district as invaluable in recording an under reported period in our history, was my greatest satisfaction. Similarly if this book is seen as pulling together a disparate history for others to browse through in future, while further popularizing Glen Tanar, that will have fulfilled all my expectations.

3

A BRONZE AGE DISCOVERY

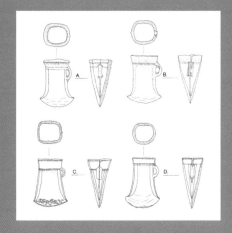

The Bronze Age is recorded as running from 2700 to 700BC. The name is related to the discovery by man that by smelting together three parts of copper with one of tin the result was a metal of greater strength than copper alone. All forms of utensils could be crafted, especially cutting tools, weapons and drinking vessels.

The Iron Age then dated from the end of the Bronze Age to the Roman invasion of Britain around 47AD. We think of the Picts as being from way back as well, but they were in fact a confederation of northern tribes dating from the Roman era into the 10th century AD.

By about 2000BC Europeans from the North West German plain had reached the north-east of Scotland and had started venturing up the valleys of the Dee and Don. Bringing with them supplies and livestock, they started clearing the great forests and raising crops of barley. It is said they had also brought bronze metal as well as moulds, casts, bellows and kilns.

Copper was plentiful in Scotland but, other than in Cornwall, tin had to be imported from the areas the new migrants had left behind. Experts maintain that this requirement meant that our ancestors were quickly made dependant on trade to survive and prosper, so ushering in a new concept of interdependence for them.

High status objects – such as jewellery made from gold and silver, amber and jet – give the impression that this society was developing an elite class of chieftains and warriors, holding sway over the labouring classes. Burials often in stone-lined chambers or cists, accompanied by expensive jewels and weaponry, suggest a belief that such material possessions might be required in the later life.

Susan M. Pearce, Emeritus Professor of Museum Studies at Leicester University, has written a detailed and influential paper on the first of our recorded treasures of Glen Tanar. The following details have been taken

View from the Knockie looking down on the old mansion house

from her article to interest the average reader, without including all the expert's intricate details.

In 1971 a Mr Oddy appeared at the city museum in Exeter with a bronze penannular armlet, one of sixteen bronze objects in his possession. The group consisted of four socketed axes, six armlets and armlet fragments, two rings, two sets of triple rings and two cups, each with a single projecting handle.

The collection had belonged to a Colin Matheson Milne Miller of the Royal Army Medical Corps – born in Nairn in 1826 and died in Eastbourne in 1895. He was the son of the Rev. Robert Milne Miller, who was the Presbyterian minister of Aboyne and Glen Tanar from 1826 to 1848. The *Aberdeen Journal* for Wednesday 29 March 1843 records, "some woodcutters in pursuit of rabbits on the hill of Knockie in Glentanna accidentally discovered, under a cairn, an ancient burial place covered by a large flat stone. On removing this, they found articles including two bronze vessels, capable of holding about two-thirds of a pint, of neat workmanship, cast in rather an elegant shape, with a handle on one side; seventeen spear or axe heads of bronze, known among antiquaries by the name of celts; from thirty to forty bronze bracelets; six bronze rings of good workmanship, of different sizes."

The Ordnance Survey (O.S.) six-inch map shows "bronze celts and

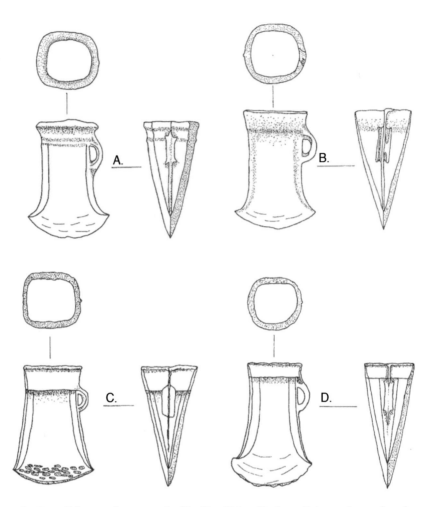

A: Axe, 7.3 cms long, probably English; B: Axe, 7.4cms long, local copy of 1; C: Axe, 7.6cms long, shaped blade; D: Axe, 8.0 cms long, more slender form.

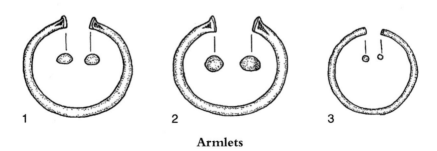

Armlets

cups found" at NJ 482953 on the top of the Knockie, overlooking what is now Glentanar House. The O.S. name book entry made in 1865, relating to the hoard, refers to two cups and six celts and adds that James Ogg of Aboyne has one celt, but that it is not known where the others are. Prof. Pearce adds that there is no reason to doubt that Mr Oddy's bronzes are part of this hoard, or that his cups are those described in the newspaper.

The two cups are the most important pieces in the hoard. They have been cast from the same two-piece mould. Both cups are 7.2cms high and measure 7.6cms across the mouth and 8.5cms at their greatest width and are flat bottomed.

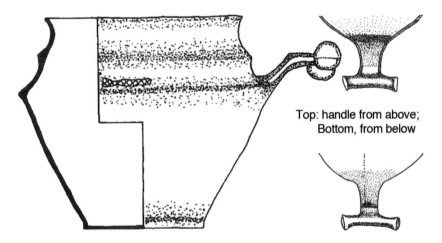

Top: handle from above;
Bottom, from below

Most important pieces of the hoard: I am grateful to Emeritus Professor Susan Pearce for allowing me to include her diagrams.

The rest of Prof. Pearce's paper, written in 1971, is highly technical; it can be viewed in full on the internet under the heading, *A Late Bronze Age Hoard from Glentanar, Aberdeenshire*. She maintains that the find was late Bronze Age, probably 800–700BC. In her summing up, she feels the hoard contained at least sixty objects of which perhaps half were armlets. These armlets are consistent with those found in the Rhineland. In addition some of the things called triple rings were thought to be pieces of horse harness. All very intriguing, but for me the real thrill is to think of all the times we as boys climbed the Knockie, right over this find and had not the faintest idea it ever existed.

In a further paper, probably written about 1978, Prof. Pearce tells about a find of amber related to the Glen Tanar hoard. Mr Oddy, who had originally brought the collection to the Exeter Museum, had lost his wife in 1976 and came across a small box of amber fragments when going through her effects. Included in the box was a written list in the handwriting of Colin Matheson Milne Miller. The description was undated but headed, 'List of Ancient Relics found at Glen Tanna and Aboyne about sixty years ago'. The list included 'fragments of amber' and conservation work has shown that at least five separate amber beads are represented; possibly the remnants of an impressive necklace. The fact that Mr Oddy was unaware until after his wife's death of the existence of the amber and the list of objects, suggests that Mrs Oddy had inherited them. That Mrs Oddy may have been a relative of Colin M. M. Miller seems a distinct possibility.

Attempting to find out more about Miller, I discovered that he graduated in Medicine from Edinburgh University in 1847 and was appointed an Assistant Surgeon in the Army Hospital Corps, later to be called the RAMC, in 1851 and was promoted to Surgeon Major in 1858. He was involved in the Indian Mutiny in the years 1857 to 1859 and retired from army service in 1873. There is no record of whether he was married and so no note of his having had any children.

Recent correspondence with Prof. Sue Pearce reveals that she also had tried to explore the association between Miller and Mrs Oddy without much success. She felt that it was possible that Mrs Oddy's mother or close relative had been housekeeper to Colin Miller. If this was the case, I jocularly commented to Sue Pearce in thanking her for all her assistance, then this relative must have been over the moon finding herself the proud owner of such a pile of apparent old junk.

Susan Pearce in her summing up suggests that from various records, the list of known objects represents only a small part of the actual hoard. Mr Oddy presented all his material to the National Museum of Antiquities, but where the rest of the objects disappeared to is open to conjecture. It takes little imagination, however, to guess that some were squirreled away by those who found the hoard. Then having been stuck in a loft they were thrown out as junk by the succeeding generation. The other question that arises is how the local minister came to acquire part of the hoard, or was it really given to the church for safe keeping. No one will ever know, but in the *Statistical Account of Aberdeenshire* of 1843 the minister writing the survey for the Aboyne and Glentanner Parish is none other than the Rev. Robert Milne Miller. Remembering that the local press wrote up the hoard discovery in March 1843 it is not surprising the minister makes no reference to the find under his record of antiquities. However, he was extremely knowledgeable and had a great interest in such matters, so it is possible that he came to treasure the objects and made sure they were passed on to his son, realising their significance.

It seems fitting to bring this chapter to a close by quoting the observations of the Rev. Miller himself, back in 1843. At Newton of Tilliecairn, which now looks down on our old Glentanar School, several urns were uncovered in 1828 and were found to contain calcined bones. One was perfectly intact, "and the gentleman into whose possession it has fallen has either lately presented it, or intends to present it, to the Museum of Marischal College". Fifty yards from this discovery the soil was noted as having a blackish appearance, with small pieces of charcoal embedded in it and the Rev. Miller suggests that bodies had been burnt there before being placed in the urns. Close by were the remains of some Picts' houses or, as they were called back in 1843, mullochies. Whether these people were Picts or further back, if not as far as the Bronze Age but to the Iron Age, could not have been accurately dated in the Rev. Miller's time.

Another discovery was made about a mile to the east of Newton in 1818 when some cairns were opened to obtain stones for house building. Under one cairn, bones were uncovered along with a small gold chain of four links attached to a pin of such size as might have been used in a brooch for fastening a Celtic plaid. Such echoes are, however, far too distant for most of us to begin to sense the difference between the ages.

The Knockie is mainly wooded now, but it is exciting just to stand on the spot where that flat stone revealed those ancient ancestors' belongings. Looking around, I wonder what else lies hidden from view that will never be revealed. To imagine those early people and their pioneering way of life is difficult, but yet so intriguing in the stunning stillness. Yes, a really outstanding discovery and a marvellous start to our journey.

4

FROM PICTS TO JACOBITES

I had a Victorian upbringing where not a particle of food was left on your plate at meal times. Those unsavoury-looking vegetables had to be eaten, with my mother's rejoinder that they would do me good. So stop pondering that Sudoko, leave your crossword, turn off the background television and renew your knowledge of our ancient heritage with this brief résumé – you know it will do you good.

The find of a Bronze Age hoard in Glen Tanar was sensational, but it has left historians toiling to fill in the years until Glen Tanar appears in print in the records of the 13th century AD. It is important for us to have memories jogged a little as to that period leading eventually to Culloden, when all Scots really begin to hear the echoes.

Tacitus in the first century AD, in his account of the Roman invasion of North Britain under Agricola, gives the name of the country as Caledonia. By the end of the Roman dominion in Britain the name Caledonii is replaced by that of Picti and in time the dwellers became Picts. These Picts figure in early Roman history as fierce and untameable enemies of the Empire. The Romans left Britain at the beginning of the fifth century AD leaving Scotland, north of the Forth, in two kingdoms of Northern and Southern Picts.

Historians see the Picts as forming a unique culture, implying a long history as an independent people. Hill forts, earth houses, sculptured stones, all known as Pictish, are thoroughly native and, in a sense, unique. Few parts of Scotland demonstrate this culture better than Aberdeenshire and especially middle Deeside.

The language of the Picts is difficult to evaluate as so few remnants survive. Some gravestones, however, bear the well-known Pictish symbols as well as alphabetic writing. One such stone is recorded in the *Glen Tanar Estate Papers*.

The Formaston stone, dated around 500AD, was discovered at the old

church of Formaston, the original church of Aboyne, about a mile east of the present village. The stone is seemingly only a fragment of what had been a cross-slab, the shaft of which is formed of Celtic interlock work. The inscription, which was complete, has been translated to read: 'Maqqo-Tall, successor of Nehht, descended from Vrobbaccene, or, of the clan Vrobbacen'. The stone now resides in a splendid glass case in Aboyne's Victory Hall, hopefully secure for posterity.

Francis Diack in the *Glen Tanar Estate Papers* says that the view of the Picts promoted by their enemies, as barbaric, is largely unfair. There is evidence, enhanced by more recent finds, that they were settled agriculturists, tilling the soil and rearing cattle in a way not so far removed from present day rural life. The *Glen Tanar Estate Papers* of the 1930s are now well out of date and modern historians appear uncertain about this period. I can, therefore, but point my reader to check such internet sites as Scotshistoryonline.co.uk while I tiptoe into shallower water.

There is still a degree of mystery and mythology about the arrival of the Gaels in Scotland. Some historians see them coming mainly from Antrim in Northern Ireland around 500AD; others maintain that seafaring Scots from Europe settled in Ireland and Argyll at much the same time. Conversion of the Picts to Christianity is credited to St Columba, while others think this is not true for our own east coast. Gradually, however, over the generations Gaelic influence increased, to the detriment of Pictish culture. The Pictish monarchs eventually agreed to unite under Kenneth

Macalpine in the ninth century and the new nation of Alba – later to be called Scotland – emerged with Gaelic as the dominant language. This produced a mixed society with every clan containing Pictish blood and this is perpetuated in many of our indigenous inhabitants today.

Angles, Saxons and Vikings played a part with their penetration of Celtic Scotland, further increasing the genetic diversity. English and Norman influences began in the reign of Malcolm Canmore (1057–1093) and were speedily felt in this district. Lords Superiors of the lands were Anglo-Normans, but the process of Anglicisation took a long time to reach down to all classes of the community. Celtic law and custom was transferred into an English-speaking community, with feudal notions from the south supplanting native practices.

Gaelic was gradually replaced by English, especially in the upper echelons of society, but pockets of Gaelic persisted until the 20th century, especially at the heads of valleys and in remote districts.

In the Celtic period the ecclesiastical unit was the monastery, from which the churches recruited their clerics. The first vague records relating to Aboyne and Glen Tanar come from the year 1014 AD, when the battle of Clontarf outside Dublin saw the Irish beating the Viking invaders with the assistance of a small Scottish expeditionary force. It is recorded that the Scots had men from Mar, and so it is possible that some came from the Aboyne district.

The territory of Aboyne and Glen Tanar was feudalised in the 12th century and became king's land. Another record of the time relates to the reign of King Alexander III (1264–1286) who, it was said, enjoyed hunting in the royal forest of Glentanar. In the 13th century, for the first time, there is a record of 'the thanage of Aboyne' – a reference to the lands of Aboyne. This infers that these lands as they are described in early documents remained practically unaltered into the 18th century.

Following the death of Alexander III a period of turmoil ensued with a loss of Scottish independence and its eventual recovery by Robert the Bruce. In 1291 Edward I of England – 'the hammer of the Scots' – was called in as arbiter on claimants to the Scottish throne. As a price, he demanded that all the castles in the country be handed over to him. Aboyne castle was one of those surrendered and an English garrison was stationed there.

However, Edward invaded Scotland in 1296 and again in 1303. The route his armies took on Deeside is a bone of contention, especially as

Cunliffe Brooks erected a formidable inscribed stone in the late 1800s on the Fir Mounth stating that Edward had invaded using this very route. Scottish history from this period makes little reference to Aboyne or Glen Tanar, and only when we get to the 1600s do national events begin to have a bearing on our more parochial interest.

Catholicism, having ruled supreme for generations, was challenged in England by Henry VIII who in 1534 made it a treasonable offence not to recognise him as head of the Church. So Episcopalianism was born.

In 1560 in Scotland, John Knox led the Reformation, which also banished the Catholic faith. However with the Episcopal Church still under the domination of bishops – and its ceremonial reminiscent of the hated papists – Scots were to eventually rebel. In 1638 the National Covenant was signed, abolishing bishops and the divine right of kings, thus bringing many Scots into conflict with both the throne and the establishment. Government troops were deployed to oppose these Covenanters, bringing terror and destruction to the district in the 1640s.

In the *History of Loch Kinnord* the Rev. J. G. Michie recalls the suffering inflicted by the opposing forces of the Civil War in 1644. As the Marquis of Argyle approached with an army of 6,000 Covenanters, the Marquis of Huntly, a Roman Catholic, disbanded his small group of followers and made off to Sutherland. Huntly, was however arrested in Strathdon in December 1647, and was made an example of by the Kirk and the Scottish Parliament being beheaded in Edinburgh in 1649.

Robert Dinnie in *An Account of the Parish of Birse* written in 1865, also outlines the effects on our district. In 1644 a regiment of Argyle's highlanders called 'the cleansers' arrived. Eight hundred footmen with their commanders certainly cleansed everything in sight – Covenanters and anti-Covenanters alike:

"The haill country people fled that could flee and left their houses desolate. They plundered and spoilzied the house of Aboyne and the house of Abergeldie with their ground; they spoilzied and plundered the haill Birse, Cromar, Glentanner, Glenmuick and left neither horse, sheep, nolt, ky, nor four footed beast in all these brave countries, nor victuals, corn, goods or gear that they may lay their hands upon; and seeing they could not live longer in these harried bounds, they got orders and removed home over again upon the aforesaid 1st of July, leaving only one of their captains with eighty men."

On the second of July 1645 the Marquis of Montrose – leading a

Royalist army in support of Charles I of England – defeated the Covenanters at the Battle of Alford. The stone at the top of the Firmounth Brae above Glentanar School is said to mark the route of his advance into Donside. This was but one of many battles at that time as the English, with the aid of not a few Scots, tried to crush the Covenanters. Yet the dates 1314 for Bannockburn and 1513 for Flodden are those most indelibly seared into our minds from those days in the 1930s, when we fought bravely in Glentanar School playground to uphold the pride of the Scots.

Eventually in 1689 a system run by elders was evolved and the Presbyterian Church, now known as the Church of Scotland, was established. In the clan system (*clann* – Gaelic for children) of the time, however, members owed their allegiance firstly to their own leaders and with so many chieftains in the Highlands still sympathetic to the Catholics or the Episcopalians, trouble was never far away.

In our own district the Earl of Huntly and his Gordon connections were foremost in their distaste for the modern religion. They were on weak ground, as those of lesser stature were quite prepared to accept the Church of Scotland and felt lukewarm towards these chiefs and their causes.

In Glen Tanar and Aboyne following the Reformation, the proscription of Catholics seems to have been effective, despite Huntly as the Superior and his chief vassals – including the Farquharsons – continuing to be Catholics. Priests were banished, but itinerant clergy continued to provide the Sacraments of the Church, passing between the parishes in disguise. By 1697 conditions had eased and Robert Seton, the first of a succession of priests, occupied part of the old building of Deecastle, under two miles west of Dinnet bridge on the South Deeside Road.

In 1795 Alexander Scott was appointed the local priest and he erected out of the fabric of the old castle a house of two storeys, the ground floor serving as the chapel with the priest's quarters above. In 1812 a new chapel was built in Ballogie and the priest went to stay there, but took a service once a month at Deecastle. In 1874 the present Roman Catholic church was built in Aboyne and the Inchmarnoch community chapel ceased to be used.

The Deecastle house originally called Chapelton, now known as Chapel House, had fallen into disrepair by the 1890s, but landowner Sir W. C. Brooks, appreciating its historical importance, had it renovated. It is described by the Rev. Michie in 1896 as, "converted into a comfortable and even elegant habitation, while the ground floor serves as a hall and library for the district of Inchmarnoch".

Dilapidated once more by the 1960s, the house was spotted, quite by chance, and the lady of the family, Mrs Mary Thomson, approached Lord Glentanar with a view to purchase. Normally this would have been out of the question, as no houses on the estate were ever sold. Being a musician, however, the lady struck up a rapport with the organ-playing laird. Lo and behold, he agreed to pass over ownership on the understanding that the house be totally renovated and the new owners pay the annual feu duty. The renovation was a giant project, as the house was a listed building, but by 1969 it was completed.

Mrs Thomson's daughter Mrs Geraldine Mucha, also a musician, has now inherited the house and although she lives part of the year in Prague, she still comes to summer here. As her son and grandchildren also love it, Chapel House seems secure. The owner calls it an upside-down house: like the priest, they live upstairs and sleep downstairs in the converted chapel.

The irony is that Mrs Mucha's grandfather was the Rev. George W. Thomson, Church of Scotland minister at the West Kirk of St Andrew in Aberdeen, and here we have his descendants living in an old papist House of God.

Mrs Mucha, a delightful lady of 92 years young, is picking her dark crop of wild gooseberries when I call. Full of energy and with a never-ending host of memories, she keeps me riveted for an hour. A composer as well as a musician, she is still gainfully occupied back in Prague. As the daughter of a professor of music and as her late father-in-law was the celebrated art nouveau Czech artist, Alphonse Mucha (1860-1939), she has enjoyed a lifetime of culture.

Marrying a young Czech pilot serving in the RAF who later became a war correspondent with the BBC, she found herself living behind the Iron Curtain for much of her life. Recalling the atmosphere of restriction, bureaucracy and corruption of those years, she feels a deep empathy with the Czech people buffeted by adversity from one century to the next.

Chapel House breathes her life, the grand piano, family portraits and examples of her father-in law Mucha's works all mingling to provide a unique atmosphere. If Lord Glentanar were alive today I am certain he would be delighted with the outcome of his generosity.

The massacre of Glencoe in 1692 is but one incident of a discreditable period in Scots history; intrigue, dishonesty, self interest, deception and clan feuds interlinking with incredible bravery and decency, making it a truly sad time in our evolution.

The 1715 and 1745 rebellions were the culmination of all parties, in Scotland and England, promoting their own causes; hoping, by way of the Jacobites, to re-establish the Stuart dynasty and Catholicism on the Scottish throne. The rebellions pitted Scot against Scot, sometimes with family members on opposing sides – a truly disheartening period which saw the end of the clan system on the savage battlefield of Culloden in 1746. But this is a tale for another chapter.

5

A LITERARY TREASURE

To have unearthed the story of a Bronze Age hoard in Glen Tanar is a wonderful start to our exploration. It is to be expected that the treasures of the valley will be mainly found in artefacts and structures from past ages, along with perhaps the odd verbal or written anecdote handed down through the generations. That we should find a whole literary work about our valley, hidden away for the past seventy-five years in an innocuous form on the shelves of two separate libraries and in Glen Tanar estate, is therefore a totally unlooked for bonus.

The *Glen Tanar Estate Papers* consist of sixteen volumes of densely packed facts about this very valley and its surrounds from the earliest times. Typed on office paper, they are presented in what appears to be a final proof copy for editing prior to being printed yet bound for presentation in a marketable form. That the pages have the occasional correction of spelling carried out in fading ink suggests that an editor or proof reader was at work. Also, there are gaps in the text with brackets around the spaces suggesting that the author had still to define a date or a reference. Their fine leather binding, however, shows that they have been valued enough to preserve for posterity. The volumes have no preface, nor yet any summing up, leaving the feeling of an uncompleted labour of love.

The writings demonstrate such detailed rigour and ability to research and reason that a very fine academic mind must have been involved; yet the volumes give not a whisper as to authorship. From my own close contact with Lord Thomas Glentanar in the 1930s to 1940s I wondered whether he could have researched this with a co-author, along with the assistance of his full-time private secretary, Norman Dain. Certainly the laird had a fine enquiring mind, but the level of references and ability to look at Celtic writings suggest a person of expertise in this field and the frequent references to the singular person "I" appear to rule out a shared work.

Why someone would go to this extent with months, if not years, of intensive research and then not formally present it as a completed concept of great substance, defies commonsense. Whether Lord Glentanar had any hand in it seemed increasingly doubtful; knowing him he would have completed such a challenge and he would have certainly required the back-up of a professional in this field to assist him. The lack of a date of writing was puzzling; in one volume there was a reference to an article in the *Deeside Field* of 1929 showing that the early 1930s was probably the closest we would get to a definite year.

Three sets of the volumes appear to exist. One is held by Glen Tanar estate, one in the Aberdeen Central Library and the other is in the Aberdeen University library. No others have been so far uncovered to the best of my knowledge. That one should be held by the University suggests that this may be where the work originated.

A suggestion that a Celtic academic might be involved led to that department in Aberdeen University. Francis Carney Diack (1865-1939) has been mooted as the author and certainly the description of him on the University website appears to uphold this. Described as a Celtic scholar, born in Aberdeen, educated in Banchory and Aberdeen University, he went on to make his career in and around the latter establishment. His eventual death in Banchory at the outbreak of World War II also gives one the flavour of someone dedicated to Deeside. He was described as precise and meticulous in his work but, on account of his scholarly caution, he only allowed a fraction of his research to appear in print during his lifetime. This fits in well with the information-packed volumes which have never really seen the light of day and knits perfectly with his character.

The guessing game was finally resolved when Michael Bruce, the present owner of Glen Tanar estate, volunteered the fact that his grandfather had commissioned an Aberdeen academic called Diack to write the history of the estate, known to the family as *The Diack Papers*. There seems to be no knowledge in the family as to the background for this unfinished work, no documentation regarding the remit given to the researcher and no evidence of a fee being agreed or paid. Could it have been that Diack and Lord Glentanar had not seen eye to eye with the direction of the research, or perhaps the time it was taking to produce it? Whatever the reason, it is most unlike the laird to abandon a project, so we are left to surmise. Nevertheless, Lord Glentanar valued the unfinished project enough to have at least three sets of volumes bound gloriously in leather and to keep one set and place the others where he knew they would be safe and treasured.

The volumes are a mine of information, not only for the researcher, but for those with a general interest in times gone by. Apart from his Celtic involvement, the author goes into details of every farm and small holding on the Glen Tanar of old. The intricate composition of the society is finely sketched throughout the ages, especially the strata of land ownership and tenancy. Detailing the individuals, their occupations, whether gentleman, wadsman, tenant or subtenant, everything is recorded minutely. The record – of crops grown, the domestic birds and beasts held, even down to the number of chickens – is stunning in its completeness. Incomes and costs are covered and the many legal squabbles showing attitudes regarding land tenure over the years bring personal animosities to bear, so energising drab detail. The author does not hesitate to propound his theories where evidence is missing. Cattle rustling, the smugglers and the trials and tribulations of the 1715 and 1745 rebellions are all covered from a Glen Tanar perspective.

The volumes then strangely stop at the beginning of the nineteenth century and so miss out on the clearances of Glen Tanar by the Huntly estates and the subsequent era of Cunliffe Brooks and his revolutionary deeds. Did Lord Glentanar consider the more recent history of the Glen too close to deserve a place in these works?

Research at times uncovers details of no particular importance, but which dove-tail into some totally different aspect of life. While looking through the records of Inchmarnoch School, I came upon this interesting occurrence. The teacher of the school, Mrs B. Wattie, had become ill in April 1892 and a Mr Francis C. Diack, M.A. was installed as relief schoolmaster from 18th April to 19th August 1892, until the appointment of a permanent replacement for the autumn term. Diack would then have been twenty-seven years old and this had been another insight into the district he would so knowledgeably write about forty years later.

6

LAND HISTORY

The history of land tenure on Glen Tanar is involved and would almost deserve a book dedicated to that one subject. King David (1124-1153) became the first feudal king of all Scotland. The king gave out land to feudal lords called 'maths' and used the term 'thanage' for such lands. These lands were granted on a tenure which may be described as resembling a feu with appropriate fee. In return, the nobles were expected to hold themselves ready to assist the King in any military operation. The King, however, held some ground back under his own control, termed Crown Lands. The territory of Aboyne and Glen Tanar was feudalised sometime in the 12th century. The effect of this was to break up the ancient tribal organisations and to bring in English and Anglo-Norman nobles, with English officials and churchmen in their train.

The first lords of Aboyne were the Bissets, probably the first non-native lords to hold the thanage. They were powerful, holding lands around Inverness and were well-connected with the King himself. Records name Walter Bisset as probably the first incumbent before 1242, but he had a chequered career. Bested in a tournament by Patrick of Athole, he took his revenge by setting alight the barn he slept in, causing Athole's death along with that of many others. Fleeing to the King's protection, he was banished to Ireland where he continued to cause mayhem.

Following Edward I's invasion of Scotland in 1303 and subsequent retreat, the thanage of Aboyne was back in the Scottish King's hands. By 1337 Aboyne belonged to a Sir Alexander Fraser and subsequently through marriage came in 1437 to Alexander de Seton, the first Lord Gordon. His son Alexander succeeded in 1441 and was afterwards created Earl of Huntly.

In the charter of 1450, James II granted the Earl of Huntly his lands as a free barony in fee and heritage. This was the highest form of feudal tenure conveying the fullest powers of possession to the Earl. The barony also granted jurisdiction over the inhabitants, with the fines and fees that came from it. Huntly kept some land in his possession to be cultivated by his own bondsmen and later by free labourers. This part of the barony was called 'bordland' and appears in Glen Tanar, with the name Bordland given to a now defunct farm near the mouth of the Auldroy burn and east of the present day Braeloine Visitor Centre. Land not retained by Huntly was cultivated by vassals, tenants and sub-tenants paying rent and rendering services to the Earl as Superior.

Vassals held their land by various arrangements. 'Lands in Feu' was the term for use of land in consideration of an annual payment in money, produce and certain services. Lands in feu were held in perpetual hereditary lease. The feuar had the right to sell his land, but had to give the superior the first opportunity to purchase. When a feu charter was granted by the superior it was followed by 'sasine'; that is the symbolic gesture of giving possession of the land to the vassal. Commonest symbol was the delivery of earth and stone to the new owner in the presence of witnesses, including tenants living on the land, so that everyone was fully aware who was the new overlord.

In 1638 the Marquis of Huntly granted the feu of Upper Bellastreen to a George Middleton. This holding is now part of the Glen Tanar home farm. Besides arable land, the pasturage and the sheilings of Auldinhervie, Tomlair and Cornmalchone were included in the feu, it being the rule for farms to have hill ground held at times in common with others. Auldinhervie is the west tributary of the Allachy shortly before it joins the Tanar. Tomlair is on the north side of the Tanar just east of the march between the parishes of Glen Muick and Glen Tanar, while Cornmalchone – now called Coire Meacan – is the corrie immediately north of Etnach.

The feuar could let what land he pleased to tenants and charge duties direct to himself. If the vassal fell into debt so that profits of his estate fell by law to the superior, the latter promised to assign them back to the vassal or anyone he might name for a consideration. This could be a valuable privilege.

As to other duties, the vassal and his tenants were bound to appear yearly at four of the superior's head courts at Deecastle or within the barony, while he himself was not allowed to hold courts of his own or judge the tenants, except for very minor offences. Other additions, such as not killing deer or felling trees except for farm building work were appended, while the vassal himself was held responsible for any misdemeanours by his tenants. Vassal and tenants were to attend the superior at all his huntings and be present at their own expense at meetings where military service was required. His assistance was also forbidden to anyone except his superior other than the King himself.

'Lands in Wadset' also relate to vassals, but here the superior had the option of repaying to the feuar the original sum advanced, so repossessing the land. This made the vassal a second-class type of feuar, thus a wadsetter. Wadset – something put in pledge. Ranked below a true feuar as to tenure, he could nevertheless be a person of important standing in the district. Middleton of Upper Bellastreen was a humble person compared with the powerful Donald Farquharson, wadsetter of Ballaterach, but Middleton had a much superior tenure.

These two types of vassals were the nearest in status to the superior in that they were hereditary owners of their land and so were 'landed men', quite different from those who held land only on tack or lease. They are invariably described as 'of' not 'in' before the name of their land. John Garden 'of' Bellamore implies heritable possession, while John Garden 'in' Bellamore is merely a tenant. Sometimes feuars and wadsetters dropped their names and simply signed themselves as, for instance, Bellamore, but this did not rate them as lairds. The word 'laird' implies a subject holding land direct from the Crown with a heritable jurisdiction over the inhabitants of his land which vassals and wadsetters never had. Later it appears some vassals, with the superior's consent, were promoted to a Crown holding and then were styled by their neighbours and notaries as 'lairds'.

'Lands in Tack' relate to a tacksman or leaseholder (tack – a lease) having no right of ownership beyond the period of his tack. Tacksmen were often men of means occupying several farms which they sublet to working tenants. They had some obligations of attendance at huntings and hostings and no doubt these obligations reached right down to their sub-tenants.

An obligation to the superior that appears to have gone on for centuries was 'carriages'. Tenants had not only to make payments in money and kind, but to provide personal services such as assisting at harvest time, or going on errands with horses on a specified number of times a year. This is recorded into the 19th century and was split into short and long carriages. A long carriage may have required a day or more away whereas a short carriage would have been the routine trip to Aboyne.

A *Carriage Book* for the years 1796 to 1804 was found among the *Aboyne Papers* and such a function may have gone on for some time after that. One entry refers to, "providing one turn at leading the lord's peats from the moss to Deecastle and to execute one long carriage of not more than forty miles from Deecastle". Carts had not come into use in those early days so loads would have been carried in creels or 'packets' slung in pairs across the horse's back. A load in this register was calculated at eight stones. Wood was carried in some sort of litter and the horses of the time were the sturdy Scottish garrons. The first wheeled carts were recorded at "Dalquhing" farm around 1800, posing the question why the Earl wasn't the first to embrace this leap forward.

Long carriages would have taken peat, slate, lime, wood and heather etcetera, to Aberdeen, and such things as wright's tools or provisions on the return journey. These carriages were demanding on time and manpower, as is well demonstrated in Etnach. A small holding here was charged with the enormous expectation of providing 80 loads of peat annually, amounting to 640 stones in weight which was far more than most other farms. Loads were taken from the Moss of Monavie, already quite far from Etnach, into Aboyne. By 1796 it was noted the holding was already 376 stones in arrears, but by the next year this was only 104; the record abruptly stops after this with the appended note, "Discharged by my hand and to pay money in time coming". It is obvious that the burden was just too much for the sub-tenant and that the tacksman could take a turn at dragging about interminable quantities of peat all for nothing.

The last heritable proprietor in feu of any part of the Glen Tanar-Inchmarnoch lands, John Garden, sold his estate back to the superior in 1756 and from that date on the lands of our district were held by tenants from him or leased. There is scarcely a farm that has not at one time or another been held in feu or wadset hereditarily.

Although pecuniary interests were tantamount, there were other motives at work in this system of land tenure. The superior's standing in the district and his security were largely dependent on the military power he had on hand in times of strife. His selection of vassals was therefore with half an eye on his own needs in the future, to have dependable able men at his shoulder in combat. Vassals selected their tenants with similar care and so often involved their own relatives. This ensured a solidarity

1957: Site of Boganlaik Farm above the Queen's Drive looking down the valley

and community spirit of mutual support closely resembling the clan closeness of the Celtic Highlands.

Diack in his *Glen Tanar Papers* examines the farming community through the ages in inordinate detail. The valley of the Tanar was very restricted in arable ground with the area around Etnach isolated from the lower valley by miles of hill, moor and forest. Through the ages Etnach and Coirevrauch appear to have been held by non-resident tacksmen letting the land to various sub-tenants. Records show that before the clearances of the Glen there were still two houses at Etnach and two at Coirevrauch. The area is of great archaeological interest. Remains of a great boundary dyke can be traced round most of the old arable ground. Specimens of the old Celtic dyke, which divides arable from hill giving it an appearance of a rampart, are described by Diack. He maintained that it was in an excellent state of preservation, a short distance from the Garchory burn, which it does not cross.

The lower valley broadens out to present moderate arable opportunities. A number of farming communities existed here through the ages making the most of the ground available. Glen Tanar ballroom probably stands in the old farm steading of Woodend. It seems probable that the Marquis of Huntly erected a shooting lodge on the site of

Woodend farm when he converted the land to a sporting estate and this is where Cunliffe Brooks would build his mansion in the early 1890s. Other buildings in the early 1800s were the farm of Boganlaik which lay just above the Queen's Drive, with Upper and Lower Bellastreen nestling below. These farms were later merged into the Home Farm which later was to control all the other land within the valley.

Across the Tanar there would have been around nine houses at Knockieside West and in Peter Harper's record he tells of a hotel, a general merchant's shop and at least three shoemakers there. Knockieside East had two houses, while down on the wide haugh was the settlement with Braeloine the main component. A fortified compound had predated the mansion house of Braeloine, the ruins of which now border the Chapel of St Lesmo. Mansion house seems rather a grand name for what was probably a modest farm dwelling, but it would have been much superior to the three wee cottages around it. The Garden family through the ages made this their residence and probably had much to do with its construction. Late in the 18th century it appears that Braeloine was involved in offering goat's milk to visitors and passing travellers when so many believed in its health-giving properties.

Back in the 1600s there is mention of the Alehouse Croft around here, but no record survives to identify its exact position. Over by the river side was the Mill of Braeloine with the line of the mill lade still obvious, running across the field from higher up river. This is where Lord Glentanar erected his turbine to drive the chapel organ back in the 1930s using the same lade. This little round structure, originally with a heather-turfed roof, is still standing today in dilapidated isolation. Further east of Braeloine and in a direct line with the Braeloine bridge was Glen of Glentanar with another four houses. Going east down the south drive and past the Fairy Lake was Birkenhillock on the right with four houses and further still what Peter Harper calls Craig of Boreland with another four houses. This is presumably the area of the old farm of Bordland referred from earlier times and where there was a fine wooden arched bridge long ago. Last recorded houses here were Mounth-side and Old Roy. None of these buildings now exist, but if you look closely there are still clear signs of past developments which a team of archaeologists is still examining.

On the north side of the river many of the houses remain as recorded by Peter Harper; this is where Cunliffe Brooks carried out his redevelopment, while allowing the south side almost to disappear. As for population size it is difficult to be accurate. In 1762 the population, over the age of ten, of the whole estate was 282. The population of the valley itself around 1850 was about 150 just before the Glen was cleared and converted to a sporting estate.

Now passing out through the Tower of Ess gates look along the south bank of the Dee at all those tenanted farms and cottages of the estate from Dalwhing to the edge of Pannanich. Most are still in existence from way back, making it unnecessary for me to go through them individually. Some of the farms are now amalgamated with their neighbours, but that is all about the changing face of a modern Britain. That many livelihoods are under strain there is little doubt, while the numbers working the land is unimaginable compared with a hundred years ago. The same canny attitudes persist, however, and the same half-mocking perception of the world around them is a breath of fresh air to town dwellers.

But something more worrying comes to light. Speaking to stalwarts such as Frank Coutts in Greystone and Neil Williams in Ballaterach there is a feeling of loneliness and fatalism towards the future of farming. The sense of community is disappearing, with no regular Friday mart to attend to oil the wheels of brotherhood and no thrashing mill to gather around to pass on the local gossip. Sons and daughters see no future in farming and many wives do not wish to tie themselves to this way of life. Surrounding cottages are more and more becoming holiday homes or are housing non-agricultural workers who come and go without ever really belonging to the community. A sense of gloom hangs over the district with a question mark over the future of nearly every farm.

Where farms are less viable the estate has taken back the houses to convert them into holiday or rented homes and let the land out to the remaining active farms.

Long gone are the days when Pannanich with its healing waters was the tourist centre of Deeside. Its nine-hole golf course long forgotten, only Frank Coutts in Greystone now farming the ground can still discern the old fairways and greens. Candycraig, Mill of Bellamore, Newton, Little Tullich, Tillycairn, Balindory Cottage, Ettrick Croft, Headinch, Burnside Cottage are but some of the well kent names of old that no longer house sons of the soil. Even Deecastle sees such a son managing to split his time between medicine and farming. Douglas Glass not only takes all this in his stride, but the onerous task of Balmoral medical duties as well.

The Glass name reminds one of the past vassals and tenants of one of

**From Ettrick Croft, looking down to Greystone Farm with the Dee
in the background**

these properties. A Donald Glass who died in 1762 was in Bellamore and
had been in Etnach as a sub-tenant in his younger days. His son followed
him into Bellamore until 1792 when the name disappears, to reappear
when Dr Glass's father came from Birse to Deecastle in 1936 to re-
establish the name in the district. *History in Birse* tells of two look-alike
Glass brothers in the years 1820 to 1830; James the honest farmer, but
John, poacher and well kent smuggler. There was much hilarity in the
district when the detested gaugers made a clever arrest, only to find too
late they had captured the wrong brother. Neil Williams, late of Dalwhing
and now in Ballaterach, is also a Glass on his mother's side, so tradition is
still very much to the fore, but sadly there is no offer of an illicit dram at
his door.

The other name of importance in the area was Garden or Gairdyne.
Diack in his *Estate Papers* gives much space to this family through the
generations, but it is sufficient here to give the outline.

The first records go back to July 1581 when a Mr Robert Garden of
Bellamore was recorded in the Aberdeen Sheriff Court. The title 'Mr', it is
suggested, depicts him as college bred and probably an M.A.. Bellamore
or *Baile mor*, great town in Gaelic, implies it was the largest township in
these parts. The greater part of the lands of Bellamore are now included in
Ballaterach, originally a comparatively small holding. It appears one of
Robert's sons acquired Bellastreen in Glen Tanar. Robert died in 1600 and
in 1638 his son John established the mill at Bellamore and had arranged,

The Mill of Bellamore as it stands today

presumably with the superior, the 'sucken'. This is the collective noun for tenant farmers bound by the terms of their lease to have their crops ground at a specific meal mill. The bigger the sucken the more valuable was the mill. In addition, the farm had the sheiling ground in Coire Meacan above Etnach with the cattle moved there in summer.

The Gardens also appear to have been involved with the Mill of Braeloine and the sucken there was named as Waternaddie, Tillycairn, Bordland, Dalwhing, Foulbog and Etnach. Foulbog sounds uninviting, but its situation is now shrouded in mystery, although it has been suggested it was an area close to the mouth of the Tanar. John died in 1648 to be followed by his son William. The Gardens, although taking their designation from Bellamore, actually lived in the Glen Tanar part of the estate at Braeloine.

Through the years there are various disagreements over rights with the superior wishing to take back the farms, but losing his case in the Court of Session in 1736. William's son John eventually in 1756 sold both Bellamore and Braeloine in the Glen to the Superior, the Earl of Aboyne for £28,000 Scots and so ends a memorable era.

Robert Smith in *Land of the Lost* goes into fascinating detail regarding the area in his chapter headed *The Rocking Stone* which makes for delightful reading.

Mill of Braeloine is now no more than a memory, but there is the consolation of being able to view the Mill of Bellamore. The farm buildings are now tastefully upgraded to a modern dwelling, while the old mill stands bleak and barren, reminding us of times when the whole district was buzzing with activity. Let us now meander past the mill and wend our leisurely way out along the Pollagach Burn into the lovely countryside beyond. If you are still breathing easily, let us take the route up the stiff climb on to Carn Beag and struggle atop the Big Stane. Now close your eyes, relax and hear again all the powerful echoes from those far off days wafting up to us from the valley below.

The Big Stane

7

THE CHURCHES OF GLEN TANAR AND DINNET

S cotland has been divided into districts and parishes since medieval times, but over the centuries boundaries have changed and amalgamations have occurred. A Scottish parish usually described a village, a group of villages, or hamlets and the adjacent lands. They were originally ecclesiastical with inhabitants of the parish paying part of their income to the Church. During the 17th century the parishes gained civil functions for purposes of taxation and the recording of such things as births, deaths and marriages. In the middle of the 19th century these civil functions gained in prominence and over the decades the influence of the Church diminished.

The earliest reference to a church in Glen Tanar appears in 1567 immediately after the Reformation with the services being conducted by a reader at a stipend of £16 (Scots). At first Glen Tanar formed a parish linked to Inchmarnoch but due to "the poverty of living they were disjoined sometime after 1666". Inchmarnoch was then joined up with Glenmuick, Tullich and Glengairn. From church records it appears that Glen Tanar formed a separate chaplainry, probably around 1696, but in more recent times it has certainly been part of the United Parishes of Aboyne and Glen Tanar. The exact dates for this amalgamation are obscure, but previous to 1763 there was a church at either end of the parish with divine service being performed in the rotation of two Sabbaths at Aboyne and the third at Glen Tanar.

The ruins of this Glentanar Church is situated a quarter of a mile east of the old Glentanar School and Cobbleheugh farm, in a field overlooking the Dee, with an enclosed burial-ground still around it. The kirk was described in 1725 as "but a little edifice and thatched with heather and without a bell and situate about the middle of the parish on a muir near the Dee". It was known locally as "the Black Chappell in the Muir". There are references that prior to the Reformation it had been Roman Catholic, but history has left us few records from that era.

In December 1696, an Alexander Gillanders was involved in burying his father in the evening. With the assistance of eight or ten fellow mourners he had removed desks to allow digging the grave under the earthen floor of the church. Someone had brought a hot coal to light the candles and left it on one of the timbered seats. After they departed the church was reduced to ashes. An action was raised to apportion blame, but there is no record of the outcome, some blaming the mourners, others the caretaker who should have checked the church before leaving. The church was rebuilt, but there is no hint as to who paid.

An interesting aside to this story is the fact that the mourners removed the 'desks' to dig into the earthen floor. In those days there were no fixed pews and the parishioners were expected to provide their own seats. Probably, in those days of interminable sermonising, they were essential to allow a quiet shut-eye out of sight of the minister.

The church served those living on the south side of the Dee as well as a number from across the water, as there was a ford close by and even a record in the mid-1600s of a ferry "neir Glentaner Kirk".

In the history of the clan Farquharson there is mention of a bell being presented in 1729 to the kirk by William Farquharson of Tarland, a nephew of the Farquharson at that time in Tullycairn (presumably the present Tillycairn) and William's wife, Anne Gillenders of Cobblehaugh.

The inscription on the bell read, *Insiptio campana Glentaner campana temple de Glentaner Exdono Gvlielme Farquharson Anne Gillenders convigis sve 1729.*

In 1886 the Rev. John G Michie, minister of Dinnet, left an interesting tale. "Of old there was a fair or market held on the moor beside the old Church of Glentanar. It was called St Anne's Fair and was celebrated by a rhyme, the following couplet is all that is remembered.

St Anne's Fair amid the flowers,
When the sun shines full eighteen hours."

It seems St Anne's Fair was transferred to Banchory about the 1840s and died a natural death. At the fair a prize was awarded to the prettiest girl within the bounds. Hosts of competitors took part, but after a time it seemed that misfortune followed the winner and Banchory was made

Old GlenTanar Kirkyard PHOTO: ANNE BURGESS

most welcome to both the prize and the Fair. St Anne is recorded for posterity as being the mother of Mary and grandmother of Jesus.

The churchyard contains relatively few tombstones considering its longevity and none earlier than 1750. The practice of sculpting and inscribing monumental stones seen in early Celtic times fell into disuse through the Middle Ages in country parishes. After the 17th century small rude slabs bearing the initials of the dead began to be found in the churchyards of Upper Deeside.

A curious custom survived until relatively recent times with burials in the parish. Gravediggers rigidly refused to break ground on a Monday or Friday. The traditional reason given was, when the parish had been ravished by a savage plague an abatement was noticed on those two days of the week, so ever after they were to be left free from the association of death or burial.

When the church fell into disuse after about 1763, the Farquharson bell was melted down to become part of a new bell for the parish church of Aboyne. Regarding the Farquharsons, it was said that in 1746 Lewis Farquharson, the son of Tillycairn, and his seven sons were all killed at Culloden. In fact, only three sons died in the battle, as if that would have lessened the grief in the family.

The gravestones in the kirkyard make sad reading for us in an age where infant mortality is so negligible. Peter Begg of Braeloine buried six of his children, the youngest eleven months and the oldest fourteen years, all around the mid 1800s. Another son died aged twenty-seven, then his wife died at fifty-eight in 1862 and eventually Begg himself died in 1867, aged seventy-four.

Around ninety marked graves exist, many with multiple names inscribed. The earliest appears to be 1750 with the bulk in the 1800s, but quite a few through to the present. Apart from the very young, many died in their twenties and thirties and one wonders about tuberculosis as the cause, but an astonishing number reached their late eighties and even nineties. It seemed that if you could survive the early years of diphtheria, scarlet fever, measles and whooping cough and then somehow dodge through early youth, a long life could be ahead. Remembering that life was an unremitting struggle for so many, only the toughest made it through to retirement, a period in life we take for granted now with the state helping to finance our ageing years, but back then no such luxury beckoned.

While considering churchyards, we should turn to look at Cunliffe Brooks' private chapel of St Lesmo. The Chapel was built in 1872 close by the ruins of the old manor house of Braeloine and dedicated to a holy hermit who lived in Glen Tanar around 790 AD. Legend has it that this recluse lived in a cave near the Hermit's Well, and preached to the Glen people as well as travellers passing through. Pilgrimages are said to have continued to the well until the time of the Reformation. The site is uncertain; although there is an area just west of the Porphyry Bridge marked on old maps as Hermits Well, no one seems aware now of either a cave or a well in that vicinity.

Apparently, the old mansion house close by the site of the chapel was built from the remnants of an old fortification. It is said that the arched gateway, taken by Brooks and incorporated as the entrance for his chapel, still exhibits evidence that it was from the old fortification.

The chapel had a thatched roof and stained glass windows, with the external walls dotted with small pebbles known locally as cherry-cocking. In my youth the ceiling was bedecked with deer skulls and antlers from the stags shot by Brooks and guests on the estate, along with gilded stars with convex centres of silvered glass. In later years, Lord Thomas Glentanar enhanced the chapel with a huge stone from the Tanar as an altar and installed a very fine organ which he had inherited from his brother-in-

Chapel of St Lesmo

law the Duke of Wellington in 1936.

My own memories – apart from always being conscious, on entering, of the font in which I was baptised in 1929 – were the silver stars on the ceiling which I regularly counted to drown out yet another dreary sermon. Also the young mind was conscious that the seats for the ordinary worshippers were very hard and sparsely covered in deer skins, while the front rows for the laird and family had thick Dunlopillo-type cushions. So were the seeds sown of realising that not all men are equal, even in the worship of God.

Lord Glentanar later had the thatched roof replaced with slates and the stags heads and gilded stars also disappeared, but after my time. In 1979 the chapel was transferred into an endowed charitable trust, but is still registered as an independent Episcopal Chapel. Inter-denominational services are held there on occasions with the blessing of the Bishop of Aberdeen and Orkney.

In these changing times the chapel has become an essential part of the financial survival of the estate. Linked to Glentanar House ballroom for wedding receptions, it forms an impressive setting for those wishing a wedding of outstanding quality. I have thoughts of Cunliffe Brooks

Chapel entrance with arch from previous fortification on this site

turning in his grave at the entrance to the chapel at the thought of such commercialism in his beloved church, but changing times demand fresh ideas.

The little private graveyard has an atmosphere of tranquillity which I find comforting when I stop there on my walks. The erect Celtic stone at the chapel entrance heads the graves of Sir Cunliffe and Lady Brooks, emanating a feeling that even in death they are dominating their Glen Tana dream. The stone is a replica of the Loch Kinnord stone dating from Pictish times, around the 9th century AD, and is described as "a cross slab richly decorated with interlacing spiral knots and rings". The cross also features in one of the stained glass windows in the chapel. On the eastern aspect are the graves of Lord and Lady Glentanar, which along with their daughter Jean and one of her sons, Robert, take up the central portion. Around the fringes are the graves of those who spent years of service on the estate. Albert Garland who came to help my father in the 1930s and went on to be Lord Glentanar's valet for many years, is a well remembered figure, while close by is the headstone to Jimmy Oswald, late head-keeper and fount of so much information, who died September 7th 2006.

Two stones built into the perimeter wall bring echoes of the Menawee

Stones and the Haunted Stag, shot behind the Knockie by Brooks in 1877. The first stone is inscribed: *Sacred to the memory of DONALD MACKINTOSH deer stalker (none better) dep. this life 30th day of May 1876 & of MARGARET his wife who within a week was also buried here.* Beside it is a stone inscribed: *in memory of THERESA b. 8 April 1874 – d 19th of same month, dau. of DONALD MACKINTOSH & MARGARET BURTON his wife.*

It is said Brooks held Donald Macintosh in very high esteem, a feeling fully reciprocated by his stalker. They spent hours on the hill together over the years and agreed the survivor of the two would erect a special stone in the other's memory. A stag, which over the years kept evading them both on the ground behind the Knockie, became an obsession with Brooks and eventually he managed to shoot his haunted stag in 1877, at 267 yards. It is sad to note that his beloved stalker had died the year before this eventual kill, a fact that must have affected Brooks. The tall unmarked stone in the graveyard, set in front of the Macintosh's burial stone is without doubt Brooks keeping his part of the bargain.

The other sad event from the gravestone is the stalker's wife's death within a week of his own and we wonder as to the cause. As if all this is not disturbing enough, the next stone marks the death of their infant child just two years before her parents, suggesting they themselves must have been relatively young. In the Glentanar School records at this time it is noted on 2nd June that the four Macintosh children are absent on the death of their father and then on 9th June there is an entry regarding their mother's death; no children are yet back at school. Human suffering and tragedy is all part of life, but some would appear to have really drawn the short straw.

The postscript to the Haunted Stag tale is left to Jimmy Oswald. Having looked up the larder records of the stag, it turned out to be only a ten pointer. Jimmy was full of derision for anyone so obsessed over such a puny head, but also suspicious about anyone, back in 1877, able to shoot a stag at 267 yards with the black powder ammunition then in use. His typical rejoinder to me when telling this tale was, "That must really have been the unluckiest bloody stag on the whole of Deeside".

Now let us look at a church lying outside the present day Glen Tanar. Sir William Cunliffe Brooks not only owned the Glen Tanar estate, but was also involved in land across the Dee and over as far as the

Dinnet moor. Whether he actually owned it or was a tenant is not clear from records, but he installed some of his inscribed stones along the north bank of the Dee and in 1899 funded a new church in Dinnet itself. That was the year before he died and the architect involved is uncertain, although in 1905 that renowned Aberdeen architect George Bennett Mitchell was responsible for repairs to the fabric.

An internet reference tells of a mission church being first established in Dinnet in 1874 with "180 attachments and the minister's salary of £80 a year." In 1876 a bell was cast for the church. A gravestone in the Kirkyard of Aboyne, however, gives us the answer in that the Rev. James McKenzie was parish minister of Glen Tanar and Aboyne from 1861 until 1902. "During his incumbency and greatly owing to his strong interest and effort, the Church of Dinnet was erected and endowed and the parish formed."

In yet another churchyard, this time the Chapel on the Muir, a headstone to the Rev. John Grant Michie informs us that he was the "first minister of Dinnet from 1876 to 1904". The Rev. Michie, prior to entering the ministry, was schoolmaster at Logie Coldstone from 1853 to 1876 and has a number of publications to his credit, including *Loch Kinnord*, *History of Logie Coldstone* and *The Braes of Cromar*.

A postscript to the original Dinnet church is recorded in the log book of Glentanar School. On 9th April 1875 all the pupils were given a half day to attend the ceremony of laying the foundation stone for the new church. Further on it is noted that on 18th July 1876, Dinnet church was formally opened by the Rev. Dr Pirie – but no word this time of a holiday for the scholars.

That the Rev. John Michie was on good terms with Sir Cunliffe is shown in a letter dated 24th December 1895 on the derivation of the name 'Dinnet'. Just as Brooks insisted on spelling Tanar without its 'r', he appeared to be trying to get Michie to agree to the name 'Dunath' from the Gaelic *Dun n'ath* – the fort by the ford. Michie advised leaving well alone, as in English the name would be just mangled to 'Dunnath' and lose any Gaelic enunciation.

Cross the Dinnet bridge from the south side and on the left before you reach the old level crossing is the church that Brooks rebuilt in 1899. Now a private residence it has outwardly been sensitively converted, but its heritage will be retained forever. On two front pillars are the separate dates of the first church in 1875 on the right and the date 1881 on the left

Church pillar: WCB – 1899

when Dinnet became a *quoad-sacra* parish. That year established the parish as functioning for ecclesiastical purposes in its own right, a separate entity from Aboyne under whose jurisdiction it had previously existed. A pillar standing proudly on its own to the left of the church tells of its mentor in the unfailing Brooks' style.

My own memories of Dinnet church relate to its minister in the 1930s, the Rev. William Sawers. I have a lasting image of this worthy, dressed in black, trundling around the local roads visiting his parishioners in his ancient and very noisy Austin 10, as he never seemed able to get out of second gear. Dinnet is now combined in the Aboyne-Dinnet Parish

The Auld Kirk, Dinnet, built 1875 and rebuilt in 1899

Church, situated in Huntly Road, Aboyne, and highlights the gradual rationalisation of churches across the country, as not only congregations fall, but do those entering the clergy. All a far cry from the days of my youth when communion was held twice a year and all the locals dutifully flocked to the kirk. Whether evidence of true faith or fear of the consequences of appearing not to conform is hard to evaluate, but the latter is certainly no problem for the present generation.

Although the final church of Inchmarnoch is no more – the river Dee took care of it many generations ago – its story is well documented in the *Glen Tanar Estate Papers*. The derivation of the name Inchmarnoch is from the word 'Innis' meaning an island or flat land by the side of a river. 'Marnoch' in English or *Mearnag* in Gaelic refers to the Celtic saint who appears in placenames across Scotland. This would have been the Celtic church of the district of those far off times and so by extension the church haugh came to be the name for the whole district.

The church was situated near the island in the Dee which is a short distance above the mouth of the Inchmarnoch burn. Around 1910 an experienced ecclesiologist examined the island and found no trace of a church. Some years before, however, a local antiquary had found a small slab sculpted with a Celtic cross, first noticed in the water and close to the edge of the island. A gamekeeper even before this had come upon a baptismal font on the island, while ancient locals are recorded as seeing a large flat stone lying on the bank just below the road, a few hundred yards west of Tassachd Cottage, bearing a cross on its surface. This stone has since disappeared without trace. In 1829 following a great spate graves were exposed; later, around 1860, when some trenching work was being carried out in the west angle of the field, more graves were uncovered, while there have been vague stories of human bones being washed up below the island.

Dating the destruction of the church has proved very difficult, but it probably occurred between the 15th and 16th centuries. It appears that a large spate had broken through the projecting haugh of land from the main channel, so probably sweeping away the church and establishing an island which has remained ever since. From the finding of the artefacts experts judge that the church was situated nearer the island than the present south bank, but this is all really conjecture.

The site can be approached across the field from the roadside houses which make up the present Inchmarnoch. The island appears of considerable size, but to the present day viewer it is difficult to visualise the church setting. There is still a record, however, that the church bell was hung on a tree just outside the entrance and that the track west of Tassachd Cottage was called Bell Brae. No sign of this remains, but Colin Espie who ghillies this water drew my attention to the fact that a very small pool just about this spot is called the Bell Pool. All very interesting.

In the mid-19th century annual games were still being held in Inchmarnoch along with other non-specified festivities, but whether they originated from old church times is uncertain. The records regarding this church are scanty but it is still an interesting memory from the past.

8

THE MOUNT KEEN ENVIRONMENT

There, tow'ring Keen o'er looks the tenfold cloud,
And shoots its conic head into the sky,
While sable mists its sloping sides enshroud,
And half way hide it from the wond'ring eye

The Tanar rises on Hare Cairn at an altitude of about 2,250 feet, about two miles west of Mount Keen. It then flows in a north-east direction for about twelve miles to join the river Dee a mile south-west of Aboyne. Its main tributaries are the rivers Allachy and Gairney which rise on the Forfarshire march to the east of Mount Keen and drain the northern sides of Braid Cairn (2,907 feet), Cock Cairn (2,387 feet) and Hill of Cat (2,435 feet).

A Mount Keen vista from above Etnach. PHOTO ALAN FINDLAY

The word 'tanner' or 'tanar' is variously spelt, but appears to have no descriptive meaning. My original understanding was that it came from the compounded words *glean-tan-ar* from the Gaelic, signifying 'the glen of scanty arable land'. However others maintain that it is the word *tana* from the Gaelic meaning 'shallow'. To me a glen of shallow water sounds less authentic and I much prefer the first explanation.

Mount Keen at 3,077 feet is an outstanding hill, both for its shape and its dominant setting. I can never think of it as a mountain despite its name and reserve that description for the likes of Lochnagar. The most easterly Munro in the district, Mount Keen stands out like a beacon from so many directions and over great distances. I have climbed it frequently and often waved my white flag vigorously around its borders as a gallant young grouse beater in the days when the bag could easily exceed two hundred

Mount Keen in early spring from the Rumblin Brig PHOTO:ALAN FINDLAY

brace. I was once briefly chased by a rutting stag near the top, but my lack of antlers stopped him pursuing me very far.

More famous people have also graced its slopes and Ian R. Mitchell in *On the Trail of Queen Victoria in the Highlands* identifies the first recorded climber as John Taylor, the Water Poet, in 1618. Taylor set out to impress the new James I of England by travelling through Scotland, depending on native hospitality. Reaching Glen Esk he climbed the hill, describing it as an "exceeding high mountaine called mount Skeene" caught in a "Scottish miste".

Queen Victoria, accompanied by Prince Albert and her entourage on 20th September 1861, came across the hills from Glen Muick on one of her "big trips". Her Majesty seems to have been quite impressed with the mountain. "Mount Keen is a curious, conical shaped hill, with a deep corrie in it. It is nearly 3,200 feet high, and we had a very steep rough ascent over the shoulder, after crossing the Tanar Water."

Ian Mitchell also adds to our flavour of times gone by, with his reference to the old Scots ballad, *The Baron o' Brackley*. The Glen Tanar involvement makes it worth browsing through this long ballad to get a sense of those scary times. The Farquharsons of Inverey were in a recurring feud with the Gordons of the Huntly lands and in this ballad young

Inverey and his band seem intent on murder rather than the usual plunder of cattle. The fight was three against thirty-three, so the outcome was inevitable, but Peggy Gordon's reaction to the murder of her husband by entertaining her husband's killer overnight scandalised the district. Many versions exist, but this one seems most relevant to Etnach and Glen Tanar, so sense the drama, cruelty and muddled relationships of the age.

Doon Deeside cam Inverey whistling and playing,
He was at brave Brackleys yet ere it was dawin,
He rappit fu loudly and wi a great roar,
Cried, cum doun, cum doun Brackley and open the door
Gin I had a husband whereas I hae nane,
He would nae ly in his bed and see his ky taen.
Ther's four-and-twenty milk-whit calves twll o them ky,
In the woods o Glentanner, it's ther thei a' ly,
Ther's goat i the Etnach and sheep o the brae
    and a will be plundered by young Inverey.

Now haud your tongue Peggy and tak care o' our son,
Ye'll see me gang oot but I'll never come in
At the head o the Etnach the battle began,
At little Auchoilzie thei killed their first man,
First they killed ane, and soon they killed twa.
They killed gallant Brackley, the flour o' them a.
She kept him till morning syne bad him be gane,
And showd him the road that he would na be tane,
"Thro Birse and Aboyne" she says, "lying in a tour
    oer the hills o Glentanar you'll skip in an hour".

Inverey is way up beyond Braemar, while Brackley or Braickley House, now the modern House of Glenmuick, is just across the hill from Etnach, in lower Glen Muick. John Gordon was obviously renting pasture in Glen Tanar at the time, which explains why the skirmish was above there. Little Auchoilzie is further up the Muick so was it a running battle or is poetic licence at work? History, according to James Mitchell, tells us that young Inverey, John Farquharson, also known as the Black Colonel, disappeared after Brackley's murder in 1666, but reappeared as a Colonel in Viscount Dundee's Jacobite Rising of 1689. He was forced once more into hiding in Glen Ey, at a place known as the Colonel's Bed, but eventually died

The Quartz Cliff seen from Glen Muick with tip of Mount Keen in the background

peacefully in his own bed in the year 1698.

Before leaving the upper reaches of the river let us tramp the mile from the end of the carriage road at Coirevrauch out west to where the Tanar and the Ault Deas burn meet at what is called the Linn of Tanar. Following up the Ault Deas in a southerly direction for the best part of a steep mile you come suddenly upon the Quartz Cliff which in places is 300 feet of sheer rock. In some records it is listed as the 'slate quarry', but this is a misnomer. The cliff is formed of pure white quartz embedded in which may be observed specimens of crystal. It is said that manganese in some quantity is to be found by the Ault Deas burn.

You will probably be greeted here by a pair of peregrine falcons who will leave you in no doubt as to what they think of your presence in their domain. In the past golden eagles used to nest, but their eyrie was too easily accessible to human marauders and none have returned there, as far as I know, since my childhood. As youngsters, driven by our egg collecting obsession, we used to come to this cliff with various bits of rope.

Coming back down to the end of the road at Coirevrauch, the chalet that existed in my youth is no more. Lord Glentanar and his family often used it as a weekend retreat, but I believe it was burnt down by intrusive

Mount Keen as seen from the ruins of the old drover's inn

hikers. Walking a short distance down the road, on your right is a wide expanse of green pasture with a jumble of stones at its far end. This was the site of the drover's inn and the area of pasture would have been partially used for the temporary accommodation of the drover's cattle in the early 1800s. Drovers bought cattle from farmers way up north and when they had accumulated a goodly herd brought them south along the well worn drove roads of Speyside, Donside and Deeside on their way to the markets of the south. It is recorded that many drove their cattle into England in times of high prices. They were a hardy breed of men who not only had to be physically fit, but also knowledgeable about their cattle's worth and prepared to fend off thieves along the way. They had stopping off points like Glen Tanar, but had at times no option but to wrap themselves in their plaids and bed down out in the wilderness.

The drove road from Ballater to Glen Tanar and then over the shoulder of Mount Keen into Glen Mark was one of the major routes of old. It takes little imagination to stand by the new metal and wood bridge across the Tanar, just beyond the ruins of the inn, and imagine the approaching noise of lowing cattle and the shouting of the herdsmen as they hove into sight, coming around the hillside above Etnach. This area around Coirevrauch and Etnach has probably been the site of men striving to

Etnach, the loneliest modern day outpost on Glen Tanar

make a living from at least Pictish times. Evidence of old dykes, quite distinctive from the dykes of later generations, still exist.

Over the ages this small area of upper Tanarside would have supported a number of families making a living from the scanty agriculture and helping move cattle to the sheilings for summer grazing. Cattle, sheep and goats were brought over the hills from the farms bordering the Dee into the sheilings of such as Glen Dui, and here in roughly built shelters with turf roofing, workers lived throughout the summer months, watching over the herds and flocks and making butter and cheese.

Cattle rustlers were prevalent and the isolated sheilings were particularly exposed, thus an event of notoriety relating to the Etnach district is the last recorded raid by the cateran. Cateran from the Gaelic *ceatharn* – troop of fighting men – were to all intents and purposes cattle rustlers. However, clan feuding could also lead to petty tit for tat thieving rather than frank professional rustling. The story is told that around 1725 a young girl of sixteen was at the lower sheiling of Glen Dui near Etnach attending to her dairy duties when the cateran appeared. With no one else around the raiders drove off all the Candycraig sheep and cattle, taking the girl with them. Some distance away they released her, giving her some trifling amount of money. Running off home she raised the alarm and a vigorous pursuit was organised. According to tradition the raiders were overtaken and the cattle and sheep all retrieved.

The main centre for the cateran was Lochaber. They travelled great distances to carry out their plunder and their intimate knowledge of the districts far from their home was uncanny. Also, often shielded by certain clan chiefs, they knew where to find a safe haven when hotly pursued. Two well-known cateran were Patrick, called Gilderoy, and his brother Robert McGregor, who were said to have used the Glen Tanar forest to

Shepherd's Hut in the 1920s with the Dowager Lady Glentanar third from left.

hide in at times. Gilderoy's career ended in 1636 on a gibbet in Edinburgh.

Peat was cut and transported down the Glen and there was some quarrying of stone. In the hey day of the illicit distilling of whisky, grain for malting was harvested, and poaching was looked on as no more than nature providing the necessities of life. The surreptitious acquiring of a choice piece of venison or hare from the hill and the odd grouse was a bonus, while the occasional salmon was never missed by the laird. The ever likely call to arms would have been an unsettling factor in their lives, while the winters would often cut them off from all contact with the lower glen. The droving years at least brought some extra revenue and the gossip of the herdsmen, itinerant workers and travellers of all persuasions on this busy route kept them abreast of life in the outside world.

Red letter day for a little boy: Shepherd's Hut 1934

Coming down the road from the drover's inn we first pass over the Rumblin Brig built by Cunliffe Brooks in 1873 and some quarter of a mile further we cross the Etnach bridge, also built by Brooks in the same year. Standing on this bridge we look northwards to the gamekeeper's house of

Glorious vista looking down the valley behind my son Peter, with the Shepherd's Hut to the left and Etnach set among the trees below.

my youth, now a holiday home, and then above it we espy the Shepherd's Hut set among pasture.

Not any shepherd's hut, mind you, but the one and only of my youth. Used by the estate through the last century as a shooting bothy, it has hosted hundreds of the nobility coming to shoot grouse in August and September. My lasting memory is of my mother and myself taken to the foot of the hut road in the estate bus carrying the beaters and dropped off to hide in the heather. After the guns had lunched my father would stand at the bothy door and wave a white towel to let us know to walk up and partake of all that had been left over. *Paté de foie gras* and cold grouse washed down with bottles of delicious ginger beer seemed like paradise to a four-year-old, and this was repeated over a number of years.

Walking on we leave behind the open country and come to the wooded part of the glen where some remnants of the old Caledonian forest still exist. There among the smaller trees, a couple of hundred yards on the left, just above the road, is an old survivor called the Admiral's Tree. The story is told that before the forest extended this far, this tree stood alone and was used by an old retired admiral to spy out the hillside for deer when he was out stalking. This must go back to the Brooks' era, as I was unaware of the story in my youth and believe it was a Jimmy Oswald tale, probably told to him by the late Lord Glentanar who seemed to cherish the tree as a historical memory.

A few hundred yards further is where I feel the environment of Mount Keen should stop. The Half Way Hut has been a milestone in my life in the valley and probably in the lives of hundreds of others for decades before that. Used as a stopping off point for shooters in the past, stalkers bringing their quarry off the hill and now as a shelter for hikers and cyclists, it is a cosy little haven, especially on a cold rainy day when a dram seems fully justified.

Queen Victoria, as she completed her big trip of 1861, came back this way via Fettercairn, over the Cairn o Mount to Finzean, Aboyne and back up the Glen. Probably stopping here at the Half Way Hut for lunch, she described it as "very pretty" but had her day spoilt when she encountered at Etnach "a wretched idiot girl – sat on the ground with her hands round her knees, rocking herself to and fro, and laughing". General Grey came to the Queen's rescue by getting between the two of them until an old man appeared to take the girl away. Really quite a sad little tale, but highlighting so well the extremes of life from the sheltered privileged few down to those living a barren existence.

To end this chapter on a far happier note is *The Perfect Picnic* as told by Isabella Wilson, late mother of Lindy Cheyne, editor of our north-east

A brake with horses and a coachman off to Glen Tanar

magazine, *Leopard*. From a private publication, Mrs Wilson recalls her early childhood, some time before World War I, and her picnics to the Forest of Birse and Glen Tanar. Hiring a brake with horses and a coachman, her parents, grandparents and friends would set off for Etnach in Glen Tanar. Her dad and grandad took their fiddles and everyone sang and listened to their music, while sorting out a huge hamper of food. Gathering wood, they would light a fire to boil their kettles with water from the burn. Her dad had a great interest in the golden eagle and would tell them about the time he had scrambled up to get a view of the young eaglets in their eyrie on 'Mount Etnach'. This was interesting for me as this could have only occurred on the Quartz Cliff as previously described.

Then on the way home in the evening, Mrs Wilson recalled, "I can still hear the echo of the cornet through the woods on a summer evening and Dad playing, *When You Come to the End of a Perfect Day.*

Yes indeed, a perfect echo.

9

A GAMEKEEPER'S YEAR

The year is 1877 and Mr William Cunliffe Brooks (WCB), not yet a baronet, has been the tenant of Glen Tanar estate for some six years. In that time he has stamped his authority over all those around him, but is viewed as a caring generous man as long as you live up to his high standards.

Nowhere is his authority more obvious than in the game larder where ten members of staff know exactly what every day is to bring. James Murray is the head keeper, with John Milne next in seniority. Milne is an old hand after years of service going back long before the coming of Brooks. Seven others will be keepers with varying years of experience, and a definite order of seniority, defining their level of duties throughout the year. Three may well be unmarried and living in the kennel's bothy, providing for themselves. The tenth member is the pony man, John Gill, whose work involves all the fetching and carrying; from bringing in the deer carcases and shot grouse from the hill, to all the odd jobs necessary to keep the larder team supplied with equipment.

No word of a kennel boy, but as his job is full-time, looking after the dogs to see that they are adequately fed and their living quarters clean, there is no need for him to appear on a roster. Watched over by the head-keeper, and with Brooks often in the vicinity, he will only be kept on if he shows keenness, and perhaps the promise of becoming a competent stalker or ghillie.

The pristine kennels in the time of Brooks had electric light and central heating installed, while some of the workers' houses were to wait until after World War II for electricity and indoor toilets. Dogs formed an integral part of the shooting scene, with pointers and setters to pin-point birds, when walking up game. Deerhounds were kept to bring down wounded deer or put them at bay, until a stalker arrived to despatch them. Flat and rough-coated retrievers were kept to bring in shot game when walking up or when driving birds to standing guns.

From the game larder book for that year we get an intimate insight into the lives of these men and their routines according to the season. The bland single-word entry for their individual daily duties is interspersed with just the hint of their separate lives away from the daily grind.

January is usually a bleak month in Upper Deeside and so it proved in 1877. At first most were involved in shooting rabbits in the forest, but on 8th January the snows arrived to stop everything. Casting snow all around the estate went on for four days, then clearing the snow around the deer fence continued as a priority.

The deer fence was of the utmost importance, built with the specific purpose of keeping deer on the estate. Jumping banks were also built, the fence cleverly sited along the contours of the terrain within the estate boundary, so that deer could leap into the estate but not out.

There is no record of whether other estates thought that this was unethical behaviour, not that it would have probably bothered Brooks one iota. That snow piling up against the fence on the Glen Tanar side could allow deer to escape was, however, totally unacceptable to Brooks. Keepers must have dreaded the sight of snowflakes and the prospect of hours of thankless, back-breaking work for the sake of a couple of lost stags. By mid-January all keepers were involved for four days shooting white hares, followed by rabbiting for the rest of the month.

The feeding of game is regularly mentioned and probably relates to feeding pheasants and partridges on the low ground overlooking the Dee On 24th January, and for the next four days, a number of the keepers are attending to "Gentlemen" shooting partridges around the Tillycairn district. On 29th January three keepers are out with guests shooting hinds, but the snows return next day to get everyone back to their shovels. Making cartridges is another job for a rainy or snowy day, along with the making of snares in the larder.

February is ushered in with WC Brooks out with a party shooting partridge and most keepers seem so involved except for two, still casting snow out at the deer fence. The next days see rabbiting high on the agenda all around the estate, except for the odd keeper cutting branches around Belrorie. On the 10th comes our first glimpse of personal matters as Moses is entered as away seeing his mother. The 12th heralds the first entry about the salmon season with two or three away every day to the river. The head keeper is now regularly in attendance to the laird on the river bank, with many others also involved throughout this month. On the 28th John Milne is out looking for foxes and others are setting vermin traps, while Moses is off work with a bad arm. It would appear that foxes are rated separately from vermin. Ground vermin consisted of stoats, weasels, martins, polecats, hedgehogs, rats and cats and the gin trap was the main method of trapping.

March sees the fishing gaining in priority with WCB active day after day, attended by Murray. The chores around the game larder and the kennels keep recurring, indicating that keepering is not always about being out in the wilds. Rabbits must be in profusion as scarcely a day goes by without someone pursuing them, while setting vermin traps is also high on the list of priorities at this time. Suddenly on 20th March heather burning becomes all consuming. Five or six keepers are out for the next five days, burning those controlled strips that give our hills their characteristic patchwork appearance. The 15th April is the statutory date to stop burning nowadays, but whether in Brooks' time is not clear. On the 30th, Power is at home "putting right his hens" while some of the others are back at the heather burning.

April starts off with three days of heather burning involving the whole squad apart from Stephen who is "attending on a gentleman fishing". Then on the fifth appears an odd entry, recurring quite often: "pulling heather at Dee". This is a puzzling entry as pulling heather is extremely hard work, so the heather must have been for a purpose. Thatching comes to mind; heather has been used decoratively, but not in this quantity.

Eoin Smith points out that as a head keeper, concerned at keeping so many men employed, they could have been clearing away heather along the banks of the river, rather than burning it. Later entries appear to have them pulling heather on the hill, making one wonder if they were stopping the heather from further encroaching on pasture land at the sheilings, but this would be a laborious way to keep it in check. Records show that heather had been used for thatching the Glen Tanar churches, so this is its most probable use. Setting mole traps also appears in the records at this time; a task appearing to fall within the job description of keepers in those days.

WCB still seems intent on clearing the Dee of salmon as Murray has to be with him day after day. On the 9th, however, Murray gets respite from the river and is involved in "breaking dogs", while Power is delegated to attend WCB. Stephen is off work unwell on the 10th and 11th, but is

Target practice

back ghillieing on the 12th. Poor old Murray gets little peace as he is back with WCB from the 13th until the 18th. On the 19th and 20th he is then listed as "at home", probably exhausted from gaffing fish, although Eoin Smith points out that salmon catches in those years were relatively small compared to the later years with much improved tackle.

On the 21st Grant is entered as "target shooting" and on the 28th he is "putting water off Forest Road". This relates to the regular flooding of these hill roads, until over the years more drainage ducts were installed.

May comes in with the salmon still dominating the work load, but seeking out foxes and attending vermin traps are also priorities. On the 18th Milne gets a break, going off to William Thomson's sale, while on the 19th Grant gets in some more target practice. Murray is back fishing with WCB, but suddenly is off "at home" again on the 23rd, 24th and 25th and you sense all is not well here; he is at home again on the 30th and 31st.

A new month and the human tragedy is revealed. June 1st and Murray's entry reads, "At home. Mrs Murray died at 7.30 am". At this distance, a hundred-and-thirty-two years later, you can feel the deep sadness having followed this head keeper so closely from the beginning of the year. Around him the work goes on as normal, but everyone must have been deeply affected by this loss in their midst. On the 4th, Murray's entry is simple, "at the Wife's funeral"; four others are listed as at the funeral, while the rest are fishing. James Murray himself is back fishing by the 6th and life just goes on.

Odd entries turn up from time to time, such as on the 9th when Milne is "making his turnips," presumably hoeing them, while on the 11th all but two of the squad are "pulling heather" again. Power is cutting peats on 12th, while Milne is also there on 13th; Thomson is entered as "getting his turnips made". On June 15th John Gill, the pony-man gets away from it all to go to a wedding. Pulling heather again rears up in importance over three days from the 18th, with three keepers involved; looking for foxes, checking the deer fence and the sheep fence all take up time. On 23rd both Milne and Duncan are listed as in the forest after crows, while on 25th Thomson is back at the peat moss. Murray is off work on 25th and 26th with a cold, coming back on 27th, but off again on 28th and 29th.

Entries regarding salmon fishing begin to decrease in July and an entry "out with dogs" begins to appear. On 4th July, Milne and Duncan are out "in the forest taking down hawks" while on 6th Murray and Duncan are "hunting dogs back of Menawee". On 10th Murray is in the "forest breaking dogs", on 11th "breaking young dogs" and on 12th "hunting dogs in forest". The head keeper continues breaking dogs, but on 18th is entered as "not well" and rather worryingly is off until 28th, having returned on 26th but felt unfit to continue. While he was off others take on the task of breaking in the dogs and hunting with them in the forest. On 28th Grant was target shooting while Thompson was at Aboyne, rifle shooting. Others were involved in cutting thistles in the Kennel Park.

A regular entry throughout the year is to get "rabbits for the House". I well understand this entry and can still see the long dining table in the servant's hall of Glentanar House. Crammed with servants, with the butler at the top, at the other end the hall boy is whispering to the bonny still-room maid, "Not blooming rabbit again".

August dawns with Murray and Duncan up the Gairney with young dogs and again on 2nd in the Fir Bog, hunting with dogs. Power was hunting the Black Burn with dogs while Duncan was doing the same in the Allachy. On 3rd and 4th two keepers are "cutting grass Glenduie"; on 6th, three keepers are "pulling tansies in the Forest" and on 7th two are "pulling tansies down the Glen". To cut tansies is said to be a waste of time, as only getting them out by the roots stops them flourishing and spoiling the pasture. Killing rabbits still involves many keepers' time while on 11th both Grant and Thomsom are "at Banchory at drill". Could this be some sort of TA of the time?

On 13th August the roster book takes on a different appearance, both in handwriting and content. The names of WCB's guests are now included; an Admiral Farquhar is out with Power hunting with dogs, and Lord Francis Cecil is out with Duncan and Grant at the grouse. Murray is in attendance to WCB and Charlie Milne, a new name, is entered as loader to the laird. John Gill is following WCB with the pony. Walking up grouse goes on intermittently throughout the month with Lord Francis Cecil and Admiral Farquhar as regular guests. On 25th the deer stalking season appears to begin with two keepers out with guests. WCB is stalking on 27th, 28th and 29th and Lord Cecil, having had his fill of the grouse, changes sport and also stalks on 28th and 29th. Charlie Milne on 28th is noted as "out with Stag Hounds" and on 29th is "leading Stag Hounds for WCB".

September has deer stalking in full swing and here we begin to sense the enthusiasm that Brooks has for this sport. For eight consecutive days from 3rd, WCB is recorded out stalking with Murray, with at least one other keeper in attendance. Among a number of other named guests at this time we find Lord Francis Cecil out almost as often as his host and you begin to wonder at the relationship between the two men, resulting in such generous hospitality. Only later do we find that Lord Cecil is Cunliffe Brooks' son-in-law.

All activity stops, however, on 12th September – the day of the Aboyne Games – with only Stephen noted as working, "gathering cranberries". The 13th sees Lord Cecil back on the hill and along with WCB is out again on 17th. From there to the end of September Brooks stalks for ten days and Cecil for nine. Little wonder the Glentanar House ballroom ceiling is enveloped with antlers, the overflow being used in the chapel of St Lesmo. Brooks at this time was not a young man being fifty- eight years old, but must have been very fit to endure the daily strain of stalking the hills in wind, rain and shine.

October has come, but Brooks' obsession for stalking deer continues. Eight days by 12th of the month, he shows no sign of exhaustion, while around him at least two other guests are out daily to swell the bag. The little things in life seem forgotten, but on 8th, Stephen is allowed off "to shift his father".

On October 9th comes the day of days for our local laird. Over two seasons he has failed to get a shot at a large stag on Duchery Beg, behind the Knockie in the hollow known as the Menawee. Time and again the fates have intervened before he has pressed the trigger. The wind has veered, the mist has swirled in, or the beast has just been bloody minded and strolled away behind the nearest hillock or into the wood. At last, however, on this fateful day the quarry stays just too long and at 267 yards Brooks eventually kills his 'Haunted Stag'. James Murray sounds fairly phlegmatic about it all, "stalking for WCB and killed the Big Stag". Brooks must have been ecstatic, as the following day he sends Grant out to start building a cairn, just where the stag fell.

Today, two pyramid cairns with large circular stones on top, known as the Menawee Stones, mark the spots where Brooks lay and to the south and uphill where the stag met his destiny. The bases are now tending to subside and tilt ominously, while the carvings on the stone balls are so weathered as to be hard to decipher.

In the year of 1778 there is an entry for 16th July: Grant repairing the well of Menawee. Did Brooks also erect a well in this area? If he did, there is no evidence of it now.

Admiral Farquhar is now stalking and one wonders if this is the admiral referred at the Admiral's Tree beyond the Half Way Hut, which was used to espy the deer across the valley. On 15th October five keepers are involved in bringing a large stone down out of the forest. This tall standing stone set up in St Lesmo's churchyard is in memory of WCB's favourite stalker, Donald Mackintosh, who had died the year before. Did Brooks suddenly remember his promise to his stalker about erecting such a stone after he himself had shot the Haunted Stag that had evaded them both so many times?

Little entries of no seeming importance are still worth recording. On October 19th John Milne is away getting birches for planting at Glen Tanar and on 29th six keepers are involved in "holing birches", which presumably means digging them up to transplant, but unfortunately there is no mention of their replanting or the site. On another occasion a keeper is planting juniper. A multitude of other little jobs are recorded such as removing branches from the Tanar, poisoning rats, draining footpaths, gathering cones, picking blaeberries and juniper berries. Reference is made to "watching around their beats", as if poachers may be suspected.

Strangely, for those of us brought up in this environment, only one reference is made to ferreting, with the keeper out the next day looking for his lost ferret. Eoin Smith points out that dogs and ferrets belonged to the estate and not to the individual keeper, so losing a ferret was a serious loss of your employer's property. Was ferreting perhaps included under "rabbiting" which, in my early years, was part and parcel of a keeper's life? John Gill the pony-man is forever carting sand, wood, posts, coal and peat, or working on the sheep and deer fences. WCB seems to keep him and his pony, frequently in attendance, often retrieving his master's carcases from almost inaccessible spots.

Of interest to ornithologists would be the fact that the ledger entries are non-specific. Destroying crows' nests never distinguished between carrion and hooded crows. Similarly with hawks, no separate species was ever specified.

Ingram was noted in May as "at Slate Quarry looking for Hawks' Nests". These were presumably peregrine falcons, whereas reference to knocking down hawks' nests in the forest would relate to buzzards and sparrowhawks. It is surprising that such knowledgeable men would ignore these differences and list them all under the broad title of raptor or vermin.

For such a heather clad estate it is difficult to find any clear indication of the regular shooting of driven grouse, which in later years was high on the agenda throughout August and September. Only two days, 17th and 23rd October, are specified as "driving grouse" and no reference is made to making or repairing butts throughout the year. All the snippets seem to indicate walked up grouse with various gentlemen guests. Twice in November and four times in December, the last on 10th, were four keepers noted as out grouse shooting, but there is no reference to them driving the birds to standing guns in butts. It begins to dawn on one that Brooks was not hugely enthusiastic about his grouse and would perhaps rather spend his days among the deer in his beloved forest, or in season, casting a fly over salmon.

Here again I turn to Eoin Smith and learn that driving grouse back in those days was seen by the upper class as relatively unsporting. From around 1870 onwards, however, estates started to build butts and gradually the pendulum swung to driven grouse being the more desirable sport. In Glen Tanar there is still evidence of some of these early butts from Brooks' era, constructed by stone masons using semi-dressed stone, with a projecting stone ledge inside for the gentleman to sit on. In late season, grouse tend to become very wild and fly off before the guns can get within range. To overcome this, artificial kites were used as a ruse. Flown over a moor, the grouse would crouch down fearing a raptor, allowing the guns to approach much closer before being flushed. Eoin Smith still remembers seeing a couple of these kites in the Game Department, from those far off days.

James Murray, along with Duncan, shot grouse in the forest on 3rd November and it was sadly to be the last time for one of them. Murray was off work on 5th, 6th and 7th November with no reason given, but departed on the 8th with Mr Brooks to shoot at Springkele. Ominously there are no entries for Murray after that until out of the blue on 30th, Power writes in the ledger, "inviting friends to Murray's funeral". Next day, 1st December, the entries have all personnel attending the funeral, except John Milne who is "at home". Milne continues at home until 5th December when the entry is "at his mother's burial" with all keepers present. Reading these entries brings home poignantly the highs and lows of life; for some the pursuit of pleasure, while for others – adversity. James Murray loses his wife and then follows her only months later. John Milne loses his mother, then goes on to lose his own life in the Allachy in 1882; shot dead at ten yards by a careless guest gun.

Life only pauses for an instant and then resumes its inexorable progress. WCB himself is in no hurry to appoint a new head-keeper, as looking into the next year no replacement has appeared by July. "Rabbiting" never ceases and before we know it Christmas day 1877 has arrived. Not a holiday in Scotland, but we find three gamekeepers "keeping Christmas" and wonder whether the Brooks English influence is encouraging such an attitude. John Gill the ponyman is certainly not getting any peace, as he is still "taking home hinds". The last day of the year sees the deer larder being thoroughly washed and cleaned out, while with the dawning of 1st January 1878 and with no obvious holiday for estate employees, what do we find all our keepers involved in yet again? Shooting rabbits of course.

10

To Culloden and Beyond

L ife in our Highland glen from the 1600s through the 1700s must have been very frugal, with much hard work and little time for noticing the world around. In this modern age, with so much TV, quality newspapers and the internet, there is no excuse for not being aware of the forces moulding our lives. Many of our young people seem blissfully unaware of even recent past events, however, so what must it have been like for tenants, subtenants and the lowly labourer of yesteryear? Travel to Aboyne would have been a big day out, so events in the pomp and glitter of the Paris and London royal courts would have seemed of no relevance in their little world. Yet before long, power politics in far away places were about to affect so many lives.

With James II (VII of Scotland) fleeing to France in 1688, Viscount Dundee deserted the Scottish Parliament when it appeared it would accept William of Orange as successor to the national throne. Proceeding north Bonnie Dundee raised an army and had a stunning victory at the Battle of Killiecrankie in 1689, but was mortally wounded. Now leaderless, the revolt petered out. Parliament viewed all territory north of the Tay as disaffected and so took preventive action by seizing places of strength. Aboyne Castle was occupied, but the Earl of Aboyne, only eighteen years old was still abroad at a Roman Catholic college. In the absence of the Earl and watched over by the Government garrison and a local laird, the Master of Forbes, few in the district would have become involved with those early Jacobites.

Nevertheless, the district suffered damage and maltreatment from the occupying forces. From the Aboyne factor's accounts, woods appear to have been burnt and the garrison looted foodstuffs. Some houses, as well as crops, were set on fire. General Mackay, the leader appointed by the Convention – the Scottish Parliament – and later by the new king William, caused devastation in Glen Gairn. As late as 1722 it was said the glen had not recovered and was still lying uncultivated "since the burning".

Commander-in-Chef General Mackay was later to write his memoirs, but in a private report to the Secretary of State he wrote: "I burnt 12 miles of a very fertile Highland country, at least twelve to fourteen hundred houses, but had no time to go up to Braymar". He continued, "I am a great believer in fire and sword."

The Jacobite period in Scottish history is dreadfully contorted and its culmination in the disaster of Culloden saw the end of the clan system. The term Jacobitism is defined as the political movement dedicated to the restoration of the Stuart kings to the throne of England, Scotland and Ireland. It was a response to the deposition of James II in 1688, when he was replaced by his daughter Mary II, jointly with her husband and first cousin, William of Orange. The Stuarts lived on the mainland of Europe after that, occasionally attempting to regain the throne with the help of the French and Spanish. Ireland, and especially Deeside in the Scottish Highlands, remained sympathetic to the Jacobite cause during this period.

The in-fighting between the various clans also caused friction with the Presbyterian Campbells, Munros, Macleods and the Macdonalds of Sleat opposing such as the Huntlys and Farquharsons in Deeside who were still staunchly Catholic. There is little doubt that personal advancement or benefit to the clan influenced many chiefs throughout these turbulent times.

In 1701 the Act of Settlement stated that any future monarch had to be a Protestant, so banishing any further hopes of a Catholic Stuart as monarch. In 1702 William of Orange died and the throne passed to Anne, the last of James IIs children and she ruled until 1714 when she was succeeded by her second cousin the Elector of Hanover – George I. The Act of Union in 1704 bound Scotland firmly to England, despite many Scots being unhappy at the outcome.

After years of famine and hardship, Scotland was fertile ground for rebellion and this led to what is known as the 'first Jacobite rising' in 1715. The Earl of Mar, an Episcopalian, with his traditional seat at Kildrummy Castle in Upper Donside, had been a strong Hanoverian and attained the office of Secretary of State for Scotland in 1713. However he suddenly changed sides when the so-called James III called on him to raise the clans, so becoming known as 'Bobbin' John'. It was said Mar rushed from London to Braemar and summoned the clans to a "grand hunting match" on 27th August 1715, when he renounced his oath of allegiance.

George M. Fraser in the *Deeside Field* of 1924 discusses whether the second meeting of the chiefs on 3rd September 1715 took place in the relative privacy of Glen Tanar. Certainly many local writers from that time have suggested the Glen as the rendezvous, but Fraser is far from certain. What he does accept is that the Earl of Mar was at Aboyne Castle on that date, so whether the meeting occurred at the castle or somewhere up the Tanar valley is now never likely to be ascertained.

Diack in his *Estate Papers* spends some time looking into the local scene, pointing out that the rising of 1715 was intimately associated with Deeside. The situation in Aboyne was that the Earl had succeeded in 1702, but was still underage. One of his guardians was Patrick Lyon, the Laird of Auchterhouse and son of the Earl of Strathmore, and the young earl's mother, the dowager Countess of Aboyne, was Lyon's sister. As a Jacobite zealot Auchterhouse vigorously raised forces in the district, but was killed at the battle of Sheriffmuir in 1715.

It is difficult to ascertain how many men were 'out' in the rising from Aboyne and Glen Tanar, but various documents suggest it was a considerable number. The district was generally sympathetic to the Jacobite cause, so making recruitment that much easier. The vassals of the Earl of Aboyne, like those in other Highland districts, were required by the terms of their charter to attend the Lord's hostings – that is to give military service providing it is not against the King. In this case, according to Jacobite contention, this service was precisely for the King.

The years had eroded some of this unthinking loyalty and so feudal service to the Superior did not necessarily meet with unanimous obedience. Some were totally loyal, while others had to be gently coaxed. Some who were craftier than the rest, sat back and waited for the heavy hand of authority to demand their adherence. Then, if things went wrong, they could plead they had been coerced to fight and were really victims themselves.

Government evidence following the uprising showed that Auchterhouse and the young Earl of Aboyne sent out directives to the tenants and vassals to meet at a named rendezvous. Only five or six did not comply with the call to arms and were punished.

There is no accurate account of the local contingent from the Aboyne area. Most of the Farquharsons of Braemar were in the army under Brigadier MacIntosh and came to grief at Preston. Charles Garden of Bellastreen was taken prisoner at Sheriffmuir, which indicates that Glen

Tanar men were there with Mar himself, along with Auchterhouse and the Earl of Strathmore's men.

James had landed in Peterhead, but suffering from fits of fever and so melancholy that he failed to inspire his followers. He proceeded for a brief period to Scone, but fled back to France accompanied by the Earl of Mar on 4th February 1716, advising his Highlanders to look out for themselves. Government troops then took over Aboyne Castle and an official enquiry was opened in January 1717 to ascertain the part the young Earl had played in the rebellion.

Various witnesses gave evidence; some giving their stories openly and honestly, while others preferred to give only the scantiest of histories. However from all these documents the "fire raising" and "driving of cattle" on Glen Tanar is intriguing. If a tenant or vassal refused to obey the superior's summons and did not appear at the rendezvous, by tradition his house might be burned and his cattle seized.

Charles Garden of Bellastreen had his house burned and his cattle driven off, as told by various witnesses. His refusal may well have been crafty in that if disaster overtook the rebellion, he could fall back on the excuse of compulsion. As things turned out he was taken prisoner at Sheriffmuir, but released on his own and others' evidence; he died at the age of ninety in 1760.

Patrick Gordon gives evidence that he was ordered by the young Earl and Auchterhouse to go and raise the men of Glen Tanar and, in the case of refusal, to raise fire. This was accordingly done at William Fletcher's house at Boginlack, high up on the brae above the present Glen Tanar house, and at James Fletcher's and James Watt's houses in Bellastreen. Patrick Gordon was tenant of Bordland and factor at Glen Tanar and was listed as 'gentleman', so we may be sure he was a witness against the Earl, only under compulsion.

John MacDonald gave witness that he saw the smoke of the fire that was raised in the town of Boginlack but, "knew not who raised the same and knew none of the men who drove that cattle. Neither I knew who raised the fire in Balnastrein land and this is the truth as he shall answer God." These witnesses were caught between a stone and a hard place with such an uncertain future and so were sensibly playing safe in their vagueness.

William Fletcher, whose house at Boginlack was burned, stated that Auchterhouse had promised to return him his cattle upon condition that he got a man to come out in his place and this he was obliged to do. During the enquiry there was much evidence of the threatening behaviour of Auchterhouse and all said they were made fully aware that if they refused their allegiance, retribution would be swift.

Auchterhouse was obviously seen as the main culprit, but it appears that no punishment was meted out to anyone following the enquiry. The young Earl went unmolested, probably because of his age, while the Laird of Auchterhouse was far beyond the reach of the victors.

Following the '15 debacle the Government was full of good intentions for Scotland's future, but little was achieved until around 1725. In that year General George Wade was appointed commander in Scotland and set about improving the road transport system throughout the Highlands and linking up to the various garrisons. He continued in post until 1737 by which time he had built over 250 miles of military roads, along with many distinctive bridges.

In the intervening years up to Culloden, Roman Catholic missionaries became very active among the clans and acquired a lot of influence. With increasing clan unrest, a number of chiefs sent an invitation to the son of James III, Charles Stuart, to lead an uprising and so launched the romance and tragedy of Bonnie Prince Charlie. Assuring him that they would rise up and fight his cause if he came from France with as few as 3,000 troops, they set about drumming up support from their tenants and vassals to abide by their contracted duty. Those clans which were Roman Catholic or Episcopalian, mainly favoured the Catholic prince, while most Presbyterian clans stayed loyal to the Hanoverians. Justifying their stance, many Highland chiefs felt that through the decades James II and his son James – termed the Old Pretender – had come to understand the predicament of the region.

An infertile, over populated land with a surfeit of fighting men owing their personal allegiance to so many different chiefs made plunder essential, to maintain their basic standard of living. The real crisis of the time was not law and order, but economics, there being a lack of cash for investment and estate improvement, a state of affairs that was set to haunt the Highlands for the next century and a half. Into this crisis came Bonnie Prince Charlie, depending heavily on these disgruntled clans, especially those of the Gaelic speaking regions. However, far too few of those he considered his natural followers rallied to the cause and it all petered out on that memorable day in Scots folklore, 16th April 1746, on Culloden

Culloden by David Morier

moor. An epic event and the last land battle ever to occur on British soil.

The rising of '45 was a very different rebellion from its predecessor. The superior in Aboyne this time did not take part and so no general summons went out to vassals and tenants. Those who did join did so of their own free will and so no "fire raising" or "driving cattle" afflicted our district. In neighbouring districts, particularly in Cromar where Gordon of Blelack and other Jacobite leaders were active, there were, no doubt, cases of unwilling service.

This was highlighted in Newton of Logie-Coldstone on the Laird of Invercauld's land. John Easson a tenant, was ordered "to go out as soldier or send one in his place". He negotiated with one "John Smith, servant to John Garden of Bellamore" and hired him as a substitute. Smith, thoughtlessly accepted a bill from Easson instead of the £75 Scots as promised. Surviving the massacre at Culloden, Smith returned to claim his payment on production of the bill, only for Easson to refuse payment and to demand the return of his bill. Smith refused and sued in the Aberdeen Court, but his case was thrown out and he was forced to pay costs of £3. Justice – what justice?

Fraser in his *Deeside Field* article is of the opinion from lists available that no one from Glen Tanar was 'out' in the '45 rebellion and that no troops made use of the Firmounth pass or the route over Mount Keen. Despite Fraser's comments there appear in the "List of Rebells" prepared by the Supervisors of Excise in 1746, twenty names of whom "Alex Smith, labourer, Dalquhing, Glentanner, carried arms at Inverury, but returned and laid hold of His Royal Highnesses proclamation. Whereabouts unknown." All the other names are from Aboyne and district except for "John Stewart, farmer, Bordland, Glentanner and his three sons, Peter, James and Joseph." The sons enlisted as "volunteers with the French and carried arms at the battles of Falkirk, Inverury and Culloden, now lurking near their father's house." It seems certain that many others were not officially listed.

The James Stewart, son of John Stewart of the Bordland, appears in the chapter on Forestry as having a contract from the Earl to cut trees in the Allachy. However his fighting days put all thoughts of cutting wood out of his head as he rallied to the young prince. On hearing that Prince Charlie had landed at Moidart he hastened south to join up with his old employer the Duke of Perth and was appointed a Major in his regiment. He was present throughout the campaign into England as far as Derby and right up until Culloden, where he had his horse shot from beneath him and was taken prisoner.

Stewart was treated very harshly, with handcuffs that were so tight that his arms became grossly swollen, making the irons invisible. He was kept like that for ten days, then shipped south to stand trial and be convicted of High Treason. He was saved by the intervention of an Englishman, Major Bowles of Hamilton's Dragoons, who testified as how his life had been saved by Stewart when he had been badly wounded and "preserved me from being cut to pieces by the straggling Highlanders". Imprisoned for a year, James Stewart returned home and seems to have taken up his wood contract again. A census of his cut trees in June 1751 appears to have been carried out on his early death at the age of forty.

Diack lists an interesting aside. From the *Aberdeen Journal* of 6th June 1826, an obituary notice: "On 27th ult near Kirriemuir, James MacGregor aged 100 years. He was born in Aberdeenshire on the estate of the Earl of Aboyne and was servant there in 1746. When, after the battle of Culloden the Earls of Kilmarnock and Balmerino concealed themselves in the woods of Glentanner, he was employed to carry the daily provisions to these unfortunate noblemen. His recollections of these transactions were distinct and very interesting." Diack, however, adds a rider in that Kilmarnock and Balmerino were taken prisoner at Culloden, but that there is little doubt that MacGregor's noblemen were hiding in the Glen Tanar woods.

The defeat at Culloden, followed by the reprisals on all and sundry, was the harsh price this region paid for supporting a lost cause. The Duke of Cumberland's savage orders to harry, burn and kill men, women and children alike in a campaign of mass reprisal after Culloden was unusual in the 18th century. All the half hearted measures after the '15 rebellion were enacted now with vigour. Jacobite estates were forfeited, while tartan and bagpipes were proscribed, except for military units of the British army. The holding of arms was prohibited and all swords had to be given up, while the military contract between clan chiefs and their subjects was abolished in the Tenures Abolition Act of 1746.

Later the same year the Heritable Jurisdictions Act removed the virtual sovereign power the chiefs had over their clan. The dismembering of the clan system brought about huge changes in the attitude of the chiefs. As they attempted to emulate the new business ethos of the Lowlands, the relationship with their tenants changed. An impersonal cash incentive to exploit their employment crept in, so replacing the paternalistic attitude of the old system.

The Highlands were about to be launched into an alien future, but many decades would pass before any great benefits would accrue for the ordinary working folk of Upper Deeside. By 1784 there was a relaxation of the ban on wearing tartan and the playing of the bagpipes; from then on the way of life gradually merged into that of the country as a whole. The population growth in the Highlands was accelerating and this along with the new drive to make estates financially viable led to another milestone in Scottish history: The Clearances. After years of failure of the potato crop in the early 1800s, thousands of poor Highlanders left for a new life in foreign lands.

Although The Clearances were notably associated with the huge estates of the Countess of Sutherland and her infamous factor Patrick Sellar, Glen Tanar did not escape. Around the 1850s the Marquis of Huntly decided to convert Glen Tanar into a sporting venture to benefit from the increasing interest of the rich in stalking deer and shooting grouse. Pheasant shooting had also become more sophisticated in that instead of walking the birds up, they were now being driven to standing guns – a much more civilised way for portly gentlemen to get their pleasure.

Almost nothing has been recorded of the moving of the population out of the Glen, but by the time Cunliffe Brooks came to rent the estate in 1871 no one remained in the valley itself who was not directly involved in estate affairs. Yet in talking to various older people there is still the sense in folk memory that eviction followed by the razing of the old crofts and cottages had been traumatic in the lives of the poor and underprivileged in Glen Tanar.

Outwith the valley, farms remained tenanted, but here again it appears that no one owned their properties, all being retained by the estate. The years of the Glen having its own varied way of life – with all sorts of different occupations and the amenities of shops and inns – was past. From now on the valley would become the playground of the wealthy, with huge benefits for many, but for the sentimental, only a sad memory.

11

FOREST OF GLEN TANAR

Forest of Glen Tanar was our postal address in my youth, and this gives the flavour of what this valley meant to its population. Lacking the outcrops of limestone present in other parts of the Dee valley, Glen Tanar is disadvantaged, its soil being mainly granite and schist. Agriculture has therefore been minimal throughout the ages, so making the area dependent on its ability to stimulate the growth of trees, especially the Scots pine. The term Forest of Glen Tanar, however, encompassed not only the forest, but the whole surrounding valley.

Despite the granite, there is something in the soil and climate of the upper parts of the Dee and Spey valleys that suits the Scots pine and the same may be said of heather. The other indigenous tree in our district is the birch, which grows to a considerable size and is to be found even above one thousand feet. Other trees still surviving include rowan, willow, elder and aspen. Oak is also indigenous, but in light soil, only growing to a moderate size. In the past oak grew much larger, as can be seen by canoes retrieved from Loch Kinnord. Canoes of single hollowed-out logs 30 feet long and 3 feet 7 inches wide have been retrieved.

It is the Caledonian forest, dating from the end of the Ice Age, that make Glen Tanar and Ballochbuie near Lochnagar almost unique in the UK. As the climate warmed the great pinewood forests gradually retreated northwards into the Scottish Highlands, now the only area to sustain them. Today less than one per cent of the original forest survives, but now that Glen Tanar is within the Cairngorm National Trust everything possible will be done to retain this remaining prehistoric forest, so long as natural conditions remain favourable.

The regeneration of the forest over the years has given rise to conjecture as to man's part in this process. Natural regeneration depends on a number of factors, including fire. Mosses around the area show evidence of many fires, and layer upon layer of moss brings on new trees.

Timber blown down in storms allows greater space for trees to mature, and there were few deer or domestic animals to browse the saplings. There is little evidence that man had a structured approach to forest management through earlier centuries, but even haphazard felling would have been beneficial.

In documents of the 17th century, the chief interest in the trees concerned their value and the supplying of timber to neighbouring districts. Tools and implements were often fashioned locally, so making their carriage to, say, Aberdeen, easier. Even then there was competition from the Norwegians who could bring their timber by sea, almost easier than overland down the valley. A comment of the time reads, "as road is too rough and cannot be entrusted with safety to the swift and eddying river".

Evidence that timbermen were carrying wood from the Highlands to the Low Country is demonstrated in 1663 when church ministers complained to the Moderator and the Diocesan Synod about these rascals travelling on the Sabbath. Persecution for working on a Sunday continued, but without success, and the Bishop and Synod changed direction by applying to have certain timber markets changed from a Monday to later in the week.

There was extensive tree planting in the grounds of Aboyne Castle when a new building was erected around 1675. From the factor's accounts of 1686-91 it appears 90,800 "fir plants were sett", the seeds being gathered in the Glen Tanar forest; the pay to the fir gatherers was at "the rote of one peck of meall as the bounty of each thousand".

The first indication of appreciation of the business possibilities of the forest comes in 1685 when foresters were employed with the payment of 20 merks yearly. The administration and supervision of the forest fell largely on the shoulders of the head forester and certainly was no sinecure. Appointed by the Earl of Aboyne, he would be kept busy with a steady stream of customers, supervising and planning future planting and felling, while taking instructions from his employer and his agents. Usually three chief foresters were employed on the estate: one for Glen Tanar itself, a second for Deecastle and a third at Headinch for the Pannanich woods. Sometimes the less important foresters were paid in kind, with oatmeal, for example. Understanding the value of the currencies around 1701 can be confusing. Values fluctuated over the years but at that time twelve Scots pounds were equivalent to one pound sterling. One merk was worth 14 shilling Scots or just over 1 shilling sterling (5p in present coinage), while 1s Scots was worth 1p sterling.

The forest was long an important source of revenue for Lord Aboyne and records suggest an annual income of about 5,000 merks (£227 sterling) around 1700, while by 1797 this had increased to between £400 and £500. The timber was initially transported by dragging, but it is inferred that floating down the Tanar and certainly down the Dee became the usual practice until the early 19th century.

In a description of the parish of Glen Tanar in 1725 the country is said to be, "mountainous, not very fertile, the people living more by traffiquing in timber than husbandry. This timber they have from the Wood of Glentanar, which lyes on the south side of the said parish and is the only ornament of the place. It is very large in extent and ten or twelve miles in circumference, tho' not full in all places. The timber in this wood, which is all fir, grows to a great height and bigness; the whole country round about it being served in fir timber out of it, to the considerable advantage of the Earl of Aboyne who is heretour of it".

In 1693, in the hope of increasing sales, the forest of Glen Tanar was let to two tacksmen – James Gairdyne in Nether Belnastreen and John Gordon in Bordland – but ten years later the forest appears to be back in the hands of the Earl. The Earl was still a minor so his tutor was appointed to run the forest. This does not seem to have been a success and the Duke of Gordon, a relative of the young Earl, went to the Court of Session to debar the tutor from cutting the woods. A factor was to be appointed along with two assessors to mark and value the trees to be felled with various other conditions, too long to detail here.

One or two of the conditions are of interest, however. The factor had to keep a sufficient number of good axe-men to call upon, ready to cut the timber for the purchaser, who had to remove his wood within two months of cutting. Another condition read, "that these that buy the firr shall be obliged to cut the same close to the ground and as to the birk or oak if any be, they must be cut close to the fogg and sloping a hand's breadth from the north towards the south with the mouth of the axe upward to prevent rain from standing upon and rotting old stock".

This explains that no young growth will come again when the birch is cut too close to the ground. Also, the taking of the bark from the root underground, "mischievously practised has the same effect". This shows that birch bark had commercial value in those days, probably for dyeing

Allachy in sunlight PHOTO:ALAN FINDLAY

and tanning. There was reference to "the frauds of some tenants who frequently pretend the necessity of timber for keeping up their houses when there is no occasion," going on to accuse them of disposing of it "in mercats and otherwayes". An entry of 27th September 1717 also shows that thieving was widespread. "To meat and drink to a dozen of men that lay out a haill nicht in the different passes to the wood and dackering for timber next day – five shillings Scots". To dacker means to search for stolen goods.

In 1732 a giant step was taken with the contract between Lady Grace, Countess of Aboyne, and Peter Coutts "in Balmorrall to build and erect a sawmill up the water of Tanar near or adjacent to the Haughs of Allachie or other place judged convenient which sawmill shall work with sawes or blades and to pay Peter Coutts the sum of 300 merks Scots money".

In agreement Peter Coutts accepts the 300 merks and acknowledges receipt of "one boll of meal which though not contained in the contract was bargained for, the same always being given in such cases".

This new method of cutting and disposing of timber does not seem to have been successful, as by 1760 the greater part of the wood was still being sold to the axe-men and to others not at the mill. From looking at old *Statistical Accounts*, the mill must have stopped functioning considerably before 1797.

In 1744, the Earl had taken over the running of the estate from his mother the Countess and had put the retailing of the trees into the hands of a middleman. He agreed with a James Stewart, son of John Stewart of Bordland, to sell whole fir trees, young and old, great and small, in the Haugh of Allachy. A total of 7,000 trees were involved over a period of six years. The Earl was not to sell any of his wood in Glentaner during the said time, "excepting fallen trees blown down by storm and back-going trees in the park of Aboyne".

The Earl was to allow James Stewart use of his sawmill and all his machinery. James Stewart was allowed to build another sawmill "for easier manufacturing the said timber and make aqueducts thereto". The price of the trees is 10,000 merks Scots.

The Jacobites rose up in 1745 and James Stewart, along with most of his relatives, went off in fine fettle to fight for Bonnie Prince Charlie. Stewart survived Culloden and returned to his contract, as an entry in the *Aboyne Papers* of 1751 notes him in that year as deceased. A review was then taken. The number of trees on the Haugh and Brae of Allachy in 1751 – the trees that had been earmarked to sell to James Stewart – were "the number of deal trees 2,175, of spar trees 1,216". There was no trace of any other contract after this in that century. In 1766 the total amount received from wood sold in Glen Tanar by the Earl's servants was £2,500 Scots.

It became accepted practice for the tenantry and people of the district to purchase in the forest or birch woods what trees they wanted and manufacture them into saleable articles of all kinds. The trees to be sold were assessed as to their value by burleymen or other responsible valuators who fixed the price on their word of honour. It is noted around 1840 that a local man was making wooden dishes and utensils and that he disposed of them annually at the Timmer Market in Aberdeen.

Tenants on the estate were encouraged to grow birch and were often directed to plant so many trees every year in their tenancy agreements. An interesting entry for October 1763 shows eighteen farmers and tenants supplying birch bark to the Earl, confirming its use for dyeing and tanning.

On 10th August 1778 a number of the inhabitants of Glenesk bought wood from Glen Tanar. To convey the trees so far meant dragging them over a very rough road to a height well over 2,000 feet. This effort is a good indication of the scarcity of timber in the upper parts of Angus. It was noted in the same excerpt, "that the axe-men are particularly alert in picking out and cutting the largest trees. But the expense of getting them out is considerable as the trees are always squared with the axe. The wood is not so economically managed as if there was a saw-mill and proper machinery for carrying the large logs from the forest." As proof of the fineness of the wood it was noted that one tree of eleven inches in diameter had one hundred and thirty concentric rings.

The bigger farmers do not seem to have taken much interest in the wood industry, but many of the population lived mostly by it; some had no other means of livelihood, while others combined it with small agricultural holdings. However, the forest was used for grazing and sheltering cattle, sheep and goats through the ages with sheilings (huts used by herdsmen during the summer months) being erected in the 16th century in the Etnach area, Auldinhervie, at the head of the Skinna burn and in Glen Dui.

The fattening of imported cattle was restricted in 1766 with an agreement with the farmers to graze no more than they could overwinter and to build no more sheilings within the bounds of the forest.

As an aside it is interesting to note that in 1796 Etnach had fifty acres of arable land, while many of the marginal areas around Coirevrauch were only viable during the 19th century because barley could be grown for illicit whisky distillation. Similarly, farming the high ground above Etnach was only worth the effort for whisky, so those few patches of land became worthless and many small houses in the district were deserted, rapidly becoming ruins by the mid-1820s with the ending of the illicit stills.

Goats featured in Glen Tanar for many centuries, being recorded from 1600 to the 1860s. The goat population reached a peak in the 18th century when goat milk and whey were extremely fashionable as a health cure. Cattle rustling was rife in the 17th century in Deeside and Diack describes the last cateran raid in early 1700s. Cattle grazed the forests certainly from the 18th century.

The earliest record of sheep is in a letter dated 1766 asking permission of the Earl of Aboyne to engage a shepherd to care for the livestock grazing in the forest. By 1850 sheep numbered 7,000 and had totally replaced goats. Numbers gradually declined, especially after 1900, and now there are relatively few on the estate. The effect of deer on the forest does not seem to be mentioned before the 19th century, but the conversion of the valley by the Earl of Aboyne into a sporting estate and the coming of Cunliffe Brooks changed all that.

The final quote from this account is: "the inhabitants of this parish by selling their wood in more distant parts of the country, at high prices, continue to live comfortably."

The rural economy lasted in this manner at least until the beginning of the 19th century.

As it was often said in those times, "such being the way of life for hundreds of years, the people of Glentanar were proverbially known for their craftsmen in timber working:

Saw an inch and rive a span
Is the mark of a good Glentanar man."

Thus the early 1800s found the Earl of Aboyne highly dependent on timber for revenue and with serious felling threatening to denude the forest his thoughts turned to alternative methods of keeping himself solvent. Developing the estate as a sporting venue to satisfy a growing demand from the affluent rich, particularly from England, seemed the answer. This initiative was to prove successful, but with mixed benefits for his own family, as will be revealed.

12

FIRES, FLOATERS AND FENCERS

The little hamlet of woodcutter's houses at the Black Ship ceased to exist by the year 1845, when all the decent timber within a reasonable distance had been felled. This must have been a worrying time for the 9th Marquis of Huntly who had depended heavily on the revenue from his forest to fund various projects, such as building the east wing of Aboyne Castle in 1801 and Aboyne Bridge in 1831.

The 9th Marquis died in 1853 at the age of 93 years, when his son Charles took the mantle of 10th Marquis of Huntly and Earl of Aboyne. With little timber left to sell and in a parlous financial state he would have been delighted to have his father-in-law to first rent and then buy the Glen Tanar estate. Squandering any revenue in gambling he became a bankrupt in 1898, owing £140,000 and with assets of only £690. By this time Sir William Cunliffe Brooks must have reached the end of his tether with his aristocratic son-in-law.

The Black Ship hamlet was probably established in 1809 when 8,000 fir trees were advertised for sale from Glen Tanar in *The Times* of 20th February. The timber was said to be of excellent quality, over a hundred years old and fit for masts, averaging fifty feet in length and many containing over fifty cubic feet of timber. A later record in 1842 reveals that a clipper ship built in an Aberdeen shipyard and named *Glen Tanar* had been built from this timber from the estate. This association with ship building may be the reason for the naming of this deep dark pool on the Tanar, but as black ships were the name for slave ships it would be interesting to know whether any Aberdeen shipyard was involved in building vessels for the slave trade. Despite the Slave Trade Act of 1807, slave ships continued to be built, while the transporting of slaves continued up to the 1850s.

A perceptive account of that period is transcribed from a diary text given to Lord Glentanar by a Mr Anderson, retired banker in Aboyne. This extract appears to have been written about 1926.

"Robert Whyte and Ann Thomson, my grandparents, went to Glen Tanar about the year 1809. He went first as manager to the Earl of Aboyne in the cutting down of the woods and afterwards for many years he carried on a lucrative wood-merchant's business on his own account in the glen. When my grandparents first went there, a village of fifty huts was built on each side of the road, on the south-west of the Tanar, about a mile and a half beyond the present Glen Tanar House. These huts were built to provide accommodation for the workpeople. During their twenty-five years' residence about a hundred and fifty children were born in this hamlet to the woodcutters and other work people.

"When my grandmother went as a bride to the glen, she planted a lime tree in the corner of their garden, and it is interesting to relate that after a hundred and seventeen years the tree still flourishes, is a magnificent specimen of great height and girth and is surrounded by a wire protection, presumably to keep the deer from eating its bark. The forest my grandfather was cutting was considered to be one of the finest in Scotland and Lord Aboyne was justly proud of it. He continually brought his guests to the glen to view the magnificent trees and fine scenery, also to partake of bread and honey and sample the famous smuggled whisky. Many a Duke, Marquis, Earl and Lord with their ladies had my grandparents the honour of entertaining in their simple house in those days.

"The quality of the trees was considered to be of the finest, and the wood was in great demand, many coming long distances to procure it. My mother told me that yearly representatives of seed merchants came from England and collected the seed of the fir trees, it being in great demand. Sheets were placed on the ground round some of the finest specimens and the seed collected in this way.

"In June 1820 a great conflagration took place and at one time it looked as if the whole forest would be consumed. Great was the consternation of the workpeople as the fire crept nearer and nearer. It was thought the whole of the huts including the saw-mill would perish. So near did the fire come to the hamlet that all the workpeople were warned out of their houses – the women and children, with their goods and chattels being deposited on carts ready to be moved at a moment's notice. It was said that such a hold did the fire get on the woods and mosses that it was never completely extinguished until the winter snow came. Exactly a century later came the great fire of June 14th to 26th, 1920. The burnt area measured over two thousand acres and the number of trees so damaged as to have to be disposed of was over seventy seven thousand."

The reference to smuggled whisky is pertinent. It was well known in the district that Glen Tanar abounded in illicit stills at one time, distilling a brew of exceptional quality. Fourteen bothies were said to be in operation around 1800. The heavy tax on malt made whisky very expensive, so with a market thirsting for a cheaper brew it is easy to understand that so many relatively poor people produced it.

Robin Callander in *History in Birse* gives a fine explanation and paints a vivid picture of the bothies only eight feet square and cut into a brae side or, as in Glen Tanar, tucked away in the middle of the dense forest beside some small burn. In the Allachy just beyond the John Milne stone is supposed to be the remnants of the last of the whisky bothies, but it is difficult to know the accuracy of this story. Smuggled in barrels slung across wiry garrons trekking southwards over mountain tracks and through barren glens in the dead of night, it would have been no easy living, but profitable none the less. Legislation in 1823 legalising more official production along with the 'Muckle Fine' slowed the backwoods liquor production, but it was when landowners were expected to evict those discovered in illegal distilling that the trade came to an end.

The final word on this period belongs to the womenfolk. Writers at the time reported that many wives were delighted to see the last of this illegal spirit as their men folk could then return to proper work and recover from living in a perpetual alcoholic haze. Also it is interesting to note the reference to a sawmill at that time and Diack in *The Estate Papers* mentions that it was situated on the Tanar near the Strone where what are thought to be old saw pits are still to be discerned.

The anxiety and uncertainties related to forest fires must have been immense for those living close by. The following are from old records and give some indication of those experiences.

The first official record is in the Aboyne Estates factor's accounts for 1688. "Received two hundredth punds Scots as the pryce of the wood burnt in Glentanner, it being comprised and sold to James Garden of Belnastrein." Again in 1719, payment to "fourty or fifty men that lay out a day and a hail nicht extinguishing a great fire that was kindled upon the skirts of Glentanner – 5/- Scots." Again in 1726, payment to John Fyfe for "watching the fire in Glentanner".

In 1748 there was a really serious conflagration but by this time the

Aberdeen Journal was in existence, so fuller particulars are available.

June 14th: "Last week the wood of Glentanner, which belongs to the Earl of Aboyne, was set on fire and has burnt in a violent manner for these ten days, notwithstanding the people of the neighbouring parioches have used their endeavours to stop its progress. Tis supposed to be kindled of design. The damage by the fire already is computed at 30,000 mks."

June 21st: "We hear that the wood of Glentanner is not yet extinguished notwithstanding some hundreds of people are cutting and clearing away in order to stop it. It is reckoned there are three miles of it consumed and incredible damage done to young trees. The two fellows that set it on fire are fled."

The fire of June 14th to 24th 1920 is probably the greatest blaze of all time and a full description is worth recording. My own father often related the drama of it, as did so many others on the estate from that era, so it must have been a time of real crisis, leaving an indelible effect on so many.

On Monday 14th June, smoke was first noticed rising apparently from about the west shoulder of Baudy Meg. By the time the estate workers arrived quite a large area was alight. The wind was from the east tending to spread the fire westward into the forest. By early Tuesday morning it was thought the fire was under control but as the day wore on the wind increased and by afternoon the fire had crossed the burn of Skinna and spread with alarming speed towards the back of the Strone. Requests for additional help brought an additional sixty extra men but despite that the fire swept forward, the flames leaping onwards from tree to tree with irresistible force to cross the Allachy and invading the Tom Dews part of the forest.

More helpers arrived and back burning operations were commenced in earnest at the Allnaharvy burn and this proved successful, so that by the evening the fire was checked there and in the Gairney quarter. By this time the main wall of flame in the form of an arc was confined to the Strone, stretching from the Skinna burn to the Glen road almost opposite Allnaharvy. The line was guarded by a line of men ten yards apart all night and by 5 am everything seemed under control

Wednesday 16th June: The wind again freshened and then began to blow strongly from the south-east. The smouldering ground in many parts broke out into flames simultaneously and again threatened to overcome the tiring workforce. An urgent plea brought fifty non commissioned officers and men along with two officers from Aberdeen in the early afternoon. During the day the flames were making towards the Knockie in the north and the ground in the Baudy Meg sector was again ablaze. Surrounding valleys were enshrouded in an impenetrable haze of blue-grey smoke and the flames in the Knockie forced the men down on to the road at the Knockie bridge close to the lake and not that far from the mansion house.

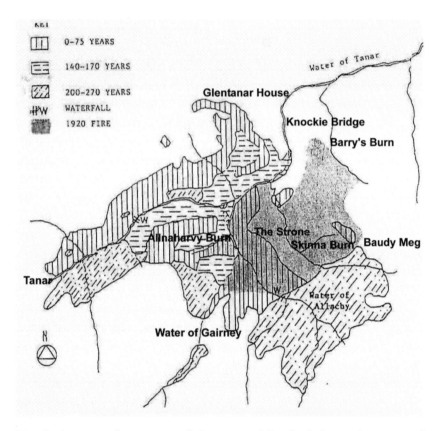

Hatched areas refer to ages of the trees while shaded area is extent of the 1920 fire.

An area east of the Knockie was now threatened and the only means of saving it was by back burning, but this in itself was a dangerous procedure. Ground from the Barrie's burn uphill was however successfully fired and the danger from that direction was over for the time being. The night of Wednesday/Thursday there were enough workers to patrol the whole boundary of the fire area and any fresh outbreaks were quickly prevented. By Friday morning it was felt the outbreak was at least under control, but for many days after, patrolling was required until heavy rain ten days later ensured that the situation was overcome. The burnt area was measured as over 2,000 acres and the trees burnt or damaged as 77,000. It is interesting to note that all these large fires have been in the month of June.

Over the years since then there have been intermittent smaller fires usually the result of heather burning when the smouldering ground has come alight after the keepers have left, or when high winds have got heather burning out of control.

My only experience of this occurred in about 1946 when aged eighteen I was a volunteer for such an experience. The fire raging through the trees on a high wind in the Gairney is something I shall always remember. All night we used the heavy wire mesh brushes to damp down the flames, but by morning my arms had lost their feeling and I was pretty near exhaustion. The ladies brought us refreshments throughout the night, but it was an experience never to be forgotten. Morning had the fire under control and a hot bath did wonders, but I can only imagine the fatigue of those fire fighters who were involved so desperately for days in 1920. 1956 appears to be the last fire of any major proportion, but the area burnt would appear to be only about a sixth of that consumed back in 1920.

Before the coming of the railways there are a number of references on the method of floating wood via the rivers in spate to the timber yards at the foot of Market Street in Aberdeen. That men termed floaters operated on the Dee and Spey in this hazardous occupation of gathering logs into rafts and steering them downstream in high water, has been well recorded as by Elizabeth Grant of Rothiemurchus in *Memoirs of a Highland Lady*.

Although using such a method on the Tanar is referred to, no actual report seems to exist of such a manoeuvre being regularly used. I find it difficult to visualise large quantities of really sizeable logs being transported in this fashion on such a small river. Rafting seems improbable so logs would have been floated individually or in small numbers held together and requiring constant supervision. Earlier it was noted that timber 50 feet long was extracted from the forest but it would have required a huge flood and been very dangerous in such a confined space to float such sizes. It is not clear what would have been considered commercial size logs although the Black Ship in the 1800s would have made an ideal loading bank for launching such timber. The construction of a dam in this area has also been suggested and the logs floated down after breaching of the dam, but again I can find no evidence of this. Depending on adequate spate conditions in any one year on the Tanar seems a very uncertain method for delivering contracted timber.

The collecting of the wood at the Tanar mouth or downstream in a spate would also have been difficult and labour intensive. That no specific record of this floating exists, but still keeps being referred to in the more recent literature is disappointing. With so many imponderables I would require some convincing that it was a viable and oft-used method on such a small river. It has also been suggested that timber further up the valley above certain waterfalls and rocky sections was left standing due to the difficulty of floating the cut timber from there, but perhaps it was more to do with the difficulty of dragging trees out of such inaccessible spots. A more reasonable explanation, still vaguely spoken about in Aboyne, was that the timber was brought by carts to the Dee at the Criagendinnie gates and taken down to the river bank where it was then rafted off to Aberdeen in high water.

In 1813 the Bridge of Potarch was in the process of being built when a sudden flood swept logs off a bank and nearly destroyed the half finished structure. Following this one episode an Act of Parliament was passed empowering county authorities to take steps for the protection of bridges from the practice of floating timber and this had a marked effect on the procedure thereafter. The coming of the railways with their convenience and safety finally terminated this hazardous age of the floaters.

Storm damage through the generations has also caused much destruction but also brought benefits both from the sale of such timber but also by opening up the forest to seedling regeneration. The gale on January 31st 1953 caused wide-spread damage on the estate, especially in the areas of Frederick's Walk, Craig of Woodend, Water of Gairney and the Allachy.

Through the ages vague references have been made of certain proprietors doing limited planting, with McGillivray in 1855 stating that there was much planting along the middle stretch of the Tanar in the first half of the 19th century.

The coming of Cunliffe Brooks brought money, ideas, development, employment and prosperity but it was at a certain cost to our Scottish environment. Not only was the face of the estate altered with English influences abounding, but there was an emphasis on boosting deer and grouse numbers. The building of the fence in 1870 to keep the deer in ensured a steady supply of quarry to satisfy a multitude of guests out stalking, but also threatened the very existence of the Caledonian forest. Increasing deer numbers, forcing the animals to forage more and more into the woodlands, meant that young saplings were soon eliminated. However, Brooks as an improving landlord was probably well aware of the danger of his policies and there is evidence that he did undertake some limited planting as well as limiting any tree felling.

Brooks was deterred by nothing in his striving to accomplish his dreams. To erect a deer fence all around his large estate in order to trap the deer within, seems a monstrous object just to satisfy a few privileged guests as well as his own preoccupation. But this was an era when numbers and size meant everything. Whether big game hunting, shooting hundreds of grouse and pheasants in one day and then being able to boast about it was the fashion of the times. Records show that one stag satisfied no one, but that a really good day depended on numbers; the more the better.

In 1871 Brooks engaged Harper & Co of Aberdeen to fence in his whole estate. This company had already been engaged in similar work on other estates such as Glenfiddoch. I am greatly indebted to retired surgeon Douglas Harper, great-grandson of the founder of the company, for the following information.

Harper & Co were advertised from about 1857 as manufacturers of gates and fences. John Harper registered his "patent device for tensioning wire" in 1864. The device in question was novel and was later developed to strain bridges.

The wire ran through the casing to be wound on to a spindle. An Allen key-type device at one end allowed tension to be applied and at the other the spindle could be fixed to the casing by a key being driven into two opposing notches, one on the casing and the other on the spindle. With three notches on the casing, but four on the spindle the strength of the casing was preserved. The posts had then to be well grounded and this was achieved by being sunk four feet into the ground, leaving six feet above ground. At the lower end of the post was a horizontal plate preventing sinkage and two fins at right angles to each other in the below ground section of the post to prevent rotation and tilting under strain. The hollow end of the post went through the horizontal end plate to allow drainage as the accumulated water would split the post as it froze in winter.

These sturdy tensioner posts would have been some hundred and fifty yards apart with two slimmer metal strainer posts between and between them, at six to nine feet, slim cast-iron posts. This was an eight-strand fence with the top wire at a height of 67 inches above ground, with three feet of rabbit wire attached to the lower section in some areas.

Deer fence tension post at Waterside

There is no record of how long it took the company to complete the work, but there is still plenty of evidence around the estate of the old fence. It even existed along the South Deeside Road and can be seen at Waterside behind the fishing hut, which was also the setting for Harper & Co. building the suspension bridge described in chapter 24.

The Coats family were in the future to turn Brooks plans upside down by reversing the use of the fence to keep deer out, but that is for a later chapter.

A recorded tale from the past referring to the use of timber as a floater comes from Dinnet. Mr and Mrs Charles Wilson, who built Dinnet House in 1890, also built the old chapel of Meikle Kinnord in the same year. Although never consecrated, the building was used to store local artefacts and in particular, one of the old Pictish canoes from Loch Kinord. When Mr Wilson sold the Kinnord Estate to James C. Barclay Harvey in 1896 Mrs Wilson was so irate that she hurled all the historic relics out on to the moor. The Wilsons took the canoe back to Lincolnshire when they flitted, but because it was too long and bulky to go on to a railway wagon it was allegedly sawn in half. So much, then, for all the Picts' hard work.

13

EARLY HUNTING AND FISHING

When the 1st Marquis of Huntly (1562-1636) built Kandychyle, now Deecastle, some two-and-a-half miles west of Dinnet Bridge about 1620, he originally called it Huntshall, so his intention for it was clear. Why should he build it on such a site, though, as somewhere up the Tanar valley would surely have been more appropriate, especially when hunting the red deer was considered the supreme sport?

Opportunities abounded, however, for roe-deer hunting in the woods and for hawking among the moor-fowl, now known by the English name of grouse. Fishing was just a few hundred yards away, but at that time it was not greatly appreciated as a sport as methods of catching were rudimentary.

Huntly appears, over the years, to have used the castle mainly as a summer residence until it was burnt down in 1641 while garrisoned by the military in their pursuit of cateran and 'broken men' – a term used for lawless troublemakers.

The 2nd Marquis of Huntly (1592-1649) was beheaded at the Market Cross in Edinburgh on 22nd March 1649 for his part in supporting King Charles I against Parliament in the Civil War, so had precious few years to enjoy Huntshall. Partially rebuilt after the Civil War it was used merely as a shooting box, the old castle having become a ruin.

Red deer and roe deer were the only game that the Superior valued and he reserved them for his own pleasure. Vassals and wadsetters had written into their agreements that they must not slay deer without licence or receive "slain deer or raes within their houses". They were also expected to attend the Superior at his huntings, although some were granted an exemption.

Middleton of Upper Bellastreen (now part of Glen Tanar home farm) in his charter of 1638 is bound, as are his tenants, to "giff thale personall compeirance and service, usit and wont, to the noble Marquis and his forsaids att all thair huntings within the boundes of Marr". Similarly in that year a charter, dated at Huntshall to James Farquharson of Ballaterach of the Mill and Mill-lands of Glenmuick, demands the same attendance at the huntings, but gives him the rights of "fouleing, fischeing, haking, hunting (except the hunting of deir and rae)".

The lairds of Bellamore-Braeloine had also to give personal attendance, but by the charter they possessed, had "the privilege of killing seven deer or rae yearlie within any part of the forrest of Glentanner, without any fine to be imposed for that Account". This is a noteworthy proviso, as the forest lies outwith their own lands and seems a generous gesture by a Superior intent on keeping others out.

The account of the deer hunt of that time makes interesting reading.

A great band of people and dogs would gather on the day. In the Earl of Mar's country his vassals were bound to supply eight followers for each davach (an ancient measure equivalent to 416 acres) of land with their dogs and hounds and "to cause to big (build) and put up our long kartis (open air fireplace of stones and sods) and make and put further tinchellis (beaters) at the samen according to use and wont".

Roe deer in Glen Tanar wood

In 1618 John Taylor, the Water Poet, on his visit to Scotland gives a factual description of a deer hunt on the Braes of Mar. He tells that once in the year, apparently the whole month of August and part of September, the nobility and gentry come to this Highland country to hunt, "and they doe conforme themselves to the habit of the Highland men who for the most part speak nothing but Irish, their garters being wreathes of hay or straw, with a plaid about their shoulders which is a mantle of divers colours with blue flat caps on their heads and handkerchief knit with two knots about their necks".

He goes on to describe 500 to 600 men rising early in the morning and dispersing over a distance of seven, eight or ten miles and chasing the deer in many herds to such a place as the noblemen shall instruct: "then when day is come the lords and gentlemen doe or goe to the said places, sometimes wading up to the middle through bournes and rivers; and then they being come to the place doe lie down on the ground till those aforesaid scouts which are called tinckhell doe bring down the deer, but as the proverb says of a bad cooke, so these tinckhell men doe lick their own fingers, for besides their bowes and arrows which they carry with them, we can hear now and then a harqubuse or a musquet goe off which doe seldom discharge in vain; then after we had stayed three hours or thereabouts we might perceive the deer appear on the hills round about us, which being followed close by the tinckhell are closed down into the valley where we lay; then all the valley on each side being waylaid with a couple of hundred strong Irish grey-hounds they are let loose as occasion serves upon the herde of deer, that with dogs, gunnes, arrows durks and daggers in the space of two hours four score fat deer were slaine. After are disposed of, some one way, some another, twenty or thirty miles and more then enough left for us to make merry withal at our rendevouze. Being come to our lodgings, there was such baking, boyling, rosting and stewing as if Cook Ruffian had been there to have scalded the Devil in his feathers".

This sounds barbaric to us, but it may not be so far removed from dozens of beaters flushing grouse across butts nowadays, so providing a sport only millionaires can afford. This type of deer hunting continued well into the 17th century until replaced by the more sophisticated sport of stalking, which became established in the 18th century.

Deer hunts in Glen Tanar would not have been on this scale, but the essentials are the same. It is interesting to note that on carvings on Celtic gravestones from before 800 AD, there are scenes involving bears as well as deer pursued by hounds and men on horseback. Taylor describes the deer being driven into a narrow ravine where they are attacked by men and dogs lying in wait. This spot in ancient Gaelic was called 'Elerc' or in more modern Gaelic 'Eilirig' – meaning to enclose or confine. In English it appears as 'Elrick' and is a common place name all over Scotland. It indicates that deer were entrapped there in a converging fence made either of wood or turf, or where natural features served the same purpose. The placename Elrick appears locally in the parishes of Newhills, Skene, Cabrach, Alford, Strathdon and Braemar.

A sequel to this brutal blood bath concerns the cost of transporting deer. In December 1719 John Strachan at the Boat of Charleston, Aboyne, took a deer carcase from Bordland, Glen Tanar to Edinburgh for the Earl of Aboyne for six pounds Scots – the equivalent of 50p today, which included maintenance for himself and his horse.

With regard to the use of dogs in hunting, there is a record in the *Aboyne Papers,* dated 15th August 1783, of a letter from a D. Morrice in Aberdeen to Charles Brown of Craigendenny, factor of Aboyne and Glen Tanar estates. The letter asks if he could procure a male and female deerhound to take to India.

"I'm told Mr Robieson, Braeline has a dog, but I must have a female also. If you could recommend anybody to find them out for me I would be obliged to you. I would not grudge a couple of guineas or so for the pair".

The first relevant reference to fishing appears in the new charter for the lands of Aboyne in 1676 when the Earl was granted the right to erect cruives in the river at Bountie (Aboyne) at a place called the Crove part, or any other part of the river. A 'cruive' was a box placed in a dam or dike that ran across a river for trapping fish. However, other references indicate that fish were mostly caught in nets – the rack net and the pock net. The rack net was similar to the ones used at the mouth of rivers, laid out by a boat and then dragged onto the bank. The pock was a kind of bag net fixed at the end of a pole.

Fish were also caught by means of a creel, but it is not clear as to the method. There is a quote from the Sheriff and Magistrates of Aberdeen in 1732 against the destruction of smolts in any way, "whether by rods, creels or any other engines". 'Pouting' or spearing salmon with a 'leister' was practical in summer when the water was low and clear.

The main season for salmon fishing was at the height of summer and extended over a number of days. Tenants were required to help, but men were also hired for the occasion. The primary object was to secure enough fish to serve the castle for a year, any surplus being sold in Aberdeen or elsewhere. The fish were mostly salted and barrelled, although some were kippered. 'Black fishing' describes catching salmon at the spawning stage, a breach of the law of Scotland. Fish spawning in the shallows were lethargic, easy prey for a nocturnal poacher using the deadly leister, his great torch of dried broom tied to a pole.

The Rev. Michie in *Deeside Tales* tells of an outing with Sandy Davidson, so well known in Crathie. "On a sultry summer's day when the Dee was low enough for pouting, a little party of us – all good well tried hands – but by the close of day Sandy had three more fish than all of us put together. His practised eyes would scan the water to a great depth with a power to detecting fish in a stream and at great depths was wonderful to behold. He would raise the spear cautiously – take quick aim, hurl it to a distance of many yards transfixing his prey, as surely as a falcon is of his quarry and sometimes when up to his neck in some dark forbidding pool."

In 1763 the Earl of Aboyne decided to make a new agreement. Instead of his traditional short summer bonanza, he let out the fishing to the tenant of Deecastle, Isaac Robertson. Perhaps he had become sick of salted salmon. The fishing season was then stipulated to last from 2nd February to 1st August. As to the rental, it was noted that back in 1732 an inventory of the Aboyne estate was drawn up which included the annual value of the fishings as £15 Scots. That works out at £1.25p sterling for 13 miles of prime water. In 1763 the agreement for the same stretch of water for seven years cost the princely sum of £1.65 sterling – unbelievable.

Salmon were so plentiful in Scotland at that time that servants bargained with their employers not to have it more often than twice a week. In 1797 a record states that the river Dee abounds with salmon and seatrout. They are, however, only to be caught by rod and sold for 3d or 4d per pound, according to the season of the year. By that time fishing with nets and spears had been made illegal and fishing licences had come into being. About 1800 the schoolmaster of Glentanar School notes in his accounts the annual sum paid for his son's fishing licence.

Sandy Ritchie from Deecastle learned to fish as a boy, becoming ghillie to a Mr Weir who lived in the Chapel House. Weir rented a stretch of the Dee for a few pounds a year and paid Sandy 8d per day. About 1850 a Dr Clark rented the river from Pannanich to Dinnet for £10 a year, to be followed by a Dr Robertson from Indigo, Tarland, who rented the same beats for £14 annually. After Dr Robertson gave up, the cost of the fishing started to rise steeply.

Sandy was a great local character with his own smuggling outlets, as well as being an excellent fisherman. The Excise were very suspicious of his activities, but never managed to catch him out or discover his store of whisky below his peat stack. Sandy continued to fish until he was well over eighty and Charles Brown of the Haugh across the river from Deecastle tells of his last visit. Calling at the Haugh after an evening on the water, poor old Sandy was so weak that the farmer had to help him home, possibly for the last time.

14

Byron at Ballaterach Farm

The association of Byron with the Glen Tanar valley is not greatly remembered by the locals as his stay was along the banks of the river Dee and over the hills from our little community. For me however there is no getting away from the romance of the poet brooding over my own early life. Coming from a working class family, thoughts of further education, even in the 1940s, never extended to the mighty city of Aberdeen. For us as children the pinnacle of achievement for the few was to reach Banchory Academy. By a quirk of fate however I was to find myself in October 1944 walking apprehensively past that imposing Byron statue in the grounds of Aberdeen Grammar School to revel, for three years, in the atmosphere of city life and its intimate educational rivalry with Robert Gordon's College.

The relationship with Byron and Glen Tanar was to remain hidden from me for decades to come. Initially it was enough to bask in the glory of having come to an institution that could not only boast antiquity but also glamour and fame. Only when browsing through the books of the Rev. J G Michie did I come to realise that Lord Byron was much closer to me than I had appreciated.

George Gordon Byron was born in London on the 22nd January 1788. His father was Captain John 'Mad Jack' Byron and his mother Catherine Gordon, heiress to Gight Castle and its estate, four miles east of Fyvie in Aberdeenshire. In order to inherit his wife's Scottish estate Mad Jack had to take the additional surname Gordon, so for a time becoming John Byron Gordon. Marrying, it is said only for the money, he rapidly squandered the family's wealth and disappeared leaving his wife to return to

Lord Byron and his mother

Aberdeen to find lodgings and enter her son for the Grammar School to be registered as George Byron Gordon.

The Robertsons of Ballaterach farm, one mile east of Pannanich near Ballater, were not considered wealthy but were however well connected; Mrs Helen Robertson being the daughter of Captain Macdonald of Rineaton in Gairnside. Along with many others in the district they added to their income by letting out rooms during the summer months to visitors. George Gordon, having been laid low with a severe illness, his mother elected to revitalise him with the bracing air of Deeside and so Byron came to the Glen Tanar environment. The area at that time had also become famous not only for its goat's milk but for the restorative powers of the Wells of Pannanich, so it is little wonder Mrs Gordon was attracted to this spot.

In a note in *The Island* in 1823, a year before he died, Byron wrote "when very young, about eight years of age after an attack of scarlet fever, I was removed by medical advice into the Highlands. Here I passed occasionally some summers" It would appear that the year was 1796 and he was again at Ballaterach in 1797 and possibly in 1798, before leaving Aberdeen. From his many excursions and also staying at Rineaton in Gairnside with Mrs Robertson's family, he must have remained out in Deeside for many weeks at a time. He certainly left a trail of memories behind him among so many of the local populace. His own great memories appear to have been an ecstatic appreciation of the countryside about him and the stirring of feelings of affection for the opposite sex.

On the 21st May 1798 Byron's great uncle died so making the ten year old the 6th Baron Byron, inheriting the title and estate of Newstead Abbey in Nottinghamshire.

Byron subsequently left Aberdeen after four years at Grammar, to enrol in the London school of a William Glennie in August 1799, before going on to Harrow in 1801. Reflected glory must have been brimming over in the Grammar School when it was reported that Byron had been in the Harrow cricket team involved in the first ever match with Eton at Lords in 1805. Despite a club deformity of his right foot, which caused a slight limp, he was nonetheless a competent boxer as well as being an excellent swimmer. He completed his formal education by going up to Trinity College, Cambridge until 1807 and then started a life encompassing nearly every excess imaginable, making him a nineteenth century celebrity, as well as poet and romanticist.

Ballaterach farm with, in foreground, Balindory Cottage

His early life was dogged by his infatuations leading many to subsequently see him as being equally attracted to both sexes. The marvels of Google illustrate how much of this might have originated from his experiences in childhood. It seems that although they were impoverished, Byron still had the services of a nurse governess while in Aberdeen and she appears to have gone south with the family on his great uncle's death. May Gray would come to bed with him at night and "play tricks with his person." According to Byron this "caused the anticipated melancholy of my thoughts – having anticipated life." Miss Gray was eventually dismissed for allegedly beating Byron when he was eleven years old.

That one of his first loves belongs to those convalescing days on Deeside has been well documented. James Robertson of Ballaterach farm had a large family of boys and two girls. Mary was the second daughter and she is said to have won the boyish affections of the young poet. Though Byron might say "It could not be love, for I knew not the name" it is clear from his future writings that this experience lived on with him throughout his adult years. However, much has been made from past records, that Mary would have been six years older than the boy and so unlikely to have enthralled him. It was considered, at the time therefore, that Mary Duff, a distant relative and playmate of Byron in Aberdeen and much nearer his own age, was most probably the "sweet Mary" from his poem in *Hours of Idleness.*

The disparity of age argument was carried on in the writings of the Dinnet minister the Rev. J G Michie in his 1877 publication *Loch Kinnord,* and it was not corrected until many years later. It was left to a Mr Charles Brown of Coldstone, an old pupil of Michie, to set the record straight. The inscription on Mary Roberston's gravestone gives her age at death in 1867 as eighty-five, but on checking her birth records it turned out she was born in December 1785, so making her just two years one month older than Byron; an age gap in my own memory as insignificant.

That this argument seemed now to be resolved locally in favour of Mary Robertson is however firmly challenged on reading *Notices of the Life of Lord Byron* by Thomas Moore in 1835. Moore quotes Byron himself, and others alive at that time, to show that Mary Duff indeed had deeply affected the young poet. Close friends also testified to Byron's acute emotional reaction to news of Mary Duff's subsequent marriage. This confusion of affections may have arisen from the poem in *Hours of Idleness* when Byron talks of his Mary in association with his climbing of Morven from the Glen Gairn residence of the Macdonalds. Our Deeside authors, keen in the past to make a direct link to our own Ballaterach Mary for posterity, appear to have been misled and so this apparent mythical romance has now been passed into the annals of antiquity. Of course there is always the possibility that Byron was attracted to both young ladies, something not too hard to imagine with our poet.

Later, Byron was to describe vistas that could only have been viewed from the Glen Gairn setting, while it has been recorded from old inhabitants that he loved fishing the Gairn. In *Childe Harold* he refers to his attachment to the people and countryside of Albania and remarks on similarities to Upper Deeside and the Albanian language resonating with the Gaelic. He also maintained that he could distinguish between the English and Gaelic pronunciations of Lochnagar. There was certainly no Gaelic spoken in Ballaterach or the surrounding district in those days, but in Glen Gairn it would still have been the current speech, suggesting again some time spent there.

Amy Stewart Fraser, authoress supreme from the Glen Gairn manse at the turn of the nineteenth century, recalls many snippets from the Byron era. In *Memory Long,* she refers to the near-death experience of young Geordie when visiting the Linn o' Dee with his mother, one fine summer's day. Adventurous as ever, the youngster would clamber down the rocks only for his lame foot to catch in a tussock of heather causing a stumble. Rolling down the bank he was luckily caught by an attendant just in time to save him from possible drowning.

This is the first verse from a poem in *Hours of Idleness* first published in 1807. For those who have witnessed the Gairn in spate in certain places, Byron's reference below is so very apt, as it can be very frightening to behold, even in my old age.

> *"When I roved a young Highlander o'er the dark heath,*
> *And climbed thy steep summit, O Morven of Snow,*
> *To gaze on the torrent that thunder'd beneath*
> *Or the mist of the tempest that gather'd below,*
> *Untutor'd by science, a stranger to fear,*
> *And rude as the rocks where my infancy grew,*
> *No feeling, save one, to my bosom was dear;*
> *Need I say, my sweet Mary, 'twas centr'd in you"?*

Lochnagar from Meikle Pap   PHOTO: ALAN FINDLAY

There is a sense from the above lines of Byron enjoying, not only the magical solitude, but also his own company lost in his own thoughts. Climbing Morven alone for a nine year old was probably well within Byron's capabilities from the proximity of Glen Gairn, but tackling Lochnagar was in a totally different league. Viewing the mountain from afar, the youngster probably felt a great urge to set foot on it, but it was not until 1803 that he achieved that ambition.

From the *Records of Invercauld* we learn of his visit as a fifteen-year-old, on holiday from Harrow; returning to his childhood paradise. This ascent of Lochnagar is faithfully recorded by the ghillie, his guide for the day. "We set out from Invercauld early in the morning, crossed the Dee by the old bridge and then up the glen of Garawalt. His Lordship rested often and looked at the scenery. He was very quiet and did not often speak to me. When we began to climb the crags of Loch-an-uan I thought he would not be able to scramble up, for he was rather lame, and I offered to assist him, but he would not have any help from me. When we got to the top he sat a long time on the edge of the rocks, looking about him, but seldom asked me any question; and we returned the same way as we went up."

The poem *Lochnagar* appears in *Hours of Idleness,* published only four years after the ascent and here in this verse Byron captures the true sense of his attachment.

> *Years have rolled on, Lochnagar, since I left you!*
> *Years must elapse ere I tread you again.*
> *Though nature of verdure and flow'rs has bereft you,*
> *Yet still are you dearer than Albion's plain.*
> *England, thy beauties are tame and domestic*
> *To one who has roamed over mountains afar*
> *Oh! For the crags that are wild and majestic,*
> *The steep frowning glories of dark Lochnagar.*

Finally, it is interesting for us to recall all those memories from the country folk who came into contact with Mary Robertson and the young Byron at that time. The Charles Brown who discovered the mistake with Mary Robertson's age had talked to a cousin of Mary. No great facts were uncovered except that Mary was of medium height, and without being a beauty, was good looking; that her hair was fair as in the poem –" I think on the long flowing ringlets of gold;" and that she often spoke of Byron, but simply in a general way. The only other fact was that the cousin spoke of him as "being a very delicate boy."

Mary Robertson went on to marry Kenneth Stewart, an Excise officer, then stationed at Crathie. On his death, which occurred very soon after their marriage, Mary moved to Aberdeen where she never remarried and had no offspring. Eventually dying in Aberdeen in 1867 she was however buried in the old churchyard of Glen Tanar, beside her parents, where there is a handsome tombstone over their graves with the following inscription:

> *Sacred to the memory of JAMES ROBERTSON,*
> *who departed this life on the 4th Day of April 1814 aged 71 years*
> *And of*

HELEN MACDONALD his spouse,
who died on the 11th Day of August 1813, Aged 60 years.
Also of MARY ROBERTSON their daughter,
widow of KENNETH STEWART,
who died at Aberdeen 2 March 1867, aged 85 years

Francis C Diack, in his early 1930s *Glen Tanar Estate Papers,* waxes indignant that Mary Robertson's birth records, having shown her to be only 82 years old, should not have been amended on the gravestone. Sternly he writes "this ought to be put right by someone." Unhappily dear Francis, 140 years having elapsed; there is now no one left to remember or care about a few lost years in an ancient graveyard.

Memories of Byron himself are often very bluntly told by those who looked on him as a bit of a menace. Someone whom Byron regarded as a friend, according to the Rev. Michie, was a William Clark who lived near Pannanich and the boy would often go over to keep him company. However, Michie also records a less positive account from a Mrs Stephen who lived at Greystone, the farm adjoining Ballaterach. She was a girl of six or seven when Byron stayed with the Robertsons and said he was "a very takan laddie but nae easily managed". He was very fond of going over to her father's workshop – he being a millwright to trade, and was particularly keen on turning the lathe. "But he widna haud his hands fae ony o' the tools, and he spoiled them completely before he would let them go. My father couldna lay hands on him and he wid tak nae tellan; so at last he always set some o' us to watch when we wid see him coman' up the brae from Ballaterach; and when he got word that he was coman' he would lock the door an' gang awa' out about. There was nae ither way o'deean' wi' him." You can almost hear the children clamouring to their dad. "Faither faither here comes hirpling Geordie noo – hurry, hurry faither." The miller at Inchmarnoch, just down the road from Ballaterach, was also deeved by the young Byron and he was said to stop the mill frequently when the youngster appeared.

Byron's tempestuous life continued right up until his early death aged 36 on the 19th April 1824 from a fever while fighting for Greek independence from the Ottoman Empire. So great was his prestige at that time that it was said that if Byron had lived to see the Turks defeated he would have surely been made King of Greece.

That his fame had certainly spread far and wide is demonstrated by another little anecdotal tale that still exists in our district. James Robertson had died in 1814 and the tenancy of Ballaterach then passed outwith the family. With Ballater booming on the back of the restorative properties of the waters of Pannanich, tourists flocked increasingly to the area. Ballaterach and its association with the iconic Byron also fascinated many and so became yet another compelling attraction. It was common knowledge in the district that the box-bed young George had slept in still existed and so strangers frequently knocked on the farmer's door. Exasperated, it is said, by this intrusion into his family's privacy, the box bed one night mysteriously went up in smoke, so putting an end to that unwelcome stream of visitors. Talk about killing the goose that might have laid him a golden egg if only he had advertised his little treasure, but this probably never entered the farmer's mind.

Let us finish however on a much more upbeat note, but with a sense that despite Byron being a man of the world he could still leave something behind for we lesser mortals to treasure. In *The Royal Dee* of 1898 by Alex Inkson McConnochie, the author repeats some of Byron's misdemeanours but then goes on to say, "In spite of his boyish tricks and perhaps on account of them, Byron is still very lovingly remembered by all at Ballaterach farm."

15

Sir William Cunliffe Brooks

A ll around the Glen Tanar estate are buildings, horse troughs and wells, inscribed with the interwoven initials, WCB. There is even a roadway called Wilcebe Road, yet another combination of the name of the man who changed a typical Scottish estate into what Ian R. Mitchell in *On the Trail of Queen Victoria in the Highlands* has termed "an English rural vernacular".

Who then was this man who affected not only his own generation of tenants and workers, but the generation coming behind? This chapter looks at Brooks mainly through the eyes of two people who came to know him well; the Marquis of Huntly and Thomas Mawson, a landscape architect who helped to fashion Glen Tanar to his client's vision.

The Marquis of Huntly (1847-1937) gives us an insight into the man who became his father-in-law, in his autobiography *Milestones*. Sir William was born in 1819 and was educated at Rugby Public School under the famous Thomas Arnold. He graduated with honours from Cambridge where he was at St John's College. He studied for the bar and travelled widely on the continent, becoming fluent in French. He then joined his father, Samuel Brooks, as a partner in the Banking House of Cunliffe Brooks & Co. in Manchester and Blackburn He extended the business to Altrincham and London, and was a man of influence in his own district. In 1847 he was called to the bar and in 1864 became sole partner of the bank on the death of his father.

Huntly goes on to describe Cunliffe Brooks as being hugely successful in business, but, according to those around him, he gradually became despotic. Unprepared to take advice from anyone, he was robbed in all directions. He loved power and was excessively proud of Brooks and Co., it being the last private bank in Manchester. A fortnight after his death the partners to whom he left it sold the bank to Lloyds Ltd.

Cunliffe Brooks' political career began in 1869 when he was elected to the House of Commons as member for East Cheshire; then from 1885 until 1892 he was member for Altrincham. He was a great benefactor to the town of Sale, where he funded the Ashton Lane Fountain – a fountain horse trough – which whetted his appetite to do the same in Glen Tanar in the future. The description of his fountain read, "Two troughs at either side of a fountain rising to stone shaft. Capital surmounted by cast iron lamp standard". He also gifted a site for the Church of St Mary Magdalene as well as money for a church tower and provided substantial funds to the Free Library in Sale.

When in 1886 he was made a baronet he must have felt that the world had belatedly come to appreciate his true worth. That he ran an estate so meticulously in the far north and still managed to represent his constituents in the Midlands beggars belief, but he was obviously a man of huge energy and commitment. He was recorded for posterity by the magazine *Vanity*

Brooks the Golden Pippin

Fair which produced caricatures both lampooning and praising eminent Victorians and Edwardian politicians, sportsmen, lawyers and other 'Men of the Day'. In the edition of 2nd August 1879, Brooks is figured as a gentleman of portly proportions with a strutting, self important pose and is labelled 'The Golden Pippin'.

Brooks married firstly, Jane Elizabeth Orrell on 25th July 1842 who died on 10th October 1865, and secondly Jean Davidson on 5th November 1879. He had two daughters by his first marriage. Amy, who married the Marquis of Huntly on 14th July 1869 and died on 13th May 1920. On 14th October 1874 his second daughter, Edith, married Lord Francis Cecil, who died on 23rd June 1889 at the tender age of thirty-seven. They had three sons and two daughters. Edith went on to marry Admiral Philip F. Tillard on 26th April 1892 and died on 9th May 1923.

Because of his close association with the Marquis of Huntly through his daughter's marriage, Brooks obtained Glen Tanar estate in 1871, on a twenty-one years' lease. With the Huntly fortunes in the doldrums, he then purchased Aboyne Castle in 1888 for £62,000, allowing the previous owners life rent of the property. In 1890 he bought the Glen Tanar estate from the Huntly trustees for £120,000 and finally in 1899 Ferrar estate, just west of Aboyne, for £27,000. These transactions highlighted the desperate financial straits of the Marquis, said to be all due to his gambling addiction.

That Brooks was a man who rated himself very highly and sent out this message forcibly to those around him, was demonstrated by a tale from Huntly's memoirs. Canon MacColl, presumably the Episcopal minister in Aboyne, had gone one day to take the service at Glen Tanar. On his return he had said to the Marquis's wife, "I was rather disconcerted with the tone and way in which your father said the responses. He seemed to be conferring a favour on the Almighty".

Despite this self belief, however, the Marquis of Huntly maintained Sir William was always in mortal terror of being shot. When a doctor peppered another gun with a pellet in the nose at one shoot, Brooks had turned to his son-in-law and said, "Fancy if it had been me, and I was next gun to him". Huntly advised him never to ask doctors out shooting again, as their presence brought grist to his mill and bad luck to the other sportsmen. The tale of a drive in Cambus o' May woods soon after this,

A day's grouse shooting on the Glen Tanar Estate. Cunliffe Brooks and his head keeper in a painting by Carl Suhrlandt

for roe deer and black game, brings a sense of the ridiculous. Sir William turned up in white flannel knickerbockers, a flaming red waistcoat and a large check coat. Needless to say no bird or beast ventured near him, so by the end of the day he had never fired a shot. He was, however, said to be a good marksman although slow and deliberate and had the odd habit of aiming at a bird saying, "Dead bird," while pulling the trigger.

In another excerpt from *Milestones* the Marquis of Huntly tells of the time in 1888, when staying in Aboyne, he witnessed at first hand Brooks' unbounded energy in planning and building. With the aid of his clever architect George Truefitt (1825-1902) the building work was all done on day labour and none by contract. Truefitt he described as a little man and although some of his work was inclined to be finicky and small in conception, but correct in design, the restoration at Aboyne Castle was done in excellent taste.

Thomas H. Mawson (1861-1933) was an up-and-coming landscape architect when he was introduced to Sir William "through a fine old Shropshire squire, Mr Frank Stanier of Peplow Hall, who warned me that Sir William would prove a difficult client, at the same time expressing confidence that I had the qualities to win his goodwill".

Mawson, in his autobiography published in 1927, gives a lovely description of Brooks. I shall quote extensively from it, as it gives us such a personal comprehensive assessment. "Now Mr Mawson, whenever Sir William takes morning prayers, look out for a squall and go very slow," was a warning from one of Brooks friends. By contrast, Lady Brooks was a joy to listen to, reading the prayers with a perfect voice and intonation.

Mawson found his new client had a passion for building and road making and kept a regular staff of two hundred and fifty workmen. In his time Brooks rebuilt not only Glen Tanar house, but nearly every farmhouse and cottage on the estate. He also, in a large measure, rebuilt or added to the village of Aboyne and carried out extensive improvements to Aboyne Castle, where his son-in-law the Marquis of Huntly resided.

Throughout his discourse on his work on the estate Mawson keeps referring to "Glen Tana", so Brooks had left him in no doubt that the 'r' was quite wrong; like everyone else, he knew to abide by the master's decision.

For a Mawson day at the Glen, he would hear, promptly at seven, the distant wail of the bagpipes and by five past, the piper was marching around the mansion house as if to waken the dead. At 7.10 a footman appeared with a cup of tea and stating his bath was ready. Breakfast was at 7.45; prayers at 8.20; the carriage and pair arrived at 8.30 and they were away to the minute, with the piper as coachman. Brooks himself started even earlier; six in the summer, seven in the winter, he was downstairs with his secretary dictating replies to his vast correspondence.

"Every day there was a big programme of work. First the widening of the Bridge of Ess, then planning, out on the ground, the lines for new roads and carriageways; then on for a mile where an important fence wall was being erected." Mawson states: "This I believe to be the finest dry walling in Great Britain, a fact on which my client greatly prided himself". An interesting comment, as at this distance it is difficult to know to which wall he was referring.

From this point Brooks would drive to where a pipe track was being laid to supply the village of Aboyne with water. Minute discussions were held at every point and alterations proposed as they came into his fertile brain. Mawson highlighted this as a drawback to every adviser to Brooks as "no finality," adding, "A poor man can't afford to change a contract; a rich man can do as often as fancy suggests".

A lunch of sandwiches and tea, always carried in a stone bottle, packed in a carefully lined and upholstered basket. Half an hour and on their way again to view farm outbuildings in the process of construction and talk to the various skilled workers about corrections to be made. Then on to Aboyne Castle in order to check on building progress and discuss the arrangement of the gardens, home policies and new avenues. Drive to Dinnet inspecting all the farms on the way, discuss sites for new schools, look at one or two fishing lodges and then stop for another cup of tea about four o'clock. The pony rested, it is off again to check on men widening a road and foresters fencing in rough land to be planted in the autumn. If Mawson was lucky, he reached the haven of the mansion house by 6.45 pm.

Mawson was obviously intrigued by this workaholic. He tells how Brooks would have a ghillie meet him at some pre-arranged place on the estate mid-morning with his mail and similarly in the afternoon. The letters were opened by the piper who handed them to Brooks, who would mark them with a blue or red pencil and then place them, according to classification, in one or other of his capacious leather pockets. Next morning, when all were asleep, apart from Brooks and his secretary, they would be answered.

You can sense a level of frustration with his pernickety client, but Mawson well realised that Brooks was a valuable contact; success with him would greatly enhance his attractiveness to other lairds in the district.

Mawson, coming from a different English background, must have found some of the dour Scots difficult to fathom. He tells the tale, when after hours of discussing and pegging out around the Tower of Ess, Sir William turned to his foreman mason saying, "Well, Donald, if I were younger and richer, I would do all that Mr Mawson advises me to do." To which Donald replied, "Weel Sir William, ye'd better get on wi' the work, for ye'll ne'er be younger and perhaps if you were richer, someone else would be aye the poorer".

Mawson comments that this was "typical of the distinctively Gaelic pleasantry of the area", so he must have come to understood and perhaps enjoy some of the canny responses that we north-easters have revelled in throughout the ages.

He speaks, too, of the unique little church of St Lesmo, contrived out of an old manor house kitchen, on which Sir William and Truefitt had expended much ingenuity. He talks of the strange Gothic effect produced by rows of stags' skulls, their antlers – many of them 'royals' i.e. twelve pointers – making a perfect forest overhead. Inscribed on each skull was the name or initials of the sportsman who had brought the stag down. He was also intrigued by a beautiful stained-glass window, depicting the Saint of the Forest, in one of the window slits. The effect was of a baronial hall or the private chapel of an old baron. The minister at the time was noted as the Rev. Cecil Nash.

At dinner on Mawson's first Sunday after arrival, Lady Brooks asked him what he thought of the chapel.

"Quaint and beautiful, but it seemed strange that you should apply the trophies of sport to the decoration of your church."

His hostess replied, "We consider these stags' heads the most beautiful thing the forest produces, and that is why we use them to beautify our church."

On a Good Friday morning, Mawson was expecting a welcome break from all this headlong work, but no; the carriage and pair arrived on schedule. Asked by Brooks if he would mind going back down to the Bridge of Ess for some more measuring, Mawson made no objection and his client added that they would go on to the church service after that.

As a number of men were driving in pegs, the Rev. Nash passed by on his way to the church and pointedly ignored Brooks. Mawson remarked that the minister looked rather annoyed and said he wouldn't be surprised if it were mentioned in the sermon. "I say he dare not do it, I pay his stipend," said Brooks, but Mawson replied that the minister was a courageous man and would speak out if he felt it his duty.

Brooks took the remarks badly and was in a foul temper by the time they reached the church rather late. Sure enough, the Rev. Nash chastised the two of them publicly about the neglect of the Holy Day. In the churchyard after the service the minister and the squire had an almighty row, the Rev. Nash giving not one inch of ground. For days afterwards Brooks was unmanageable; Mawson took the opportunity to make an excuse and left for home.

On his many further visits to Glen Tanar over the years Mawson seems to have established a good working relationship with Sir William. He maintained his client was the best raconteur that he had ever known and tells some of the tales in his autobiography. It was, of course, not all work and the running of the mansion house intrigued him.

Each evening the ghillies deposited, in the dining-room, the kill of the day, whether of rod or gun, and the guests rose ceremoniously to compliment Bailey, the head ghillie. One evening something went wrong, with Bailey in disgrace and Sir William calling him a fool. "Do you know you are a fool Bailey?" "Yes, Sir William," replied Bailey, touching his hatless head.

The next evening it was Parker the butler's turn to be vilified for something not his responsibility. So impatient was Sir William that he would not allow Parker a chance to explain. Later, someone pointed out to Brooks what had really happened and he decided to offer Parker an apology at the end of the dinner.

"Parker, stand here, for I wish to explain as publicly as I made my charge against you, that it was wrong. I wish to say, you are not as great a fool as I thought you were. Does that satisfy you?"

"Yes Sir William," was the docile answer.

Mawson maintained these were but foibles and that the irascible old martinet had many lovable qualities which endeared him to a wide circle of friends. He was, for instance, a most considerate employer and a generous landlord. However, the quality that most intrigued Mawson was Brooks' fondness for children – he carried a supply of sweets for those he met on his travels, and children's hospitals gained much over the years from his generosity.

In his final paragraph on his Glen Tana experience Mawson admires Sir William's remarkable ability to master all that was set before him and deal with it in a twinkling. No expense was spared to ensure that plans were correct, but the final product was usually a travesty of the original ideas of Mawson and his partner, Daniel Gibson. Mawson sounds despondent here, as the only things that turned out as he had visualised were the Bridge of Ess, the layout of the roads around it and the Ladywood feuing plan at Aboyne. His imaginative layout for new avenues and entrances, extensive lawns and gardens and a new carriage court at Aboyne Castle never materialised. Workers were always too busy with other ambitious projects and so Brooks, master of all he surveyed, died in 1900 with much yet to be completed.

We owe Thomas Mawson our gratitude for giving us such a personal view on a man who achieved more on his estate than a dozen others put together did – and set a gold standard for farms and cottages to be judged by.

In 1898 the Marquis of Huntly began to see a great change in his father-in-law. His vivacity and bonhomie disappeared and he was obviously depressed. He tended to quarrel with people for no good reason,

1899: Brooks with a house party at Eagle's Eyrie at Porphyry Bridge

which was unlike him, despite his well-known temper. The two men seem to have been at loggerheads over plans to have an isolation hospital established in Aboyne. Huntly had sold a piece of land to the County Council, well away from other houses, for this purpose, but Brooks objected strongly, declaring the risk of contagion would affect the value of his property, although the nearest part was a quarter of a mile away.

Brooks lost his appeal, then declared that he would sell his property and alter his will. Huntly paid no attention. Oddly enough, it was in the year 1898 that the Marquis of Huntly was himself up in the Bankruptcy Court in London, owing £139,698 with assets of only £690. You would have thought that in the circumstances he would have been only too sensitive as to what his father-in-law might do with his will.

The Marquis of Huntly in *Auld Acquaintance* tells of the death of his father-in-law on 9th June 1900. "The news had reached Aboyne on the 5th of the battle of Paardeberg, and the capture of Pretoria by the British forces under Lord Roberts. Sir William insisted on having a huge bonfire on the Green of Aboyne the following day, and went down there in the evening, and harangued the crowd on the importance of the victory. With his back to the fire he baked himself, drove back to Glen Tanar in an open carriage with only a light overcoat, went to his bed, and could take nothing; he died three days later.

"A victim of his own foolhardiness," stated the Marquis.

Huntly concludes his assessment of Sir William with these words:

"Whatever the faults of his later years, he deserves to be held in grateful remembrance for his many acts of kindness and generosity, for the improvements he made to the roads, buildings and cottages in the district, and for the liberal employment he gave to the labourers and tradesmen around him."

THE BROOKS' ERA

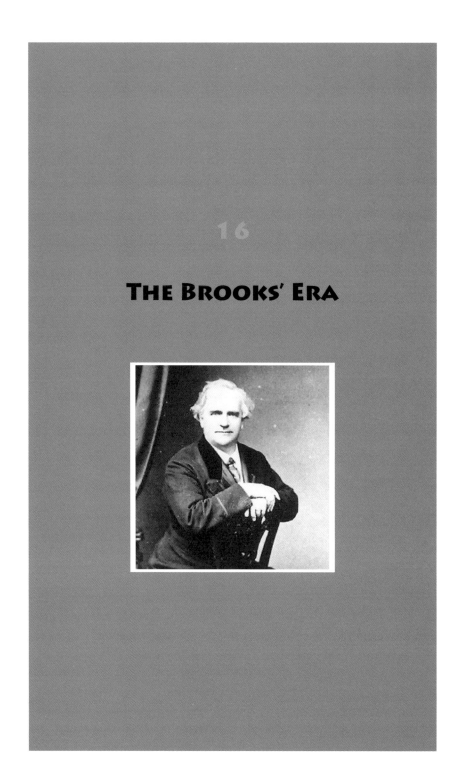

Writers through the ages, covering that period in the affairs of Aboyne and Glen Tanar, have their own slant on Brooks. This ebullient character brought a ray of sunshine into many lives, but to others a veritable hurricane of change.

Queen Victoria had come to Deeside and taken the lease on Balmoral Castle in 1847. In 1852 the estate of over 17,000 acres was bought from the Fife trustees for 30,000 guineas, which allowed work to begin on a new castle. This new Balmoral was completed by 1855 and so commenced an association with Royalty that has had an immense effect on the area ever since. Having the social scene so elevated must have had the local nobility preening with delight. Brooks may not have been directly influenced in taking the Glen Tanar lease because of Balmoral's proximity, but his subsequent revelling in the association becomes apparent through the years. The coming of the railway to Aboyne in 1859, then on to Ballater in 1866 also increased the desirability of the district in his eyes.

Looking back, his major project was the construction of his mansion house on the site of an old farm dwelling. Commissioning the architects, Fryers & Penman of Largs, he set out

Sir William Cunliffe Brooks

to build a dwelling of character and importance. The principal rooms on the ground floor included a dining room of some grandeur, drawing room, morning room, billiard room and a magnificent ballroom. The ballroom, 60 feet long by 27 feet high, with its high-pitched open timber, ornamented with stags' heads, is even today something to be admired. In

Glentanar House: A mansion of turrets, roofs and chimneys

addition there was a large entrance hall, bowling alley and all the usual amenities.

On the first floor were 23 bedrooms, dressing rooms and bathrooms for the family and guests, as well as 15 servants' bedrooms. In the servants' quarters, in addition to a big airy kitchen, was a large hall, a housemaids' sitting room, the housekeeper's room for the senior staff and all sorts of 'below stairs' requirements for the running of a palatial residence. Cunliffe Brooks had stamped his presence on the neighbourhood.

All this activity arose from his having bought the estate in 1890 instead of renting it, so becoming his own lord and master, able to do with it as he wished without seeking the approval of his aristocratic son-in-law.

In association with Mr George Truefitt, an architect from Worthing, and Mr Thomas Mawson, a landscape architect from Windermere, Brooks set out to transform this backwater Scottish valley into something to startle the natives. A striking entrance lodge in the shape of a tower at the Bridge of Ess served notice to visitors that they were approaching an establishment of some importance. The imposing pillars at this north entrance to the Glen gave the impression of a private establishment, when in fact the road was still for public use. The carvings on the pillars and the quality of the embellished masonry shows that Brooks and his workers were interested only in workmanship of the highest standard. Glen Tanar School, with its oast-house roofs, is perhaps more in keeping with Kent, but is nevertheless most appealing.

Much has been made of the fact that Brooks showed no sensitivity to

Scottish architecture and simply imposed his English designs, regardless of convention. Having been brought up in the glen and having lived my young years in his very adequate accommodation, I have no quarrel with Brooks and find most of his initiatives very attractive. Not that we as scholars, sitting in his lovely school, were ever aware of its uniqueness; it is only now, in my senior years, that I appreciate all that he accomplished.

The centre of our personal universe was the stable-yard, with the estate office and other surrounding buildings forming the core of a functioning establishment. What is now called the Butler's Lodge, at the top end of the stable-yard, was my home, with the head joiner's house semi-detached round the corner. Adjacent to us on the estate office wall was the hooter point with the infamous hooter on top of the highest building at the foot of the yard. That siren signalled mid-day on a Saturday, but its main purpose was to summon help in case of fire, especially out on the hill when immediate assistance could prevent an inferno. Over the years that siren's ominous wail could shatter the silence of the night as the forest erupted in flames… and when little boys naughtily tampered with the switch they got more than they bargained for in more ways than one.

The large kitchen and flower garden abutted the stable-yard while four hundred yards away was the model home farm. The concept was a cosy nucleus of buildings to give the feeling of community, without crowding in on one another. The fact that the mansion house was close by, yet completely sheltered from this working environment, was cleverly achieved.

The extensive use of Glen Tanar's granite from its own quarries – coarse and coral pink in colour – gives the buildings a rugged, quality feel. Because of its grainy texture the masons often left it bull-faced or rusticated. For those with an interest in architecture, it is worth pausing around the estate, not only to appreciate the stone work, but to admire the wonderful designs on the slate roofs, and the many leaded windows.

Having completed his nucleus, Brooks turned to providing decent houses for the outlying workers and also launched out on improving his tenanted farms. Scarcely a farm house and its outbuildings were overlooked in this mammoth task and although many are now sadly in disrepair, this was never a half-hearted project for the sake of appearances. He was not shy in proclaiming his vision, as many buildings have been embellished prominently with his WCB monogram and the date picked out in granite on gable ends.

There are still a few stories told in the district relating to all this building work, especially to the farms. The rebuilding of Ballaterach farm was progressing well and Brooks had just seen his well-known insignia placed on an outbuilding when the tenant farmer and he had a slight altercation. The farmer, it is believed, pointed out some minor adjustment to the building which would make it more efficient, totally upsetting Brooks who walked away from the project leaving it half finished, as it remains today. Like a little child deprived of his toffee apple, he stormed off to sulk and never ventured near that farm again.

Neil Williams of Ballaterach recounts another tale relating to the building of Corntulloch farm house. The architect had in his plans a front and back door, but when Brooks saw the project progressing he stopped the work, insisting that two doors so placed encouraged through draughts and heat loss; he stated it was to be one or the other. I checked on this ancient story and sure enough, the Corntulloch farmhouse has only one door facing north to the winter storms.

Brooks carried out extensive remedial work on Aboyne Castle, as well as completing a number of buildings in the village itself, including the Birse Lodge, and in the Aboyne Square where his monogram can still be found. His building of Fasnadarach House just west of Glentanar School is interesting, as this came to belong to Lord Francis Cecil, his son-in-law. That it may have been a wedding present is possible, but with Lord Cecil dying in his thirties, it appears that one of his sons, Ean Francis Cecil, owned it up until his death in 1942.

Brooks delighted in building roads, introducing a modern water supply and drainage system for the estate, so dispensing with the 'green patch' in front of the cottage door. He also erected miles of iron fencing to keep his deer from straying outwith his territory. His development of the artificial lake with its cosy boat-house is a feature which those of us brought up here treasure from our childhood. Below the level of this lake Brooks constructed a number of smaller ponds, in what we now term 'the policies'. It is believed that in some of these ponds he was involved in the culture of salmon, hatching many thousand from spawn obtained from the Tay. It was said that this produced a superior product in both quality and appearance, adding to the acknowledged excellence of the Dee salmon.

As regards the policies, these were various 'Wander Walks', arranged to be readily accessible from the mansion house, which meandered through a setting of imported rhododendrons and unusual trees, giving one the

1884: Brooks was never all work and no play and was always a very popular host. Sir William seated on the right

impression of a natural maze. As children we delighted in running through them, never quite sure where we would appear next, but with a lovely sense of adventure. This was of course done when we knew the laird was away on his travels.

It was in this setting by the river that the dynamo was installed to provide electricity to the mansion house. Above the dynamo was constructed a lovely little house of untreated wood with the bark still in place, Miss Jean Coats' doll's house. We loved peering through the windows at all Miss Jean's toys and marvelled at how someone could be blessed with such good fortune.

Sir William was an eccentric, with a habit of leaving his imprint on all sorts of features, the most common being the embellishing of horse troughs and wells along his roads and pathways. His monogram was often used, along with various quotations, some of which are far from clear to us in this modern age, but his dislike for too much alcohol is evident. Here, too, you begin to feel the influence of his Royal neighbour as so many inscribed stones pay homage to that formidable lady of Balmoral, Queen Victoria.

It is possible that Queen Victoria paid a visit to Glen Tanar in Brooks' time and he certainly paid tribute to her in his Diamond Jubilee fountain at Glentanar School and around various stones, both at Pannanich and in the Knockie area. His renaming of the road that runs in a semicircle around the centre of his development and the mansion house, from High Road to Queen's Drive, shows the influence of his Royal connection. Who are we to disparage this attitude, over a hundred years later, when our own generation is so blatantly celebrity conscious?

To say that life was all work for our laird would be quite erroneous, as photographs and stories exist to show him in a different light. He relished the mantle of mine host and entertaining lavishly during the season on Deeside. The most extraordinary tale, however, cuts across all that Sir William stood for, as someone with devout Christian morals.

The Prince of Wales, later to become King Edward V11, was renowned for having gathered around him a rather wild and perhaps loose-living group of the young nobility called the Malborough House Set. Among their ranks was the beautiful Lillie Langtry, the acknowledged 'it' girl of that generation. Born Emilie Charlotte le Breton in Jersey in 1853, she was the daughter of the Dean of Jersey. With five brothers as company, she described herself as an incorrigible tomboy and practical joker. At the age of twenty she married Edward Langtry, then thirty, and went to live on the mainland. After a bout of typhoid she moved to London to recuperate and her good looks attracted attention. She was painted by Sir John Millais and feted by many other artists, gathering a host of admirers.

**Lillie Langtry
by Millais**

Introduced to the Prince of Wales, she was said to have become his mistress in the mid-1870s. Her prestigious connections led her to be accepted into the realms of the upper classes and so she became a guest of Sir William himself about this time. Life was dull in a mansion house for a feisty young woman with all the menfolk out killing things and boredom had her tobogganing down the main staircase on a silver tray. This was almost unimaginable behaviour in such a setting; but for her royal connection, she would have been banished. That Sir William simply instructed his butler to hide away all the silver trays in future was a telling response. When I remember that my father used to regularly check his footmen's fingernails to see that they didn't scratch the silver, I wonder how he would have viewed the lovely young Lillie's antics.

The local Aberdeen press appeared to rate Sir William very highly, as this quote from the journal in 1893 shows. Not how a modern reporter would pen it, but then those were the times when forelocks were always being firmly tugged.

"Sir William Cunliffe Brooks and his friends have had excellent sport in his splendid forest of Glen Tana. Some very fine heads have been got. Sir William does not return south until later in the season which is fortunate, as the district does not look itself when he and Lady Brooks have left it. They are extremely popular with all classes and pleasant evidences of their kindness and consideration are everywhere apparent. So Sir William has expended a great deal of money on the Glen Tana estate since he acquired it and to good purpose. The contrast between the farmhouses and cottages on the estate, as compared with estates in some parts of the Highlands of Scotland is very marked indeed and all in favour of the very popular laird of Glen Tana."

An interesting detail of life at that time is the almost complete absence of any reference to the Brooks' ladies. The only reference appears to be in Mawson's book when he refers to the second Mrs Brooks having a pleasant voice. Among the mass of detail about Sir William, not one other commentator is found referring to either of his two wives. It is also interesting to note that he had two children to his first marriage, but none to his second. Yet when Brooks married Jean Davidson in 1879 she was only 27 to his 60, but throughout those years no son was born to carry on his work.

Following her husband's death, Lady Jean Brooks moved to a house in Aboyne that she had specially built, called the Neuk, now known as Ladywood Lodge. Not to be outdone by her dominant husband, Lady Brooks had the engraving JCB 1904 emblazoned above the front door and this is still in situ. She lived in Aboyne until her death on 27th July 1946 at Altdinnie at the age of 94 years. She was laid to rest beside her husband at the entrance to their much loved Chapel of St Lesmo – the magnificent Brooks' era had finally come to an end.

At the back of the game book of Glen Tana is pasted a card with a neat little poem of thanks to them both. This appreciation from Sir Arthur Grant, dated 11th October 1891, eventually pays tribute to this overlooked companion in Brooks' well documented accomplishments.

Where the brawling Tana tumbles,
Around Sir William's walls,
You'll find the warmest welcome,
Within Sir William's halls,
So happy days unceasing,
Through all the years of life,
God sends unto Sir William,
And to his bonnie wife.

17

THE COATS' DYNASTY

n the year 1760 George Coats, aged seventeen, left his father's small farm in Lanarkshire and walked to Paisley to become an apprentice weaver. From this beginning, after decades of trial and tribulation, arose the mighty empire of J.&P. Coats, fine thread manufactures, the first multinational business in the world.

George Coats married Catherine Heywood and in due course had two sons one of whom, James, born in 1774, was to follow his father into the business. Gradually making progress and profits, James built a fine two-storey house at Ferguslie on the western fringes of Paisley, where he went on to establish a small mill. The next generation of two sons – Peter and Thomas – took the firm to new heights, developing the factory space to cope with the ever-increasing demand for their products.

A private publication in the possession of the family, *The Coats' Story* by David Keir, dated 1964, plots a fabulous account of the empire through the ages. The publication was commissioned by the last Coats to serve on the board of the company, Lord Thomas Glentanar. It explains so much that I have only partially understood in the past.

In 1873 the brothers Peter and Thomas Coats – along with their own sons – shared the firmly-established empire equally between the two families. The family was untouched by scandal and respected by the townsfolk – some indeed loved and revered them. All shared a deep sense of religion, a distaste for immoderate habits and a liking for work. They were happy and humorous – far removed from the caricature of the Victorian employer.

Thomas Coats had five sons, James Junior born 1841, Thomas Glen born 1846, George born 1849, William Allan born 1853 and Andrew, born 1855, who became a Major and won a DSO in the Boer War.

James Junior, a bachelor, was a man of fine physique, wise in council, but seen by some as an eccentric. A philanthropist on a grand scale, he is said to have called at every lighthouse around our shores in his yacht to say thank you to the keepers and no doubt leave a little something behind in gratitude. He provided various churches and communities with libraries, along with a host of other services. He extended his library service to schools throughout many parishes and this links in with references in the records of both Glentanar and Inchmarnoch schools to receiving The Coats' Library, which meant nothing to me when I first read it.

Keir's history records James Junior's other gift: "Then there were the children. Touched by the number of poor Scots schoolchildren going to school in bad weather without satchels to protect their books and personal belongings, he arranged a nation-wide distribution of satchels. In Paisley itself he was always so pained by the sight of poor children going about in the rain or snow with bare feet that regularly over a long period he spent more than £1,000 a year on buying them boots and shoes." James died in 1912 and was remembered with great affection throughout the whole of Scotland for all his generosity, not least by the Glentanar school pupils.

George Coats was eight years younger than his bachelor brother and is described as being hugely outgoing and of a very happy nature. Keir sums up his character very well: "Though he was naturally proud of the business made possible by his ancestral namesake, George, there were times when this more high spirited George could have been seen in his working clothes trying to slip past the Ferguslie gatehouse on his way to the stables. But even in his maturity there are sporting stories to be told of him – how once, for instance, a visitor to Ferguslie knocked at his office door, heard footsteps cross the floor inside and then saw the door open just wide enough to show George Coats' face in the opening as he welcomed his guest with the jolly cry, 'Come in, come in quickly. I've got a terrier in here and some rats'."

By 1873 George was feeling his way in the business and working hard. He was also playing hard and making hosts of friends, for he was sociable by instinct and a lover of good company. *The Paisley Daily Express* on 29th December 1877 reported: "It is a fortunate fact for Mr George Coats that he is by nature a modest young gentleman otherwise his head would get turned a bit just at present. He has this week made the biggest score in the social life of Paisley Society that has been made since the river Cart ran rowin to the sea. Apparently George has invited his friends to a Calico

Fancy Dress Ball which was not only a venturesome idea but in the event a great success."

Lillie Langtry, whose antics in Glen Tanar House in the 1870s shocked Cunliffe Brooks, was by 1883 an actress of great renown. A rival cotton thread maker to J.&P. Coats at that time was Kerr & Co. who had seized the initiative over their opposition by an imaginative piece of publicity. Kerr persuaded Lillie to give a glowing testimonial and she wrote to them from Coney Island Hotel as follows:

> Gentlemen,
> I am so pleased to find your cotton this side of the Atlantic. I have used it always on the other side; it is vastly superior to any I have found here, and I prefer the shape of the spool.
> I am Gentlemen, Yours faithfully,
> Lillie Langtry.

This trivial episode made the Coats Board wake up and realise that they didn't have things all their own way… and we can smile to think how all these odd strands are linking in to our own little story. However, in the years ahead Coats were to take over Kerr & Co., so they had the last laugh after all.

Again I quote Keir directly. "In 1880 after a whirlwind courtship he (George) married Margaret Lothian Black, daughter of James Tait Black who was the son of Adam Black the famous publisher and a Lord Provost of Edinburgh. In 1884 George bought the estate of Belleisle near Ayr where he took special delight in entertaining his wife's family at that notable time in their career when they were publishing the *Encyclopaedia Britannica*. George Coats was universally liked; always down to earth, he brought a practical mind to bear on mill or Board room problems without losing his natural *joie de vivre* and contagious enthusiasm. It might be some new scheme for Ferguslie, plans to go yacht racing, fox hunting, shooting and deer stalking or the painting and sketching of water colour pictures or caricatures in pen and ink. Into each and every one he would put his heart and soul. Great ability to delegate he was often heard to say, it's no use keeping a dog and barking yourself."

In 1901, following the death of Sir Cunliffe Brooks, George Coats took on the tenancy of Glen Tanar estate from Lady Brooks, finding the stalking, shooting and fishing hugely to his taste.

George Coats' dream of owning the valley of the Tanar and its

1904: The years of tenancy before purchasing the estate in 1905

hinterland to the north around Deecastle came to fruition in the auction rooms of the Mart in Tokenhouse Yard, London in June 1905. Here Mr Bamford, a stoutish gentleman with a most persuasive tongue sat on the rostrum. His description of the estate was graphic. He commenced by pointing out that it was of a magnificent size, being 35 miles square and pierced by private roads as good as any in the country. The low ground was very good for pheasants; and, "gentlemen, pheasants are only a matter of expense – you can have as many as you like on such a place". There were in addition eleven miles of fishing and the Dee, he said, was one of the best salmon rivers in Scotland.

There was a grouse moor, too, and all this within easy reach of London. Even today this seems an exaggeration, but no, Mr Bamford went on to justify his comments. "You can leave London at eight o'clock at night, sleep all the way to Aberdeen, and have breakfast and be out shooting at Glen Tana at ten o'clock next morning." With the present state of our railway system and with Dr Beeching having eliminated the Deeside line we certainly seem to have taken a backward step since 1905.

The mansion was promoted as being exceedingly comfortable and its late owner, the auctioneer went on to say, had spent money on the estate wherever it was possible to spend it. He had erected farm buildings at a cost of £7,000 and let the farm at £32 a year. "The buyer will not have to spend a penny in putting the estate in order. Why? – because so much has been lavished upon Glen Tana that there are even stained glass windows in the piggery."

Mr Bamford proceeded with the sale and it was reported in the Aberdeen press next day that the proceedings were witnessed by a member of the Student's Representative Council of Aberdeen University. He was flabbergasted at the levels of the bids, rising by £10,000 each time, until the estate was knocked down for the princely sum of £155,000 to Mr George Coats of Paisley.

In a later edition there was a lengthy report that Mr George Coats, who had leased Glen Tanar for the previous few seasons, was now the new owner. A fuller description was appended giving the breakdown of the acreage. The total was 29,200 acres of which 22,000 acres were deer forest, 6,000 acres grouse moor and 1,200 acres agricultural land. A full description of the estate boundaries then followed, including its geographic highlights. A telling sentence was that it was four-and-a-half miles from Aboyne and twenty miles from Balmoral – no word of Ballater, Banchory or Braemar – just the Royal residence.

George Coats

The gardens were described as being very pretty and the house, which was lit by electricity, contained handsome public rooms and a magnificent ballroom. The stables were large and fitted with all modern appliances. In the kennels there was accommodation for fifty dogs and the article went on to describe the kennelman's house, ghillies' bothy and extensive game larder. The home farm contained ninety-one-and-a-half acres of arable land and was splendidly equipped with buildings, including a steward's house.

The report further extolled the deer forest, the grouse moor and the salmon fishing, with the comment that several pools were regarded as the best on the whole of the Dee. Large areas of the estate were covered with larch, spruce, Scots fir, of which about 120,000 were fully mature. The rental, including the mansion house (furnished), shootings and fishings was

The Shepherd's Hut in George Coats era of the early 1900s. Car numbers SA 398 and LN 2959

£6,037.0s.7d and the burdens £601.5s.5d. The article concluded that there was much satisfaction on Deeside at the intimation that Mr Coats, the present tenant of Glen Tana, has purchased the estate. "Mr Coats and the family have endeared themselves to all classes of the community and are very popular." I wonder where we have heard all that before?

George Coats, in addition to Glen Tanar and Belleisle, also now owned 11 Hill Street, off Berkeley Square in London, where he was wont to entertain quite splendidly. This house had a marble-paved loggia adorned with the choicest works of Italian artists. There was a Louis Seize ballroom with reception rooms and tapestried Empire suites with sunken marble baths.

Coats' wife Margaret has been described as a petite, energetic person who loved entertaining and being entertained. She was very supportive of all her husband's hobbies and took an interest in the affairs of the company. George Coats was a keen sailor who appears to have owned a variety of yachts; it has been said he won more races to his own helm than any other man of his time. He also hunted hard in the winter in Ayrshire with the Eglinton Hunt and later in Leicestershire where he was proud to represent Scotland when he was admitted to the Quorn Hunt – the most prestigious, elitist hunt in the country at that time.

The most astonishing discovery, when I was given access to the Coats' records and diaries, was George Coats five volumes of watercolour paintings and pen-and-ink sketches. They range from portraits, and sailing and hunting scenes, to skittish social interactions and must have involved him in hundreds of hours of quiet occupation in a hobby at which he was no mean craftsman. This has indeed been one of the highlights of my research as I was totally unaware that these treasures existed.

George and Margaret Coats had three children. In 1904 their eldest

**A hidden talent: Some examples of George Coats' work in five
volumes of watercolour paintings and pen-and-ink sketches**

daughter Charlotte married the Hon. William L.C. Walrond, son of Lord
Waleran, MP for Tiverton. Five years later their youngest daughter Maud

married the Marquis of Douro, son and heir to the fourth Duke of Wellington. Their son Thomas Coats, born in 1894, was to get caught up in World War I, but that is for another chapter. It is an interesting custom of the time for the new moneyed aristocracy to cement their place in society by marrying their sons, and especially daughters, into the old established families of the realm, so ensuring their future status.

The estate of Glen Tanar during the George Coats' years does not appear to have stimulated much further development, as it probably fulfilled all that its owner required of it. The most prestigious initiative of George Coats came about in 1907 when he funded the erection of St Thomas' Episcopal Church in Aboyne, which equalled in quality the buildings of the Brooks' era. The Glentanar School headmaster writes on 4th October 1907: "Scholars of Glen Tanar absent at laying of the Memorial Stone of the Church of St Thomas in Aboyne".

In August 1914 George Coats made a donation of £50,000 to the Prince of Wales Relief Fund and during the war is recorded as making many other donations. In 1916 Mr Asquith's Government rewarded him with a peerage. This fact is taken from Lady Glentanar's diaries and raises the question as to whether the title was bought or gifted. My father always said that the title had cost George Coats £40,000 from Lloyd George's drive to sell titles for the war effort while he was Secretary of State for War, prior to his becoming Premier later in 1916. This is borne out by the book by Michael-De-La-Noy, *The Honours System,* in which he records the costs of various titles at that time. However, I talked to George Coats' granddaughter many years later, who understood from the family that it was in recognition of his open-handedness over the years. Weir in his history adds:"Having neither false modesty nor false pride, George Coats wore the elevation easily and being indisputably a happy man, he had felt especial pleasure when so many of his friends and relatives expressed theirs."

George Coats went on to make the most of his estate even throughout the war years and despite failing health would insist on getting out to his beloved horses and riding as much as possible. Lady Glentanar records on 26th June 1918:"George rode for the first time since his illness. Aeroplane came down at the dining room window. The pilot Mr Macleod had to lie down for an hour." Two days later she writes "George rode. Mr Macleod got away in his aeroplane back to Montrose."

Another light hearted episode appears in the diary of 31st July 1918:

"Visit from Harry Lauder and had a big luncheon." Harry Lauder seems to have made himself popular with the family as he appears on other occasions, as on 26th September 1927: "Harry Lauder stalked – got none." On 16th of August 1918 George Coats shows his stamina by going grouse shooting and his wife demonstrates the incongruity of life at home and on the Western Front by writing: "Grouse drive – George got six birds with seven shots. Terrible number of deaths among our friends".

By 1918 George Coats' asthma, which had increasingly dogged him over the years, saw him now more and more dependent on regular oxygen and in November 1918 he quietly passed away, just sixteen days after the Armistice. Keir in his history of the Coats family is obviously a great fan of George, as he pays him this final tribute. "Lord Glentanar himself had the gifts of being as happy with ghillies in the Highlands, or with spinners and spool turners in Paisley as with his peers at Westminster, which largely explains his popularity both inside and outside business." As for his wealth it was reported at the time as being worth £4,642,263, with £2,000 left to St Thomas' Church.

That he should have died at this time when his young son was just returning from the fighting in France, with no other experience of life, was very unfortunate. His wise council would have been appreciated by young Tom, there is little doubt, and the tenor of his son's life may have been totally different. However, like a dealt hand of cards, you must play them as chance dictates, so the estate was to find a quite different laird in place for the next forty-one years.

In this postscript to the Coats Dynasty chapter, let us take a quick glimpse at two of George Coat's other brothers, Thomas Glen Coats and William Allan Coats. All three brothers shared a common interest; that of collecting fine paintings. George and Thomas Glen were relatively modest collectors, but the same could not be said of William Allan. Through the years he bought up, not only the old masters, but many of the moderns who were to become famous and priceless. He owned, for instance, twenty Corots and no less than thirty-one Monticellis. He also supported Scottish artists, and owned forty-five Crawhalls. The Glasgow art dealer Alex Reid, who had been responsible from the 1890s for the Impressionists being absorbed into Scottish collections, greatly influenced Coats' taste for art. Coats, in fact, for many years was Reid's most prolific client. William died in 1926 and his collection was sold by Christies in 1927. Sadly, as with all things in our lives, nothing is for ever.

18

THE DOWAGER'S DIARIES

"On 22nd of June 1880 I was engaged to George Coats at 19 Atholl Crescent, Edinburgh. We went out to St Catherines to see my grandfather Lothian who was very ill." So commenced the Dowager's diaries, continuing uninterrupted until 1935, the year of her death. Born in 1854, the young Miss Margaret Black was twenty-six and her betrothed thirty-one. They were destined to enjoy a way of life in which every minute was meant to count.

When George Coats died in November 1918, Lady Glentanar was only 65 years old and still hale and hearty. That her son had just returned from the Western Front and never had any form of training, having had to leave Oxford due to the war, must have given her some anxiety. Tom Glentanar was a headstrong man – certain of his own capabilities and not too fond of taking advice. The bond between mother and son, however, was strong and endured throughout her life, to the benefit of the maturing young man.

Born in the age of deference, the Dowager Lady Glentanar, although not of the aristocracy, was brought up in a household conscious of its importance in Scotland's society. Her grandfather had held the office of Lord Provost of Edinburgh, a tremendous honour in those days, guaranteeing the family recognition. Young women of that era were educated to fit into the social scene rather to have any meaningful occupation, so preparing her meticulously for the life of a lady.

Left behind to mark her life are five volumes of diaries, beautifully bound in leather with the gold embossed initials 'MC', and now preserved among the archives in Glentanar House. The diaries appear to have been laboriously typed out, probably from the hand-written originals, then bound into these volumes. Inked in additions, in her son Tommie's hand, are presumably where the typist failed to decipher the details. That her son should have taken the trouble to preserve these records, I believe, demonstrates his appreciation of his mother's life.

The diaries are a wonderful window into the social world of the leisured class of that era. They are essentially a record of events and names showing little reaction to or opinions of either the people or happenings. There must have been people Margaret really liked, including the Royalty, and admired more than others. Not a whisper of what she really thought comes through from her journals, so does this demonstrate great forbearance or just a reluctance to record those aspects of life? This approach makes it impossible to ascertain what was passing through the mind of the diarist; emotion is reserved for her husband's death and the anniversaries of it through the years, with some touching poems.

The Dowager's diaries from 1918 onwards show her carrying on her life unrestrained, in a constant social whirl, but always with an element of concern for her son and his lifestyle. Either entertaining or being entertained is a daily ritual, even the thought of which is tiring as one leafs through the years. The frequent dinner parties are striking for the nobility involved, where frequently not one untitled person is listed; the feeling persists that the whole point is to be seen with only the most prestigious in the land – and the closer to Royalty the better. Only in the latter years does this seem to tail off a little, as she seems to appreciate the joy of having her grandchildren around her.

**The Dowager
Lady Glentanar**

That Deeside and Balmoral fulfilled the prestigious ambitions is seen with such entries on 9th September 1919 – "The Queen comes to tea," or the regular references of going to Ballater railway station in the autumn to see the King and Queen depart for London and present them with flowers. At other times there are references to being entertained to tea, or attending balls at Balmoral. A typical entry here is "28th September 1927 – went to the Balmoral Ghillies' Ball. Maudie and Lottie danced with the Prince of Wales and George. Tommie with the Queen, while I sat on the dais with the King." Two days later it is time for the Glen Tanar Ghillies' Ball with the following entry: "Ball a huge success. The Prince of Wales and Prince George dined and danced in the billiard room after the ballroom." Little wonder that the entry for the following day showed the after effects: "Maudie rested in bed all day and Lottie had headache." However, her other guests must have got the message and all went off to

Queen Mary & Dowager 1925

Finzean to view Mr Joseph Farquharson's pictures.

There is a poignant photograph taken on the steps of Balmoral castle in 1928 with the tall, imperious Queen Mary surrounded by a bevy of ladies in hats with a petite dowager at her left shoulder. Even as late as 27th November 1934 the diary records: "Went to the Buckingham Palace Evening Party – the Queen, The Duke and Duchess and Princess Marina all spoke to me and also Princess Margaret of Greece."

Today this may all seem trivial, but it has to be remembered that back then many would rush to the roadside to wave to Royalty as they passed, something few would bother with in this less subservient age.

To transmit the full effect of the diary and sense history in the background we should pause, and read some entries for part of the last year of World War I in 1918:

20th August – Young Colin Mackenzie is wounded

23rd – Lottie arrived. Douro shot rabbits.

26th – Terrible news came that George Black had died of wounds. Struck by a shell when returning from seeing his tanks into action at 4.45 am. Died in a clearing station at Warfusie, Abacourt near Villers Bretteneux. Buried that night in the Cerlay Valley.

27th – George and I go to Glasgow. News came that Eric Coats' body had been found shot dead through the head.

28th – Douro left for London. Betty arrived at Aviemore.

29th – We returned to Glen Tanar. News came about Colin Mackenzie Jnr. being seriously wounded.

30th – George hunted with Hope in morning and rode in afternoon.

1st September – Service in St Lesmos. Mr Cooper sang 'Oh Lord'.

2nd – George in a lot of pain. Went to bed at dinner time.

3rd – I felt very CD. Lady Robert and her daughter fished. Tom Heywood went off to war.

4th – Billie fishing. Lottie returned. Hope brothers left. I felt very CD.

6th – Billie shooting. Manners fishing. George rode.

7th – Pencil line from Tommie. Lottie, Billie and the Manners went to Glassel.

10th – Maudie left for London. Dinner with Zia Wernher *en route*. George riding. Billie caught a salmon. Arthur Jones – 2 stags. Sir Arthur Farquharson – 2 stags.

11th – Lady Tweedsmuir arrived. Lottie very CD. Spagnum moss party.

17th – Duke of Wellington arrived & Violet Hay Drummond.

18th – The Duke stalked. Humphrey off to school. Bill to Eton

19th – The Duke, Col Jenkins & Marjorie stalked. The Duke got 3.

23rd – The Duke got a fine stag 19st 4lbs – 10 pointer. Col Jenkins got a fish. Violet & Marjorie fished. George better.

A further two entries for that memorable year highlight the highs and lows, the celebration for some and anguish for others:

11th November – Peace declared at 11 0'clock. George had another good day. Mr Walker's (the Glentanar School headmaster) son killed at the front. Tommie busy with flags and bonfire on the hill.

26th – Found my darling dead at 9 am.

The entries are so intriguing that it is difficult to ignore them.

28th September 1925 – Lady Keppel & Victoria lunched. Her Majesty the Queen, HRH Princess Victoria, HRH Princess Helena Victoria & Lady Elizabeth Hasketh Prichard came. Her Majesty planted a tree & 10 Boy Scouts assisted.

Now totally *blasé* about our Royals, it is interesting to note that there was a scout troop in the Glen at this time.

Other entries through the 1920s show the Dowager at her most regal, dispensing hospitality to a vast cross section of the upper classes, both at Glen Tanar, Hill Street in London and at the Villa Gal in the South of France. Her son looms large in her writings, but his engagement to Grethe Thorenson seems to take her by surprise. Only twice does Grethe appear before the announcement of the engagement in Oslo on 28th October 1927. A reassuring meeting with the Queen of Norway at that time, however, seems to placate her as the Queen informs her that Mrs Thorenson is her greatest friend and that Grethe is really charming, as well as being a beautiful young lady.

It is at this stage that my parents arrive on the scene. Grethe Thorenson having no lady's maid, my mother is asked to come to the Villa Gal to meet up with the newly married pair, until the young Lady Glentanar can employ a permanent handmaiden. The following excerpts appear lead on to another problem:

16th December 1927 – Fearfully cold weather. Tommie, Alan, Mr Dalziel, Fouin & Madame arrive." That the Dowager refers to my mother as Madame is interesting – not a term she ever uses when referring to a servant or anyone else.

19th December 1927 – Tommie and Arthur depart for Oslo.

The wedding takes place in the Frogner Kirke in Oslo on 20th December 1927, with Alan Arthur as best man. A lovely day, but -20 degrees centigrade. On that day, however, the Dowager is at the Villa Gal in Beaulieu, while her son travels to Copenhagen for the first night of his honeymoon.

23rd December 1927 – Lovely day. Stella lunched with the Duke. I lunched with Adam and Louise at the Brestat. Fouin and Madame arrived. Much worry about F's military papers. Tommie wired from Lyons.

25th December 1927 – Tommie and Grethe arrive from Paris.

4th February 1928 – Stella and I lunched with Tommie and Grethe at Camarelles and went to Monte Carlo. Heard Fouin was free. Bothered with a headache.

This little episode related to my father being called up in 1914 by the French, but deemed physically unfit for service. He then heard in London that the British were desperate to find interpreters and he volunteered for

1931: The Mansion House Front Door. Father watches a departing guest manfully using that dangerous starting handle.

this post with the British army. Turned down yet again, he was employed by George Coats; but on returning to France for the first time in 1927 he was arrested as a deserter and imprisoned until Lord Glentanar's lawyer was able to supply proof that he had indeed been rejected by both armies. Weeks of worry ensued for my mother attempting to fulfil the needs of a newlywed in a French villa. But with the Dowager and my father never the best of pals, is this welcome news of his release perhaps the cause of her headache?

Before World War II the Ghillies' Ball in the autumn was a time when the Royals graced the Glentanar ballroom. Over the years the Prince of Wales, later the Duke of Windsor and the Duke of Kent, destined to become George VI, were frequent visitors along with the local nobility. There is little doubt that Glen Tanar through the 1920s and 30s was the venue to be invited to. That the Dowager was the backbone of this prominent and extravagant lifestyle there is absolutely no doubt.

The other marked feature of the diaries is the amount of illness recorded. Scarcely a week went past that someone was not in bed with a cold, a chill, headache or simply CD, while doctors were frequently summoned. In London at times pairs of doctors were consulted and on one occasion three were in attendance all at once during a serious spell of illness.

In the 1920s the Dowager had fought a battle with the County Council to keep charabancs from going beyond the area of the mansion house up to Mount Keen. As she won her case, no public transport could pass the end of the public road, so the privacy of the Glen was saved from nasty weekenders defacing this hallowed ground. I totally agreed with this ruling, as a selfish person treasuring my own privacy, but when the Dowager was hailed as a saviour for her action, I could not but smile as I perceived her self interest to be exactly the same as mine and nothing to do with preserving the heritage of Scotland.

There appear to have been frequent squabbles through the years from Cunliffe Brooks onwards about access to the Glen, relating back to Huntly's clearances a century before. Over the years many local people, including farmers, felt pressure on them to recognise estate boundaries. Since Brooks' time the Tower of Ess gates had maintained the impression of privacy, despite the road being for public access. Even in my youth many in the district were left with a sense of intrusion if they proceeded beyond those imposing Ess pillars on to private land.

The total disdain with which some people treated others at this time was common, with the male-to-male use of surnames coming not only from servility, but also from the public schools and the army. The young Lord Glentanar would have thought nothing of it, nor would those employed by him. His frequent reference, when out shooting, to Strang being in attendance, ignored the fact that he was referring to his head keeper; his keeper would have accepted this as perfectly normal. When the laird was in a foul temper I have even heard him bellowing outside to know where the devil is Young. Mr R. D. Young was his factor and second in importance to the laird himself among the employees, so to be addressed as such so publicly brought home to us that no one was exempted. That the family, apart from the Dowager, referred to my father by his anglicised Christian name of Francis, I believe dated back to the days of George Coats, with whom my father had a very close relationship.

Women adopting this tone of communication always made me bristle with indignation and here I have to give some credit to the Dowager. The fine demarcation as to who were servants and who fell between two stools is well demonstrated in her diaries. Whereas she scarcely deemed to name a servant, she did call the laird's secretary Mr Dain, and similarly with her own nurses and secretaries. All of these fell into that no-man's land of semi-professionals, worthy of recognition.

**The Dowager and guests in the early 1930s. The chauffeur is
relegated to the back seat.**

The Dowager's loftiness did not stop her from visiting some of the
employees. Mrs Herriot and Mrs Warburton were called on occasionally,
as were the Camerons in retirement. Mr James Cameron was George
Coats' trusted head keeper through the halcyon days of that era and his
portrait is still in the ballroom today. She never called on my mother, as
these two feisty ladies would have had little time for one another. One
other area of interest for the Dowager was St Thomas' Church in Aboyne,
built so lovingly by her late husband. She continued an interest and
attendance at it throughout the remainder of her life and was eventually
buried there beside her husband, the 1st Baron Glentanar.

The Dowager appears to have kept in close contact with her two
married daughters. Lottie, the eldest, married to the Hon William L C
Walrond, son of Lord Waleran, was described as a vivacious and active
person who was an extremely good horse woman. She competed at show
jumping at Olympia, as well as driving a four-in-hand and a tandem.
Riding to hounds also loomed large in her recreational life. Her husband
followed in his father's footsteps, becoming the MP for Tiverton. Joining
the army, he died in November 1915 from the effects of serving in France
as a lieutenant with the RASC. Lottie was then left with the responsibility
of running the Waleran estate in Devon.

Maudie, the Dowager's younger daughter, married to the Duke of Wellington, was a gentle and artistic person who wrote music under the name of John Orange. Her husband died in 1941 and her son, the Marquess of Douro, succeeded to the title. Known to the family as Morny, he was serving as a captain in the Commandos, bearing the title Duke of Wellington. At the battle of Salerno in Italy in 1943 he died in a burst of German spandau fire and is buried in the British Salerno War Cemetery.

Through the 1930s the Dowager gives little impression of ageing, except in an increasing involvement with her grandchildren, especially Anne and Morny. Seeing that they are introduced to the right people becomes a priority for her, Anne being introduced to the Queen at the Braemar Games in the early 1930s.

The contacts with Royalty were to continue even after the Dowager's death, but were all established due to her diligence in that field over many decades. I have my own memories of Princess Elizabeth and Princess Margaret Rose driving out in the donkey cart with Miss Jean in the late 1930s, while my father was so well used to Royalty through the years that they never ruffled him. On Miss Jean's eleventh birthday in 1939, both princesses were invited for tea and the laird showed a coloured film of Robin Hood as a special treat. Among the archives is a lovely brief letter from Balmoral Castle written in a childish hand and dated 23rd August 1939. Princess Margaret Rose would have been nine years old on the 21st August and this letter is obviously a well mannered young lady's dutiful response.

> *Dear Jean,*
> *Thank you so much for the jokes and beautiful roses. I have played the jokes on lots of people and they have been completely taken in. I had a lovely birthday with quite a nice day too. I hope you are very well.*
> *With love. Margaret.*

The last entry in the Dowager's diary is dated 31st December 1934: "Adam lunched with us and we went to see Greta Garbo in *The Painted Veil*. Ruth Peppercorn, Anne, Morny and David Godfrey Faussett dined with me at Claridges to see the New Year in." In her 82nd year she sounds as spry as ever, still prepared to hit the society high spots. But time was running out and on 27th July 1935, at her holiday home at Frinton-on-Sea, she quietly slipped away. Love her or detest her, no one could ever say she had not lived her social life to the full.

She had an endearing habit of remembering her husband in her diaries by writing a tribute to him on the anniversary of his death. Despite being brought up thinking of her as a battleaxe, I end this chapter with one of her own verses and a salute to a game old trooper.

Dated 25th November 1927.

And yet dear heart remembering thee,
Am I not richer than of yore.
I cannot feel that thou art far,
Since near at need the angels are.
Shall I not see thee waiting stand
And white against the evening star.
The welcome of thy beckoning hand.

An interesting comment on this chapter comes from the Dowager's great-grandson, Michael Bruce. "I wonder if you are being a little harsh on the Dowager? While I cannot dispute the class context I think she had a very, of-the-time 'British' attribute – namely don't reveal your emotions. We are in the post-Diana age where emotions are to be publicly displayed."

Finally, a telling postscript highlights the tragedy of war. To parents and wives it must have seemed a travesty of justice to lose their loved ones just as the trumpets of peace were sounding. The reference by the Dowager to the death of Mr Walker's son on 11th November 1918 exemplifies this.

Signalman 365688 Robert Shand Walker, 35th Royal Garrison
Artillery Siege Battery. Born Glen Tanar, Aboyne on 27th May 1898,
died aged 20, killed in action on 4th November 1918. Buried Ruesnes
Communal Cemetry, France.

Son of William and Isabella Walker, Glentanar Schoolhouse, Dinnet.
Father headmaster at Glen Tanar. Robert was a distinguished student at
Aberdeen University. In the city Roll of Honour and Aberdeen University
Book of Remembrance. Roll of Service in the Great War: page 103/4
where there is a photo.

19

TOMTANAR – THE SINGING PEER

"The estate of Glen Tanar, thanks to the efforts of the second Lord Glentanar, has attained special distinction for its forestry and hill-farming enterprises. It was thanks to him that despite the heavy pressures of national need during the war years, when 3,200,000 cubic feet of timber was felled, the remains of the indigenous pinewoods were spared and their natural regeneration which had made little progress in the century before 1940 was encouraged and has made a significant advance. The hill-farming venture in Glentanar is also making history. The hardy, out-wintered cattle are of special crosses, based on the Highland breed, crossed with Shorthorns, and at a later stage with Herefords."

This summing up by Cuthbert Graham of much of the enterprise of Thomas Coats is highly important, as he followed in the footsteps of a father who had been lauded to the skies by all and sundry.

Despite all the plaudits, George Coats never appeared to consider the estate other than a sporting venture, whereas his son was to take a purposeful interest in all aspects of land management for most of his life. As George died ten years before I was born, I have no first hand knowledge of the man, but I was very aware of his son over a lengthy period. The image of George being as much at home with his ghillies as with his peers was something his son was never to aspire to. Loud in voice and almost imperious in manner, I doubt whether anyone on the estate from his private secretary Norman Dain or his factor R.D. Young down to the most humble employee could ever have felt totally relaxed in his company. He was probably unaware of the overpowering effect he had on people; if his father had lived I am certain he would have counselled it out of him. In his later years he was left without a friendship network to fall back on, but that was, unfortunately, only to be expected.

Thomas Coats was born on 14th December 1894 and in 1910, while at Eton, he was very ill with what was probably rheumatic fever with cardiac complications, or so we gather from entries in his mother's diaries. He made a slow recovery but then gained admission to Christ Church College, Oxford University, in October 1914 before the Great War intervened. Volunteering for service, he joined the Black Watch as a Second Lieutenant and his mother's diary notes on Christmas Day 1914, "Tommie's uniform and his new Colt arrived today." Reporting for duty in January 1915 he was stationed around the UK until January 1916 when he was offered the post of A.D.C. to General Sir Colin MacKenzie, C.O. of the 61st Division.

This period of life at home, with generous leave and time to go stalking, seemed a long way from the battle front. Also the cosy relationship with his new C.O. is highlighted, the general frequently dining with the family in London and enjoying stalking on the Glen Tanar hills. The division moved to France in May 1916, but the Dowager's diaries only mention Tommie when he comes home to go stalking and partying. Then there is a note that the divisional headquarters is in Abbeville in February 1918, the only hint of her son's war.

A portrait of Lord Thomas Glentanar in 1916

Officers during this war required chargers and it appears that many horses were supplied to his son's unit through the generosity of George Coats. Tommie became the proud owner of Captain who survived France to be buried in the round field below the mansion house. In a press cutting I saw many years ago it stated that Thomas Coats had been 'Mentioned in Despatches' and this has recently been confirmed by the Black Watch archivist. There is no record of this in his mother's diaries, however, which seems very odd when references to him in it are so frequent and so concerned. Perhaps under all the bravado of normality, here was a mother dreading the worst for her only son and concealing her true anxieties by keeping a stiff upper lip.

There is no record of how the young Thomas viewed the death of his father within days of the Armistice in 1918. Inheriting the title at the age

Lord Glentanar, kneeling on far right, was in his element acting, singing and directing in the early 1930s.

of 24 must have been a huge undertaking, as he had little or no experience. An intelligent young man, he showed no hint of apprehension and with a strong-minded mother behind him, he was launched into his new life. On 23rd September 1919 his mother hosted a belated but grand coming-of-age party in the Glen Tanar ballroom, attended by a plethora of guests, employees and children.

Much of Lord Thomas Glentanar's life at this time is viewed through the diaries of his mother and the title of this chapter comes from this period. In 1919 she suddenly introduced this character Tomtanar and it took me a little time to work out that she had a new name for her son, Tommie – a name that persisted for about two years. I was so intrigued by this name and also by this woman's playful sense of humour that I have captured it for posterity.

The Coats' era, through the 1920s until the Dowager's death in 1935, centres around the musical and theatrical. Having an organ installed in the ballroom – at a cost of over £12,000 around 1927 – and putting on a number of plays both in Glen Tanar and Aboyne, Thomas Glentanar was doing what he most enjoyed, surrounded by artistic friends. He converted the ballroom into a private theatre with a modern stage. and personally championed Sir Ian Whyte who was to become the conductor of the BBC Scottish Symphony Orchestra. Renowned for his powerful singing

**A GlenTanar favourite: Harry Lauder at the Aboyne Games with
Lord Glentanar in 1922**

voice Tommie was dubbed 'the singing laird' by the press.

The national newspapers, having to prepare an obituary for their
archives in 1942, held this description of Lord Glentanar. "If he had not
been born to riches, Lord Glentanar could have earned a handsome
competence in a score of professions. He had great business talent, he was
an artist, architect, actor, playwright and singer, to be often called 'The
Singing Peer'. Also, having been a soldier he was now a sailor with a
mariner's certificate to his credit. He was a philanthropist too, one whose
good deeds were done without ostentation. He was a well loved laird and
to the youth of Scotland and especially the Scout youth, the best a man
should be."

Yes, the press remained in thrall of the aristocracy, but there is no doubt
there was a substantial element of truth in this description.

The laird was very proud of his involvement in the building of the
Victory Hall in Aboyne. The foundation stone of the Aboyne & Glentanar
War Memorial Building, as it was called, was laid by his mother, the
Dowager Lady Glentanar, on 7th May 1921 and the building was formally
presented to Aboyne and Glen Tanar on 9th October 1921. It contained

not only the names of those who had fallen during the war, but a record of all those who had served – a unique commemoration which was greatly appreciated in the district, with the laird himself mentioned as a Lieutenant in the Black Watch.

Lord Glentanar personally designed and supervised the building of a recreation hall for his employees, on a piece of ground overlooking the stable yard. Opened on 31st December 1926 his mother was presented with a golden key to it by the contractors, while the laird received an engraved cigarette case. He was keen to involve his workers in the plays and Gilbert & Sullivan operas he put on in the ballroom. In 1932 Lord and Lady Glentanar gathered a notable array of distinguished house guests along with many on the estate in putting on what the press termed the "most memorable gathering ever held in Deeside." People flocked from near and far to the ballroom to view the production in which the laird acted the policeman in the comic opera *The Policeman's Serenade* and Lady Glentanar played Judith in Gertrude Jenning's *The Bride*.

Despite his lack of knowledge of the thread industry, Tommie was appointed to the Board of Directors of J. & P. Coats in November 1919, a rapid promotion obviously due to his inherited holding of equity in the firm. He remained a director continuously for a period of forty-five years and seven months, establishing a record unlikely to be exceeded in modern industry.

The laird cemented his presence from an early stage, taking a close interest in the young employees and helping to start a training programme for university graduates in the mid 1920s. For years he toured worldwide visiting Coats' factories and my father had many vivid tales of his exploits, including crossing the high Andes in South America. He got out of Germany in the nick of time just before the outbreak of war in 1939. His retirement in 1965 from the board of the now Coats, Paton & Baldwin Company was marked with a dinner given by his fellow directors at which he was presented with several elegantly bound volumes "on forestry, one of the many subjects on which he has expert knowledge."

Lord Glentanar followed in his father's footsteps with his love of yachting, but not in the competitive sense that dominated his father's involvement. Through the years he had a number of boats including *Pliosaurus* in the 1920s, *Elk* in the 1930s and *Pamela* into the 1950s. Of these the most impressive was *Elk*, described in the press as "reputed in

Pliosaurus **in the Med in 1926. Lord Glentanar in front and my father
in the middle at the back**

the thirties to be one of the most luxurious that ever sailed the seas. The
panelling of the cabins and state rooms was timber selected from the Forest
of Glen Tanar in Aberdeenshire. There was more of Aberdeenshire than
even the timber, for there was to be seen inside a perfectly original
fireplace built of granite, something so novel that it had not been thought
of up to that time, even for luxury liners. There was, moreover, a telephone
and radio set in every cabin".

Young people interested the laird, as is shown by his involvement in
the Boy Scout Movement and his appointment as Commissioner for
Scotland in 1923 at the age of 29. He continued in post for thirty years
in which time he travelled the world, attending jamborees. During the
1920s he had formed a scout troop in Glen Tanar which lasted into the
early 30s – many of the workers on the estate in my youth had
belonged to it. A cub pack was introduced in 1937 with a young Lady
Glentanar as Akela. The running of the pack was left essentially to her
secretary, but nevertheless the involvement of Lady Glentanar gave us
many happy memories. The cub pack blossomed into a scout troop as
we grew older, strengthened by the influx of Glasgow evacuees during
World War II. A Rover Crew was formed in 1945, but petered out in
the early 1950s; Lord Glentanar retired from active participation in
scouting in 1953. He was chairman of the British Legion (Scotland) from

Cub Pack 1937: back row, from left, Ronnie Gillanders, Davie Brand, Miss Robertson, Lady Glentanar, Jimmy Hepburn, and Jock Strang. Seated, Ean Mann, Pierre Fouin, Douglas Young and Willie Archibald

1923 until 1929, WW1 obviously having made a deep impact on him.

Lady Grethe Glentanar

Lord Glentanar must have been a hugely eligible bachelor for countless ambitious mothers throughout the 1920s, but he escaped their clutches and found romance across the North Sea in Scandanavia. As a guest of Lord Salvesen he met the strikingly beautiful Grethe Thorenson, daughter of a Norwegian shipping magnate and their marriage in December 1927 in Oslo was described as the most brilliant of the year. The new bride was a very good skier, loved sailing and was a fine shot. They had one daughter, Margaret Jean Dagbjørt Coats, born on 11th October 1928.

Life for the new mistress of the house, with a very strong willed mother-in-law, could not have been easy. The Dowager may have made her home in Craigendinnie House after 1927, although she often talks of spending her leisure hours in the Wander Walks — those intertwining woodland paths between the mansion house and the lake. In July 1935 at the age of 83 the Dowager died peacefully at their house in Frinton-on-Sea.

The young Lady Glentanar, in common with so many of that generation, had suffered from tuberculosis which had probably left her with impaired respiratory function as she seemed prone to infections from time to time. There is a sense in the records that she never really enjoyed robust health. Having had a large Norwegian-type log cabin built for her at Headinch, she obviously got great pleasure from it as she is frequently noted to be staying there. On a visit to London in 1940 she developed influenza and succumbed to its complications on 19th March. Her tragic early death caught all on the estate by surprise and there was genuine mourning for a lady who had always appeared to have more in common with them than with her Scottish family. Of her husband's feeling of deep loss, however, there was never any shadow of doubt.

Cunliffe Brooks had a mania for building fences to keep deer within the estate so that he and his guests could enjoy plentiful sport. Lord Thomas Glentanar stood this idea on its head in the 1930s — the spread of the tick and subsequent decreasing grouse numbers, and the fact that deer browsed young trees, required a different approach. Repairing the deer fences to prevent entry, he built a stockade at Kildoo to entice the remaining deer in so that they could be culled. Cycling to school in 1938 we witnessed keepers lying on the bank above the stockade shooting the trapped deer that had followed the trail of turnips to their doom. Whether this theory to halt the spread of tick and promote reforestation was credible was never fully tested as the war intervened in 1939 and priorities changed.

The image of a young man always keen to get out to the hill to stalk and quite enthusiastic about shooting grouse gradually recedes over the years. My father maintained that the laird lost his enthusiasm for the kill in favour of the gentle pursuit of the arts. The stories from this era of the Coats' tale are now thin on the ground. One that still persists regards the laird and his later equivocal approach to shooting.

While most of his guests, asked to a driven shoot on the prestigious

1934: The Laird in his heyday shooting grouse

Glen Tanar moor, would bring a pair of guns, Lord Glentanar was quite happy to potter along with one. He required a loader, however, so the head forester, Duncan Ross, was at times called in to do this service. The laird, having fired off both barrels, would snap open the breech and turn to Ross to insert two fresh cartridges. In the heat of the moment this required a precise dexterity from the loader, what with the laird jumping about demanding speed, and birds hurtling around his ears. As he snapped the breech closed too quickly, poor old Duncan lost the tip of a finger. A roar of disapproval came from the impatient laird, "For God's sake Ross, keep your fingers out of the b—— mechanism," as he went on banging away merrily.

The laird was surrounded in his earlier days by talented men – such as his great friend Sir Stanley Davidson, Professor of Medicine at Edinburgh University – who stimulated in him an interest in diverse fields. Contact with these individuals gave him the expertise to voice opinions in the House of Lords, at times on rural subjects, but also those related to health, showing his broad interest in national affairs.

He had a positive attitude in the running of the estate with a keen

Glen Tanar Girl Guides, 1943: Miss Jean, far right, back row while the local girls are Marigold McHardy, third, left, back row, Mary Brand, third left middle row. Front row, left–right: Londie Brand, Sheila McKay, Sheila Gillanders, Jean Young, Lily Hepburn and Annie Hepburn.

involvement in agriculture and forestry. He was a founder member of the Soil Association which partly followed from his early chemistry training. He banned the use of organo-phosphate pesticides and practised bio-dynamic farming at Glen Tanar long before this ever became fashionable.

High living ground to a halt in 1939 with the outbreak of war. The young men disappeared to enlist and the surfeit of labour on the estate shrank. The superb Cadillac and the big black Buick disappeared under dust sheets for the duration and the Rover 12 became the recognised work horse. The pristine drives around the house looked unkempt as the daily routine of raking paths and roads faded into memory. My father lost three footmen overnight to be replaced by one parlour-maid; the mansion house sank into silence as the wealthy guests disappeared and my father's gratuities became a thing of the past.

The east-end Glasgow evacuees arrived and for the rest of the war many remained in the Glen to turn our serene way of life on its head. The laird was threatened with the prospect of his lovely mansion house being turned into an army barracks and quickly took action to foil that exercise.

Registering the house as a school, he enlisted a number of his daughter's friends and some more local girls of good breeding, to keep the army boots at bay. This gave him a renewed interest in his theatricals and his young scholars must have given him many happy hours as he directed them in various public presentations. Girl Guides were launched – a very successful manoeuvre in knitting the wealthy and the commoners into a homogeneous unit, if only for a short period. Both sides learnt that their differences were minimal – a useful lesson to those whose antennae were sensitive enough. This era is so well covered in my previous book it is unnecessary to go into any further detail.

Peace returned to Europe in 1945 and following the atom bombs on Japan in 1946. The situation had changed on the estate, however, as the returning young men had raised their sights both as to occupations and a fair wage. Communistic ideas began to surface following a wider appreciation of the world; I well remember one of the workers, Dougal Brand, being sniffed at for his ideas of equality and being branded a revolutionary, so in our childish minds he posed a threat to our way of life. The laird was focused on reconstruction and planted 100 acres of forest every year until the 1960s. Even up into the 1980s the bulk of the forestry squad was made up of old soldiers from World War II.

A very proud father: The Laird and Jean in 1949

The laird himself seemed to have less inclination to entertain now and no desire to follow his theatrical and musical lifestyle of the 1930s. Business had become harder with so many factories in Eastern Europe shut off behind the Iron Curtain. International Scout Jamborees still took up his time and he took his daughter Jean with him when he attended the first one after the war in 1946.

Because of his irritation at the nuisance of gates to a motorist in a hurry, the laird developed what we called his 'bumper' gates; these were opened by a car pushing them with its bumpers and driving through before they closed behind it. Very effective for the confident driver, but a disaster for the uncertain, so they never gained a market. The south drive was kept for his personal use and he had a fancy covered gateway built at its Tower of Ess entrance. Again, getting out to open this gate was tiresome, so he had a pulley system rigged up across the Tanar to the Tower of Ess sitting room with a big wheel. Ean Mann recalls his mother having to run to the toot tooting of an impatient laird wanting her to turn the wheel to open the gate and then shut it behind him. For this round the clock service she received a shilling or two a month, says her son Ean, laughing at the memory. After the war the laird's enthusiasm led him to experiment with a small electric car which could travel to Aboyne and back on one charge of electricity, but at a very modest speed.

Running his own home farm on organic lines led the laird to be much in demand for his expertise. In addition to the Soil Association, he served as a Governor of the North East of Scotland Agricultural College. 1956 saw him created a Knight Commander, Order of the British Empire, and a member of the Queen's Bodyguard for Scotland. In 1966 Aberdeen University made him an honorary LL.D. while he also became an honorary Fellow of the Royal College of Music.

His sailing was now restricted to the much more modest yacht *Pamela,* berthed at Kerrara off Oban and he sailed less frequently. With his daughter away at boarding school the laird appeared lonely. His fall-back love was music and when sleep deserted him we would often wake to hear the booming noise of the mighty organ shattering the silence of the night. The Highland brew was also becoming a doubtful comforter and I became aware of my father's anxieties at leaving him alone at night in the large impersonal mansion house. When his daughter Jean married The Hon James Bruce, 2nd son of the Earl of Elgin in August 1950, the person closest to him departed to Balmanno Castle at Bridge of Earn to lead her own life and to bring up four children. That he did not live to see his daughter's marriage end in divorce in 1974 is probably fortunate in that such events bring their own unhappiness to the elderly.

The laird died on 28th June 1971 aged 76 years and was laid to rest beside his young wife in the Chapel of St Lesmo's churchyard. The sense of the ending of an era arrived with a catalogue of mansion-house furniture, oil paintings, water colours, silver, bric-a-brac and other effects to be sold (on the instructions of the Trustees of the late Lord Glentanar, K.B.E. D.L. J.P.) by auction in the Glen Tanar mansion house on 8th &

9th May 1972 by Robert McTear & Co. The curtain dropped on the final act in 1972 with the demolition of most of the mansion house he had lived in, improved and loved throughout his varied life.

Whether the laird would have rated his life a success is open to debate. He had almost too many attributes and due to circumstances never really followed any of them to fruition. That he left Glen Tanar in a parlous state was not his fault, but was due to a number of factors including the demise of the family business and the escalating expense of running such a property. With death duties of £1 million coming as a hammer blow Craigendinnie House was sold. Life for his daughter Jean, now a life executor, became much more difficult. The estate was increasingly required to produce revenue from its fishing, shooting and other fresh initiatives to plug the expenses gap.

In the introductory chapters I outlined how this new age is being tackled by Jean's son Michael and his wife Claire. I am sure the enthusiasm and initiative of this new generation would have resonated with him and been generously applauded by all those innovators who had established the mighty J. & P. Coats.

An interesting footnote to this chapter relates back to World War II when Norway was overrun by the Germans. My young friend from our days at the Glen together and an outstanding graduate from Aberdeen University is Alastair Strang, youngest son of the head gamekeeper at that time. Alastair after retirement from Courtaulds went back to his studies to take a PhD in Archaeology and to publish *The Distance Slabs of the Antonine Wall* in 2007. In July 2002 he brought to my attention an excerpt from a letter hanging outside the Glentanar Restaurant on the Fred Olsen cruise ship, *The Black Watch*. Fred Olsen and his family left Aalesund in Norway on May 1st 1940 aboard *HMS Somalie* and docked in Thurso. There, met by two officers from the Black Watch, Fred's father asked permission to make a phone call, but the senior officer insisted on calling the number himself. Answered by Lord Glentanar he passed the phone to the Norwegian; the officers heard their new guest addressing the laird as 'Tom' and immediately came to a smart salute. Transported to Glen Tanar, Fred Olsen remembered the experience in the following words: "Glentanar – What a place! Little canals off the river Tanar, full of salmon; Clydesdale horses the size of elephants pulling huge timber wagons with rubber tyres; rhododendrons as large as small trees. The house and the great ballroom with an organ on which Tom, Baron Glentanar played."

Fifty-six years later Fred Olsen was to ask the Hon. Jean for permission to use the name Glentanar. She in turn asked her son Michael who was intrigued with the story having himself served as an officer in the Black Watch. The letter was dated 1996, the year of refurbishment of the vessel, and signed by the owner himself, Fred Olsen.

20

EDUCATION

Education has been an important component of Scottish life now for generations, so how far back can we trace it in Glen Tanar? Scotland's First Education Act was in 1496 when James IV ordered that the eldest sons of barons and freeholders should study Latin, the Arts and Law in order to ensure that local government lay in knowledgeable hands. Two hundred years later and a further Education Act ordered that a school be established in every parish to be provided by the local heritors – the landowners. Such schools were established slowly, but by the end of the 18th century most parishes had at least one school. During the 18th and 19th centuries some private schools were also established.

Doon the Firmy Brae to school
PHOTO: ANNE BURGESS

The Scottish Education Act of 1872 set up a system of education for the whole of Scotland, but with its overall administration in London. Compulsory education was enforced for all children between the ages of five and thirteen along with fees which were not abolished until 1890.

The Church of Scotland, from the time of the Reformation, had been empowered to supervise all education. This included not only the appointment of teachers and the subjects to be taught, but also ensuring that the landowners assumed their responsibilities in placing a school in every parish. With this new act the Church lost official authority over schooling and in future locally elected school boards would be in charge.

The Scottish Society for Propagating Christian Knowledge – the SSPCK – had been formed by royal charter in 1709. Its purpose was to found schools "where religion and virtue might be taught to young and old" in the Scottish Highlands and other "uncivilised" areas of the country, to counter Roman Catholic missionaries and a growing Highland Jacobitism. These schools provided a valuable addition to the Church of Scotland's programme of education and from having five schools in 1711, there were 25 by 1715; 176 by 1758 and 189 in 1808. They were strictly Presbyterian and only the English language was permitted, in an attempt to stifle Gaelic with its tradition going back to Catholicism.

For generations we in the North-East have prided ourselves on the sturdy interest of even the most humble in education. It was therefore surprising that when I started to look into the part education had played in the lives of the inhabitants of Glen Tanar through the ages, there was a dearth of information. The earliest positive record relates to a paper written by a Peter Harper (1859-1950) some time prior to 1940. In it he discusses the population, houses and road system of early Glen Tanar. His educational comment concerns the first schoolmaster in Glen Tanar. Talking about the houses in the Glen, he refers to the mine of information in the books and papers "that were left by that remarkable man who opened the first school in Glentanar, Murdoch M'Farlane, which date back 150 years and more." He also quotes from the diary of M'Farlane in 1762 and running through to 1812, which suggests a span of

Geanbrae old school

fifty years, some of which must have been spent as the local schoolmaster.

Peter Harper, also writing about the roads up the Glen, refers to men, alive and dead, who told him of a Mr Ogg, "the old schoolmaster of Glentanner" who had surveyed the road to Etnach. As we know from later records a Mr W. Brebner retired as schoolmaster at the school in 1874, so it can be assumed that Mr Ogg taught through the middle years of the 1800s but where does M'Farlane fit in?

Eileen Bailey, Archivist of the Birse Community Trust, adds further to our knowledge of the time by drawing my attention to a gravestone in the old Glen Tanar churchyard. On a flat stone, almost now unreadable, we can just discern the following. "This stone was placed here by Murdoch M'Farlane, schoolmaster in Tillycairn, and is sacred to the memory of 6 of his children who are interred in this place. And also in memory of James M'Farlane & Isabel Bowman his parents, who both died in 1764 aged 82 years each." A six-line verse follows, but cannot be made out, followed by the date 1793.

Another reference in the chapter on *Early Hunting and Fishing* mentions the Glentanar schoolmaster in 1800 recording the payment of his son's fishing licence, but no name. Yet someone has had access to that schoolmaster's records to quote from them, or perhaps they just appeared as an aside in the *Aboyne Papers* and somewhere out there they are still waiting to be uncovered.

An intriguing read is Ian Simpson's *Education in Aberdeenshire Before 1872* and here we find three references to Glentanar. In 1721 a pupil from Tullich school set up as a teacher in Glentanar, "but got so little from the parents that the minister asked the Committee to settle two or three pounds on him". In 1727 it was noted there were no parochial schools in Glenmuick, Tullich or Glentanar, while for the SSPCK schools, "even in 1840 salaries were at little more than the 300-merk level – at Birse the schoolmaster had rather more while at Glentanar rather less".

Diack's *The Glen Tanar Estate Papers* went into the family history of nearly every farm tenant, including the minutiae of farm lettings and every conceivable listing of animals and costs, but when it came to education scarcely a sentence was forthcoming. References to past schoolmasters did occasionally occur, but in the most abstract way and never with a name attached. This seems strange as in another chapter it was recorded that Diack himself had, for a few months, been a relief teacher at Inchmarnoch School in 1892. That various schools did exist there is little doubt, but where they had been situated seemed of no consequence to our past historians.

Steadfastly looking for the original Dinnet church site we found that Brooks had built the present church in exactly the same place as the first one built in 1876. Had he, I wondered, done the same thing with the school and built on or close by the present Glentanar School site on the South Deeside Road? I was advised to look up the old maps on the internet in the Scottish National Library and lo and behold there is the old school marked only four hundred yards south, up the Candycraig farm road. Called Burnside on the map, I now find it called Geanbrae, so very appropriate as it was exactly at this spot we used to climb the trees for the wild cherries on our way home, in those early balmy summer days.

Now with the bit between my teeth I find that the Aberdeenshire Archives in Old Aberdeen House, Dunbar Street, Aberdeen, hold all the registers and records of the years since the Education Act of Scotland of 1872. Viewing these wonderfully preserved books, a whole new world opens up with a wealth of information recorded. Yet all is still not settled, as where are the history and records back another hundred years?

In the *Statistical Account of Aberdeenshire* of 1843 it is recorded that: "In the Glentanner division of the parish, there is a school established by the Society for Propagating Christian Knowledge, SSPCK, with a salary of L.16, and the usual accommodations from the heritors. The average number of scholars, 60: but their fees do not amount to much." The fact that this SSPCK school accommodated so many children seems to indicate that it might have acted as the parish school for the area. With such institutions dating back to 1711, this school in Glen Tanar could have been established in the 1750s, to link in with the Peter Harper reference and also with M'Farlane, aged possibly in his thirties. With only 29 years between the *Statistical Account* of 1843 and finding the school at Burnside in 1872, it could also be the same school. Yet there is a nagging feeling that there are almost too many teachers to fit into this era, so was there another school as dominie Gauld hints at in chapter 22 and was it around Tillycairn?

Reading over the weekly teacher reports of this Burnside School from 1872, the overwhelming message is the untiring determination of these masters and mistresses to educate their young flock. The sense of commitment is wonderful and under such challenging conditions. The old Glentanar schoolroom was 27 feet long, 22 feet wide and 11 feet high. Through the years the school roll rose from 30 pupils to over 80 a couple of years before the new school opened in 1897. In this one room the master was coping with children from ages five to thirteen and at so many different stages.

In addition to the three Rs were taught English grammar, Geography, History, Latin and French, Singing and Sewing for the girls, with Shorthand being added latterly. HM Inspectors were regular assessors and despite the conditions, demanded a punishing performance and were never slow to condemn. Discipline with these tough children never seemed a problem and time and again the masters praised the industry of their young charges. How the children viewed the situation is not chronicled, but I remember well the pressure to perform and under conditions which were palatial compared to those of the earlier years.

In the records throughout the 1880s it is obvious that the heritor, Sir William Cunliffe Brooks, is far from satisfied with the school, neither its amenities nor the accommodation. During these years he installed fresh water from over 500 yards away, improved the offices (toilets) for the children and put in a ventilation system. Even then he seemed unhappy and so it is no surprise when in the early 1890s he decided to build a new school. The Glentanar School of my generation was situated on the South Deeside Road, where the Candycraig farm road joins the main road and just four hundred yards down the brae from the old school at Burnside. It was fittingly opened on 31st December 1897 by Sir William and Lady Brooks, the children being paraded from their old school to the new one, then followed the welcome festivities.

My own memories of this fine Brooks school jump forward to 1934. Trudging the two miles across the Belrorie hill at age five to Glentanar School was not considered a great hardship by anyone. My mother came with me on that first day, but was warned off by me from returning as no other parent or adult was ever in attendance on any of the other scholars. As an only child of elderly parents I was already grimly aware of possible loss of face. I dreaded being seen as a mummy's boy and having a silly name in a very basic Scottish setting, I realised I could be in for a hard time here. My trials and tribulations have already been well documented in another publication, save to say that those years at the Glen school are indelibly imprinted in my brain.

The uniqueness of the school building never dawned on us, as our teachers and parents made no reference to it. Queen Victoria's jubilee fountain at the roadside told us the era of the school, but that in the mind of a small child could have been hundreds of years ago. The inscriptions on the wooden partition doors between the two classrooms and over the fire places simply underlined the harsh reality of having the three Rs thrust down our throats, either passively or by force. It was up to us individually how we chose to respond, but there was no escape either way. Interestingly, in these times when illiteracy seems prevalent, I cannot remember anyone not being able to read, write or do their sums, from the brightest to the slowest. True, some made extremely heavy weather of it but they all seemed to learn, even if it was at the end of the teacher's strap. I hated that method of teaching, seeing it as demeaning to those not blessed in being able to understand easily, but perhaps it did pay off for many in their adult years.

Having just enough comprehension to keep me out of harm's way in this field I was to suffer ignominy from being left-handed and colour blind, which left me sorely lacking in self confidence. My infant mistress

Glentanar School

was Miss Kate Pirie who ruled her class with a rod of iron – or a ruler across my fingers if I picked up my slate pencil with the left hand. The learning was by rote and that has stood me in good stead throughout my life. Reading the teacher's school records throughout the decades, I am left with no sense of the harshness I experienced. I have always thought of it as a really tough environment, but this does not come through the writings of the schoolmasters. Perhaps I was too sensitive, coming from my background, whereas the sparseness of life for so many others was typical in those days. Through in the dominie's room Mr Gauld held sway with the older pupils and he seemed much more tranquil than our fiery Miss Pirie. However until I left for Aboyne School in 1937 I never came into contact with him as a teacher.

The weather conditions in those days seemed much harsher than now. Snowstorms were frequent, but I can scarcely ever remember not making it to school. Trudging through the snow drifts was exciting despite being hard work, but being allowed to take off our wellies and gather around the fireplace to do our lessons was a thrilling experience. I still recall watching the large snowflakes silently falling outside and thinking, "Yes, keep going and we shall get out of school early". Sure enough, the dominie would come into the infants' room and mutter a few words to Miss Pirie and then announce closure for the day. We were out in the playground like a shot and snowballing all the way home.

Having been brought up in the actual valley of the Tanar I have remained largely ignorant concerning that part of the estate lying to the north and bordering the south bank of the Dee. Only since I began the research for this publication have I travelled widely, from Pannanich in the west to Dalwhing in the east, to familiarise myself with this territory. Discovering another school in Inchmarnoch, therefore, was a bolt from the blue. Wandering around that cluster of houses by the roadside I came upon a wilderness of undergrowth behind them, with a wall running along the middle and ruins at the end.

A lady resident enquired if she could help and pointed out that the wall separated the girls and boys playgrounds, while the ruins at the far end were the children's toilets. Turning round she then showed us this delightful little schoolhouse attached to the school – now used as her studio. The building she showed us around was still in a good state of repair, but when had it functioned as a school? Its history among the locals was scanty, although there were vague memories of people who had known of old folk who had been taught there, coming across the river from Cambus o' May.

Reading George M. Fraser's *The Old Deeside Road*, first published about 1922, I noticed he referred to the valuable help given him by a number of people, including a Miss M. A. Stuart, late of Inchmarnoch School, GlenTanner. Then while looking up Glentanar School in the *Aberdeenshire Archives* I turned my attention hopefully to Inchmarnoch and there were all the records from 1872 until closure in 1923. A vivid picture of school life back in those years was at my fingertips.

From these records comes a fitting tale to close this chapter, relating to the wife of Sir William Cunliffe Brooks. There were many distinguished teachers at Glen Tanar, one of whom was George Murray who taught there from July 1879 to March 1882, before taking up a post as English master at Robert Gordon's College in Aberdeen. While acting as an enumerator for the census of 1881, he had an amusing experience with Lady Brooks. The criteria for inclusion in the census report related to where the person had slept on that specific Sunday night and their particulars, including age. Lady Brooks, not wishing to divulge her age, told Murray that she had not slept anywhere that Sunday, as toothache had kept her up all night and so she must not be included in his return. No record of how the good master resolved that one.

21

School Life

The *Aberdeenshire Archives* boast two full ledgers for Glentanar School and one for Inchmarnoch, so for those who are interested there are hours of happy browsing.

The first schoolmaster recorded in the Glentanar files is Mr William Brebner who retired in August 1874 to be followed by Mr Alexander Brown who held sway until his death in July 1879. From the Aberdeen Grammar School came George Murray (who had the interesting contretemps with Lady Brooks) to hold the post until March 1882. Charles Stuart followed until 1885 and for the next two years William Reid ruled the roost. Thomas Laing to 1894, J B Anderson until 1897, when my well remembered old dominie William Walker graced the school with his presence until he retired on 30th September 1933 and became a school's inspector. I seemed destined to be at my scholastic worst in his presence. Incidentally the school roll was recorded in 1876 as 21, to increase to 37 by 1877 and to rise steadily thereafter.

Two factors play a recurring theme in school life through these early decades. The winter storms are frequent and severe, with snowfalls far heavier than in my memory. The recurrent epidemics of measles, chicken pox, mumps, scarlet fever, whooping cough and the dreaded diphtheria play havoc with attendance. The word consumption never occurs, although some of those off for long periods were presumably suffering from this. Even in my childhood this was a malady associated with something quite degrading and not for decent conversation, so one wonders if this prevents any mention. Cough, colds and influenza epidemics also rage from time to time, so childhood was hazardous before all our preventive measures were introduced.

The occasional death intrudes to bring home to all the sadness of such a loss. The deaths of stalker Donald Macintosh and his wife one week later in 1876 is heightened by the entry: "the family of four children are still off school following their parents' death". May 1878: "another fatality from diphtheria and some off school for fear of catching it". 25th November 1887: "Robert Mackie died this morning of a fever. His death has cast a gloom over the whole school. He was a bright promising lad and much liked both by teachers and school fellows. In consequence of the fever there has been a great falling off in attendance today".

Many interesting little comments show the priorities of the time. May 1875: "many pupils are off to take charge of the cows at grass". June 1877: "many off sowing turnip seeds". On 16th June 1885 Mr Reid notes on the poor attendance of the girls: "it seems to be the practice in this part of the county for girls to act as herds, hence the difference between the number of boys and girls attending school". 1886: "poor attendance at harvest time in October".

On the last day of 1880 each child is presented with an orange and sometimes with a biscuit. 7th January 1881: "only 10 put in an appearance on Tuesday and ever fewer on Wednesday so school dismissed. Appears to be due to the observance of Christmas 'Old Style' by all in this district".

August 1884: Mr William C. Brooks is recorded as giving all the scholars a picnic so school was closed that day. This is the first entry of the local landowner really taking an interest in the school and from then on he proves a great benefactor.

30th December 1887 – "Lady Brooks invited all the children to a Xmas tree."

On 6th April 1888: "school closed for a week with scarlatina and Mr Laing being prevented from officiating by scarletina breaking out in the house he lodged in." Following many outbreaks, the school was closed and not reopened until extensive cleaning of classroom had been carried out.

Although the schools had been removed from the jurisdiction of the Church after the act of 1872, local ministers still attended regularly and the Rev. Michie of Dinnet was often mentioned. Preparation for Fast days and Thanksgiving days form part of the recognised school year and holidays are taken at these times.

On 6th December 1889, for the very first time, the school is recorded as being decorated with holly, but yet again the schoolmaster is complaining about the divisive effect of some pupils celebrating Christmas day while others continue to celebrate Auld Yule. Since this complaint continued over the years, it is worth considering the background for this persistent problem.

The derivation of the word 'Hogmanay' is still disputed, but a strong case can be made for its link to the Vikings and their word 'Hogg-nott'. This word describes a feast before the mid-winter festival of 'Yule' which celebrates the renewal of the sun and is taken from the Nordic word 'Jul' which means wheel of life. Traditionally still celebrated in the Shetlands it has over generations become diluted in our district to merrymaking, first footing in the New Year, raising a glass or two of our own potent brew, all to the singing of Auld Lang Syne – for old time's sake.

Following the Reformation the Church of Scotland viewed Christmas as a papist festival, so until modern times celebrating the 25th December was discouraged. While the rest of the UK became ever more focused on Christmas, our kirk still remembered that date in 1560, so strict Presbyterians dug their heels in and kept their children adhering to the old ways.

In January 1890 Mr Laing is bemoaning the school roll being up to over fifty pupils, saying that he cannot give adequate time to various classes. Yet on 31st March that year HM inspector writes, "The energy and sympathy displayed in the teaching of this school throughout all the classes have been productive of particularly good results, alike in work and discipline. The children are treated with kindness and are very responsive. Higher grants for Class Subjects are unhesitatingly granted".

In June 1890 with school numbers steadily increasing the School Board resolved to consult with the Glenmuick Board about building a combined school at Dinnet. Whether this was a threat or a genuine suggestion is unclear, but in November Sir William intimated that with the school roll now up to 59, he proposed building a new school on a different site.

Despite the increasing number of pupils, outside gym was started and shorthand was added to the curriculum. December 1890 saw Lady Brooks hosting a Christmas tree party "where the children were loaded with valuable presents and spent a most enjoyable day".

Academic prowess begins to be reported in March 1892 with HM inspector praising standards including "one girl made a highly credible appearance in Latin and French". The pressure on the school, however, increases throughout 1893, with numbers climbing from the high 50s to 70 by the year end. The Brooks' Christmas party this year includes for the first time a Magic Lantern show. In October 1894 progress now sees a pupil admitted to Robert Gordon's College and another to Banchory School.

It was a proud day on 31st December 1897 when pupils trooped to their new school. The Jubilee Fountain of 1897 was erected in recognition of Queen Victoria's 60 years reign.

On 11th of November 1897 Mr William Walker takes over as headmaster. That first day is ominous, however, as his first entry in the register reads, "The bookcase accidentally fell and rather severely injured a little boy". Brief and to the point making one wonder who was most shocked, but this episode was to prove no hindrance to those Walker years of achievement. On 31st of December 1897 the entry reads: "Today (Friday) the old school was quitted and at 2.30pm the children were in their places in the New Building". Sir William handed over the building to the School Board, and Mr Sandison as chairman accepted it.

By August 1898, with a school roll of 79, an infant teacher was appointed. Miss Elsie Forsyth, a pupil teacher, stood in until replaced by Miss Lizzie Main; by December the roll had reached 82. At Christmas that year the pupils were invited to a Cinematograph Exhibition in Glentanar House. The Brooks continued to lavish gifts on the children and improvements and equipment on the school.

On 2nd March 1900 the Relief of Ladysmith in the Boer War was greeted by the singing of the *National Anthem* to "impress in the children's minds the historical event". The children were excused home lessons that night, which was probably more significant to them than any singing.

On 10th June 1900 Sir William died quite suddenly and there was a request from Lady Brooks for the children to attend the funeral and to sing *Rock of Ages* in memory of their benefactor. Many families left the estate on Brooks' death and for a time school numbers decreased. In the outside world Queen Victoria died on 22nd January 1901, and the Prince of Wales succeeded as King Edward VII.

On 6th January 1902 Mr Walker adds his disapproval to the low school attendance due to the Auld Yule festivities; in March Herbert Mackie returns to school having been absent all winter. The fact that Herbert lives at Etnach and has nine miles to walk to school every day has softened the authority's heart and the attendance inspector does not hound him.

The South African war comes to an end on 2nd June 1902, greeted by loud cheers throughout the school. On 26th June a new era dawns for the school. Mrs Coats, the wife of the new tenant of Glen Tanar estate presents a handsome Coronation mug to each pupil and the Brooks' presence is no more.

The Walker age of achievement is also about to dawn. In July 1902 in the County Council Bursary Examination for the Deeside District, four out of the first six places are secured by pupils from the school. In October of the same year, James Fraser gains first place out of 1300 applicants in a Civil Service UK Examination; the school roll increases to 94.

The school has a joyful holiday for the ordination in Dinnet of the Rev. William Sawers in July 1903, but in January 1904 a sad holiday for the funeral of the Rev. J. G. Michie in Old Glen Tanar churchyard, after years of dedicated service to the school.

In January 1905, due to the generosity of Mrs Coats, Mrs Barclay Harvey of Dinnet House and Lady Cecil of Fasnadarach, a building and equipment were gifted to provide hot dinners for pupils. Mrs Smith of Dinnet was appointed as cook and farmers were to supply potatoes and vegetables. The cost was to be one penny per day or one-and-a-halfpence for two of a family, with further discounts for the larger families. Not content with this, Mrs Coats and Lady Cecil donated slippers and stockings for use in cold wet days.

In April 1905 in the Angus Bursary Competition, all pupils entered get a bursary with 1st, 2nd, 3rd, and 5th places going to Glentanar. That the school must have had a number of talented pupils goes without saying. A particular family stands out, Davie Austin leading the way followed by his sister Anne and younger brother John all achieving distinctions. Like a passing breeze, however, they waft through leaving behind no hint of their subsequent lives. Did Mr Walker's dedication pay dividends for them through the years or were their talents wasted in those harsh times?

The open-handedness of the Coats' family is marked on 28th May 2007 with the arrival of The Coats' Library. Mr Walker writes, "Inaugurated the handsome library presented to the School by Mr James Coats of Paisley".

In July 1907 comes a change of scene with the annual picnic for the very first time taking all pupils to Aberdeen beach, along with the pupils of Inchmarnoch and Kinnord schools. My own memories of that great experience in the 1930s must have been as nothing to those youngsters venturing into this totally new world. A Miss Jeffcock of Worksop, Notts., holidaying regularly in Profeits Hotel, Dinnet, provides picnics for Glentanar and Inchmarnoch pupils over many years, while an ex-pupil, Mrs Cuthbert of Glasgow, gives many school prizes throughout the same era. In 1908 Mrs Coats instigates an annual Empire Day Essay competition, which continued throughout my time at Glentanar and Aboyne Schools.

In September 1907, for the first time, the headmaster writes, "Some pupils left to go to Aboyne Higher Grade Public School". Aboyne offering a wider curriculum with a greater variety of teachers is the first indication of a shift in the local educational scene.

Raising funds for the Hot Dinners' Scheme in November 1908 has the pupils performing the Kinderspeil, *Old Friends with New Faces*, in Dinnet Hall and academic success seems unstoppable. The Angus Bursary Competition of April 1909 must have cemented Mr Walker's reputation with five more top bursars; Patrick Austin of the Dinnet Stableyard, gains a top junior award. This success was exceeded in the following year with six more awards coming to the school. The Aberdeen annual visits now take in educational venues such as the Art Gallery and Marischal College Museum, as well as relaxing on the beach.

In June 1910 a proud headmaster father writes: "Robert S. Walker leads the list of competitors under 12 years of age for the Foundation at Gordon's College, Aberdeen. His percentage of marks is 92 and the value of the scholarship gained is £12.12/- per annum for 4 years, with free education and free books".

"On 13th of October 1910 the Chairman of the School Board handed out handsome school bags, also to the teachers travelling bags, to the district Nurse a travelling rug and to the school cleaners a gratuity, all the gifts of James Coats Jnr. Esq. of Paisley." Other independent records state that this benefactor of the Coats threadmakers of Paisley had handed out

Inchmarnoch Schoolhouse directly attached to the school on the left

schoolbags throughout Scotland.

It gets quite boring, but in the 1911 Angus Bursary, four pupils were successful with "James Fleming heading the Junior List, his marks showing the excellent percentage of 94". To complete this record of success, it is perhaps excusable to quote from William Duncan, Chairman of the School Board, to get a measure of the achievements of this small school. "I have pleasure in referring to recent successes of former pupils viz. Gordon Fraser who has gained great distinction in his classes at Aberdeen University, Bessie Walker, Burnroot, Silver Medallist and Dux of Miss Ferriers School, Aberdeen, George Leys, Glentanner, Dux of Class III Intermediate Dept. Aboyne H G School and Robert Walker, Schoolhouse, Bronze Medallist and Dux of Class IVA Gordon's College, Aberdeen."

How long could such a tiny school sustain this academic success? In April 1912 Margaret McGregor, Joseph McGregor and Minnie Morrice were successful in the Angus Bursary Comp. with the first two standing 1st and 2nd in Order of Merit. In April 1912 an innovative course was approved – the School Gardening Scheme – which proved popular into the second half of the century. The outbreak of war in 1914 was a watershed for our schools.

Let us look at how Inchmarnoch School had fared since those early records of 1872. Mrs Betsy Wattie opening the register on 10th March 1874 with a school roll of 14 pupils. The pattern of weather, illness and school closures follows almost exactly that of its larger neighbour, but there was an undercurrent of lesser expectation, in part due to the frequent absences of pupils and therefore lack of continuity in teaching. In October 1880 a new school is opened, but whether this was an up-grade of the old school or a new building on a different site is not clear. The number on the roll has by now increased to 30, perhaps necessitating a larger building.

In April 1892 a Mr Francis C. Diack MA – who wrote *The Glen Tanar Estate Papers* – acted as a relief teacher until mid August, due to the illness of Mrs Wattie. Mrs Wattie's health caused her to retire at this time to be replaced by Miss Jane Reid.

We sense the march of time in December 1893 when the children attend a Magic Lantern Party in Glentanar House, being taken there and back in an omnibus. The winters are horrendous and in February 1895 it is so cold that a bottle of ink in a desk is found to be frozen solid.

Interesting little snippets of history are recorded. In September 1896, "Some children are off to Ballater to see the Tsar of Russia". In 1897 the Queen's Diamond Jubilee, Sir William gifts a book, *Victoria and Her People*, a mug and a medal to each child, while the School Board presents another medal and *A Life of the Queen*. The cold of the winter is balanced by scorching hot days in July when the children are listless and uninterested.

Personal problems come to the fore as when a number of children are off ill for days having eaten acorns. The teacher Jane Reid suffers from chronic bronchitis and is frequently off; so often, in fact, that she would be considered unfit today, yet HM inspectors are supportive and give her good assessments. Other comments show the priorities of the times and also the odd reference, "Herding bees and hoeing turnips seems to be the most engrossing occupation just now". Children are often off helping at home, involved in the seasonal aspects of farming or assisting with the Hunt, while some degree of truancy may also be playing a part.

In August 1901 Jane Reid retires and Margaret D. Campbell is appointed in her place. In 1903 Catherine T. Forbes succeeds until 1906 when Mary A Stuart takes on the post and goes on to give sterling service until 1921. In 1907 we hear that the teacher is moving to the new schoolhouse, presumably built on to the east aspect of the school, as it appears at the present day.

On 8th of August 1907 Mary Pithie from Cambus o' May passed all her subjects at Aberdeen University Local Examination in Aberdeen. This is one of the only references to academic attainment over all the years of Inchmarnoch, whereas Glentanar was steeped in such achievements.

In November 1907 Miss Stuart receives a cheque for £3 from Mrs Coats of Glentanar House to provide Bovril at midday for those who don't get home for lunch. The postscript reads, "This boon is a result of correspondence between Mrs Coats and the teacher". Remembering that Mrs Coats and others had in 1905 provided buildings and fittings for Glentanar School for school lunches, perhaps there was a sense of unfairness that the wee school was being overlooked. Well done, Mary Stuart.

February 1908 sees the arrival of The Coats' Library, noted by Mary Stuart as being very helpful to her. On 26th October 1908 Mrs Coats visits the school and presents a Union Jack and a £3 cheque towards the Hot Dinners' Fund, while in March 1909 tea and fruit are sent to the school by Mr & Mrs Coats on the marriage of their daughter Maud to the Marquis of Douro. The £3 cheque appears again in October 1909, the school roll rises to 36, and Mrs Coats has a flagstaff erected. On 28th January 1910, 42 degrees of frost are recorded and the ink is again frozen in the bottles.

On 19th May 1910 the flagstaff and Union Jack come into use when George V is proclaimed King; Master Thomas Coats presents prizes and addresses the scholars. "Gifts were of watches, scarf pins, etc." In November the school bags gifted by Mr Coats arrive and the surplus is stored away.

The routine of school continues almost unchanged over the years In April 1914 "Mrs Coats and party called today when a demonstration in teaching and singing of Scotch songs was requested by a German professor." Empire Day was celebrated with enthusiasm in both schools, as in May 1914, "By generosity of Mrs Coats the scholars were driven to Glen Tanar on Saturday and spent the afternoon celebrating Empire Day and partaking of a bounteous feast".

Cambus o' May pupils were often noted for their absence. With no bridge until 1905, the pupils were ferried across the river, a hazardous undertaking in times of spate. Even in December 1914, after the coming of the bridge, there is this entry. "Yesterday the pupils from Cambus o' May were afraid to cross the bridge. The river rose so far as to go into one of the houses."

Inchmarnoch being much smaller than Glentanar, one might expect more individual tuition, yet academic prowess never seemed a priority in the teaching. It is unfair to make a judgement after all these years, but it is interesting to speculate on the factors that may have brought this about, including the expectations of the parents, as well as those of their children.

22

WARS AND PUPILS

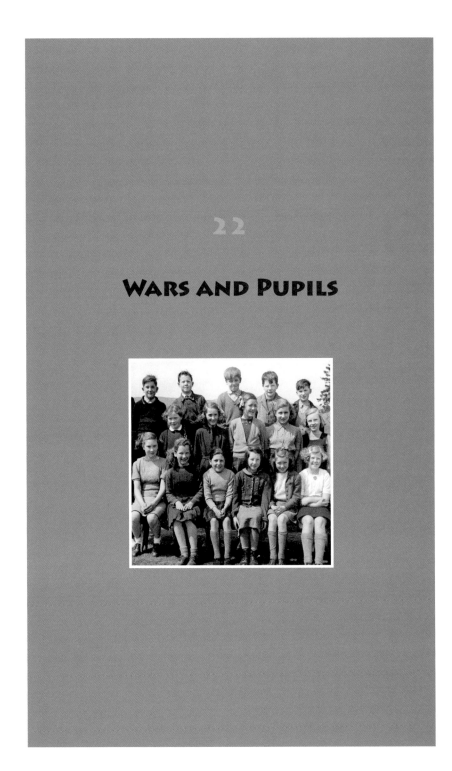

On 28th June 1914 the Archduke Franz Ferdinand was assassinated in Sarajevo, a distant city in a distant land that Glen Tanar schoolchildren had probably never heard of in their geography lessons. But by August that year Britain was at war and the educational face of our little schools was about to change for ever.

At Glentanar School in 1914 Miss Maitland, who had been an assistant for a number of years, resigned to be followed for a short time by Miss Hart. On 26th April 1915 Miss Kate B. Pirie takes up her post, to stamp her authority on decades of local youngsters. By then the Great War has been having its effect on schooling, and senior pupils are knitting scarves for the troops with wool supplied by Lady Cecil of Fasnadarach House.

On 4th December 1914 eight Belgian soldiers recovering from war wounds at Bona Vista, the Red Cross Hospital in Aboyne, accompanied by Private Cattanach of the Gordon Highlanders, wounded at Ypres, are entertained by the children at the school. The Belgians join in by singing their National Anthem and other traditional songs.

On 16th April 1915 Mr Walker is still able to announce that three pupils have gained awards in the Angus Bursary Competition, despite the war. The emphasis from here changes, however, to providing foodstuffs in the form of eggs, cocoa, jam and tea which are sent to the VAD Hospital, while the knitting gathers pace every month. Over 1,000 sprigs of heather are prepared and sent to aid the funds of Aberdeen Royal Infirmary, while sackfuls of sphagnum moss are collected for hospital and field dressing purposes. On 17th of September 1915 Mr Walker is appointed a collector of eggs under the Red Cross Scheme and this takes up a considerable amount of his time.

Busy or not, the Walker production line of scholars goes on. In April 1916 four more scholars shine in the Angus Competition, including Oliver Mackie from Etnach whose nine-mile walk to school does not seem to have drained energy from his brain cells. That same month a School War Working Party is set up to co-ordinate the production of socks, scarves, helmets, mitts and gloves.

The casualties of war are now being felt acutely within the district, but still the school carries on stoically with two more awards in April 1918 in the Angus Competition

On that wonderful day, 11th of November 1918, the carnage ceases, but what do we find in the headmaster's report? "Great European War – Armistice signed by Germany." Terse and to the point – no cheers, no exuberance in those lines. Perhaps it was an unwritten sign of exhaustion. Little did I realise at the time that Mr & Mrs Walker's talented son has just been killed, less than a week before silence descends on the horrific Western Front.

A return to normality on 3rd September 1919; the Aboyne Games are restarted and the children have a holiday. On the 23rd Lady Glentanar invites all the children to be transported by brakes to the belated 'coming out' party for her son, Lord Thomas Glentanar, home from the war. This was followed the next day by a tribute from Dr Sinclair, County Medical Officer, who remarked "that without exception the children were the cleanest he had anywhere examined".

The year 1919 sees the start of the Scottish War Savings Committees Appeal – the emphasis firmly on thrift through these difficult times – while business is as usual in April 1920 with two more awards in the Angus Competition. The great forest fire in June has everyone in a state of excitement as thousands of acres of forest go up in flames, while on 8th April 1921 the pupils are said to have a fine view of the Eclipse of the Sun.

On 13th November 1923: "Memorial to 14 former pupils who fell in the Great War was this afternoon hung in the schoolroom. It is the gift of the Dinnet Curling Club and was handed over by its President, C. M. Barclay-Harvey, Esq. of Dinnet". In February 1926 we read: "Case of birds donated by Mr James Cameron of Tower of Ess, retired Head Deer Stalker, Forest of Glentanar."

In 1929 Mrs Cuthbert, the donor of so many prizes over 30 years, dies, but is replaced by her nephew Dr Charles Ritchie of Nelson, Lancs. As a pupil living with his grandmother at the now derelict Burnroot Cottage, he came to the school in May 1880 and left in 1883. He graduated in medicine from Aberdeen University and came to spend his holidays in

Deeside and so began his second association with the school.

May 1929: "Albert Ogston, Patricia Anderson and Lena Porter gained Angus Bursaries of £7.10/- for 3 years and will pass on to Aboyne after the summer vacation". So it appears that Mr Walker's best pupils leave him early which must have been disheartening, as he could no longer be involved in advancing their careers. In April 1931 the same happens with Gladys Ogston and James Ferries gaining Angus bursaries and departing for Aboyne. The school roll is noted at this time as 56.

When we were scholars, no adult ever referred to the uniqueness of the school or marvelled at its roof.

There comes a memorable day in the history of Glentanar School on 29th September 1933 when Miss Pirie, on behalf of the school, presents Mr and Mrs William Walker with parting gifts. The Walker era, 35 years, has produced nigh on 40 bursaries, many of his pupils taking the top awards on offer and making the name Glentanar School synonymous with academic excellence. Neither before nor yet after this is this word 'bursary' mentioned.

Anecdotes from the Walker era are few, but Ian Hepburn, youngest son of the Hillhead keeper, still recalls one related to his older brothers Alan and Ronnie. I always thought of Dominee Walker as a mild inoffensive man, but Ian's brothers remembered him for wielding a cutting from a broom bush which he would switch around the legs of the boys who made mistakes with their sums or spelling.

On 3rd October 1933 Mr Charles E. Gauld, BSc Agri. takes up the post of headmaster. Because of his background, the school garden becomes one of the main interests for the senior boys, as well as wood-working handcrafts.

In October 1934 there is a scarlet fever epidemic and there is public unease over the treatment of it in Aboyne Hospital. Many Glen Tanar families, including my own, are quoted as keeping their children at home as they have lost faith in the hospital. Letters are written to all these parents to point out that their children should be at school and satisfactory replies are received from all, including mine. The Medical Officer of Health is required to reassure the headmaster that facilities and treatment in the hospital are considered satisfactory. In the Dowager Lady Glentanar's diary for that period, her ladyship is very worried about this outbreak. As it apparently originates among staff in the Huntly Arms Hotel, she bars any employees domiciled in Aboyne from coming to the estate until the danger is over.

In February 1935 Mr Gauld is investigating the history of Glentanar schools and finds that his school cost £7,000 to £8,000 to build. He also notes that there were two previous schools – the one vacated in 1897 and a previous one in an unknown situation. In December that year there is a curling bonspiel on Clarach Loch – the first for several years.

In May Mr Gauld is quite upset at one of his most promising pupils, James Jaffrey, being off school with suspected tuberculosis. Apart from one pupil noted as being in Fraserburgh Sanatorium some years previously, this diagnosis has never been whispered, right from 1872. Are people now realising that this disease, although very serious, is no different from all the other epidemics so frequently encountered?

In 1936 the abdication of Edward VIII to marry the commoner and divorcee Mrs Simpson arouses comment from Mr Gauld and appears to be causing some excitement, even among the scholars. By June 1937, however, the scholars are more thrilled by their annual outing, this year to Dyce Aerodrome, while the master is really delighted with the state of the school garden.

About this time the headmaster felt it necessary to strap three boys for their misdemeanours. One boy refused to hold out his hand and the master struck him around the legs instead. Faced with an irate father the next day, the master still felt he had been justified and that the punishment had been reasonable. This episode is well remembered locally, but old scholars disagree over the identity of the culprit. Two families seem associated with the event, but whichever one was involved both had frightening fathers and the master was being either very brave or extremely foolhardy to stand up to them. Another incident, when stones thrown over the school wall smashed some glass vegetable covers, hints at hooliganism among the pupils. Yet another occasion when two boys fighting or wrestling in the playground resulted in Peter Strang, the head gamekeeper's son, suffering a broken leg confirms my own feelings about the level of aggressive behaviour at that time.

By 1938 Mr Gauld recognises the darkening clouds and he gives much space to the crisis in Czeckoslovakia; he finds the children interested in Hitler and the Sudetanland, which quite astonishes him. By September he sounds mildly optimistic: "Europe situation more hopeful due to the energetic action of the Prime Minister Mr Neville Chamberlein. An anxious feeling still in minds of most adults". By 3rd of November he states: "the tension of last week has completely settled". Air raid precaution classes were started in Aboyne, however, and the pupils had diphtheria injections.

August 1939 tells of the distribution of gas masks, while by the end of the month it is notified that Glen Tanar is to receive 200 evacuees from the Townhead district of Glasgow. On 1st September the children arrive at Aboyne railway station, and Mr Gauld notes, "general appearance not very prepossessing with five evacuees in the school house". By 9th September the school is opened on a two-shift basis – with locals in the morning and evacuees in the afternoon – but within a week there is a rapid drift back to Glasgow. The master also notes that a number of the incomers have impetigo.

By September the Kinord School evacuees are transferred to Glentanar bringing the number up to 50. However this decreases to 36 by October, 29 by December and 22 by January 1940. With the numbers so depleted the senior room comes back to full day attendance with the suggestion of shared teaching. Mr Gauld is against this as teachers of evacuees have a rapid turnover and he feels that lack of continuity is unfair on the children.

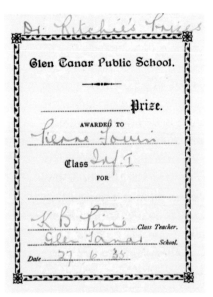

On 13th of March 1940 the school notes the passing away of Dr Charles Ritchie. Now, holding my first school prize dated 27th June 1935, the presentation label reading *Dr Ritchie's Prize for Infants One,* I realise that I have followed directly in his professional footsteps. Mrs Ritchie continued to supply the prizes for at least another year.

By June 1940 not only was knitting in full swing, but the collection of scrap metal was resulting in piles of scrap rising on various sites, while evacuee numbers continue to drop. By August there are 52 local children and 19 evacuees in the school. Cloth gauze is provided for putting over the windows to prevent shattering if bombing occurs and Mr Gauld and Miss Pirie spend hours fixing it in place over the multiple panes of glass.

By October 1941 only five evacuees remain in the school and the last of the Glasgow teachers is withdrawn. The records from here on are concerned with making the garden and surrounding lawn produce enough vegetables to supply the school kitchen. Waste paper is collected each week and the school report becomes more of a general diary than ever before. Mr Gauld also records the progress of the war and the sense of the turning of the tide comes over strongly into 1943. Education vies with other needs; senior boys are working in the garden and even planting and lifting potatoes for school in the fields. The feeling comes across strongly that this headmaster is happier in the agricultural setting than stuck in a stuffy classroom. However, his old pupils talk warmly of his teaching abilities, especially in history as he appears to have travelled widely in Europe. Inspectors' reports remain positive regarding the standard of education – reports usually written by that past master at achieving bursaries for his pupils, Mr William Walker.

On Tuesday 8th May 1945, VE Day is underlined in the report and the school gets two days' holidays, whereas the end of the Japanese conflict goes almost unrecorded. In September 1945 an Act is passed to provide transport for pupils under eight living over two miles from the school. Great debate whether the Stableyard, Glen Tanar qualifies, as by the Piggery short cut it is fractionally below two miles, but by using the Bungalow Brae it is just over. Common sense eventually prevails and transport is provided, but is this the first symptom of our molly-coddling modern age? Life settles into this new era and a parents' committee is appointed to raise extra funds for the school.

Miss Kate Pirie completes a marathon service of over 40 years when she retires on 24th September 1953. Mr Gauld dies in post in June 1962 and the now one-teacher school is led by Mrs G. Gardiner, as an interim teacher from August 1962 to the end of March 1963; she is followed by Mrs E. Milne up until April 1966. The final teacher is Mrs Newhouse, who held the fort in Brook's fine old school until it was closed on 1st of July 1969.

Readers may feel I have dismissed the last 25 years of this school in a few lines, but with the necessity of confidentiality intruding, the records are increasingly censored from 1937 onwards. It is difficult to imagine what details would require censorship as nothing in the previous 65 years

Mr Charles E. Gauld with his senior classroom 1947-48. Back row, left to right: Mr Gauld, Peter Brandie, D. Watt, Jock McGregor, Ian Hepburn, Jimmy Henry, Dougie Ross. Middle row: George Archibald, Alison Gauld, Alice Livingstone, Eveline Dawson, Teddy Beattie, Freda Silver, Ronnie Anderson. Seated: Sheila McKay, Mabel Archibald, Mary Brandie, Margaret Hepburn, Lucile Chalmers, J. Corbett and Liz Stuart

would have warranted this. Some old pupils may resent teachers' comments, though, so the researcher must wait some years yet for the truth to emerge.

The World War I does not rate highly in the teacher's records in Inchmarnoch School, although in 1917 there is this quote: "The scholars are now bringing in large quantities of sphagnum moss which is cleaned, dried and sent to the Ballater Depot". Also that year appears: "Due to the shortage of paper written exercises are frequently done on slates".

Unlike at Glentanar, Armistice is recorded on 12th November 1918. "Word of Armistice came as school was dismissing last night. Flag was hoisted and saluted and the school will close at 2.30pm for the rest of the week."

The world wide influenza epidemic, said to have killed upwards of 50 million around the globe, comes to our little school on 18th November 1918. "Due to the severity of the influenza epidemic school has been closed by order of the Local Authority until December 2nd." In fact the school remained closed for a month. The Spanish flu as it was called, killed 250,000 in the UK alone, but in neither school was any fatality recorded.

Life reverts to normal with Empire Day celebrated on 25th May 1919. "Lord and Lady Glentanar and a large house party came in the afternoon and after a short display by the scholars, her Ladyship awarded several prizes. Saluting the Flag and singing of the *National Anthem* was followed by an Empire Day address by Lord Glentanar and school was dismissed by 3pm."

"On the 2nd of September 1919 Bertha Stewart aged almost 14 years has been entered at Aberdeen High School for Girls." For the Inchmarnoch teacher this must have been a highly unusual, but welcome experience.

On 1st July 1921 Mary A. Stuart retires and is replaced by Margaret J. Ingram. The school roll stands at 16 and falls to 11 by the following year; closure looms. In September 1922 many boys are off school at "the game beating". In the past they would have been away "at the hunt", but now modern terminology is appearing and old ways and habits are fading. On 28th June 1923 modernity closes the doors of Inchmarnoch School and its pupils disperse to Ballater and Glentanar.

Reading quietly through the records there is the sense that the Great War sapped enthusiasm in the grind to survive the hardship and sadness that must have pervaded the whole district. Despite this, at Glentanar Mr William Walker still managed, along with Miss Pirie, to keep the conveyor belt of bursars flowing. The rise of Aboyne School as the bridge to higher education must have frustrated teachers who were left, in the higher classes, with only those children waiting to leave school at the earliest opportunity.

As a pupil at the school from 1934 to 1937 I was very aware of the harshness, and at times the brutality of the scholars. Bullying was rife and terrorising the younger pupils was common. I learnt very quickly to keep out of harm's way but others suffered badly, as I recount in *Glen Tanar Exile*. My friend Alfie Dawson recalls how he had to cover miles in detours with his schoolmate Willie Archibald, to evade those lying in wait to take vengeance on Willie for some misdeed. When I changed to Aboyne School I found the senior boys totally supportive of the young, and remember almost no bullying.

The records of Glentanar School end on a sad note. The then Director of Education in 1969 is obviously perturbed as to the future of this historic building and appears to do his best to have it preserved. The correspondence peters out in defeat; he is firmly advised that the school belongs to the Glen Tanar estate and the Local Authority has no power of interference – so endeth the County's interest.

The ledgers of these two schools make enthralling reading for those who want a glimpse into the past, but be prepared for thousands of references to the weather, while the epidemics that raged regularly make us appreciate our modern prevention and immunisation schemes.

Nature and Recreation

For a countryman I am amazingly ignorant about much of what goes on around me. Flowers have never really excited my interest and although my father loved his dahlias, which he planted annually outside our little house in Glen Tanar, I never could muster much enthusiasm. Only flowers or plants that intruded on our childhood interests or fired our imaginations do I remember with fondness. The memory of the wonderful yellow broom on the Firmounth Brae on the way to Glen Tanar School at times brings a nostalgic lump to my throat. The fields of yellow tansies – a scourge to the farmer but the source of a caterpillar at its root which was deadly to sea trout – is a lasting echo from my all-consuming fishing hobby.

Carle doddies will ring a bell with many; we tried to knock the heads off the plantain stems in a conker-type dual on our way to and from school. Amy Stewart Fraser has the greatest fund of stories imaginable and *In Memory Long* she tells us that 'Carle' was Bonnie Prince Charlie and 'Doddie' was his enemy King George II, so we are back to the 1745 rebellion once again. However like *Ring a Ring o' Rosies* being thought by some to refer to the Great Plague of London in 1665, so the game of carle doddies may also fall into this dubious category.

My interest in trees is also rather limited and I used to get very irritated in not being able to name them all for strangers. I have, however, always treasured the birch, especially on the Dinnet moor, in the woods of Cambus o' May, or on some barren hillside gulley where only their stunted, scattered forms transform the landscape. Pine woods, along with the open moor, are my natural habitat and nothing gives me greater satisfaction than to meander through them, even in my senior years. The alder, with its branches hanging over some of the best pools on the Tanar, was a constant annoyance, as when trying to creep up unseen to drop an inviting worm without tangling the hooks in foliage.

Holiday cottage West Lodge – a wonderful situation to appreciate the beauties of the natural world.

As children we loved the horse chestnut, as playing conkers was a seasonal game through many years. The wild cherry was often the cause of our late arrival at school in July, as we clambered among the branches to pick those succulent dark red geans. The sycamore with its winged seeds intrigued us, while the oak with its acorns reminded us of those ships of oak from days gone by.

The copper beech is a magnificent tree, but this one failed to survive the impact of a two-seater *Fairey Battle* light bomber in 1940. Developing engine trouble as it came down the Tanar valley, the pilot saw the golf course dotted with posts to prevent German aircraft landing there. Over-shooting the fairways the plane crashed over the Tanar, just above the Braeloine bridge, and came to rest at an angle across the public highway. One wing was wrenched off by the beech tree, but the pilot and navigator amazingly climbed out unhurt. The sight of an aeroplane blocking our route home from school was an event never to be forgotten. The beech tree seemed to have survived, coming into leaf next season, but later it came to be but a ghostly silhouette to be felled many years later.

The mountain ash or rowan is yet another tree with memories, as when we were very young and playing with the girls, we would pick its berries, along with those of the elderberry, when playing 'housies'. In later life one would spot a solitary, sad rowan standing guard over the larach (ruins) of some ancient cotter house, still trying to keep ill luck at bay. One

The huge Linden Tree, now over two hundred years old

linden or lime tree is now two hundred years old, but still stands proudly on the south bank of the Tanar at the Black Ship. It was attributed the same mystical properties as the rowan, that of combating evil spirits. Now, huge of girth and height, it has certainly thrived, but of all those woodcutters and their bairns that it was to keep safe there is not a single memory.

Only in my senior years have I become aware of the trees Cunliffe Brooks planted around the estate, like the massive Wellingtonias within the policies and alongside the farm roads he laid out over the hill, from Belrorie down to the South Deeside Road. The Wander Walks we played in so often in childhood are not only a maze of rhododendron bushes but contain huge specimens of more exotic trees planted way back in the 1890s. Many still have the species names recorded on lead markers attached to ancient posts. All there for us to learn about in our childhood, but no one ever realised their significance. As with so much on the estate, the uniqueness of our surroundings passed straight over our heads, seemingly of little interest to employees or their offspring.

The juniper seems to have been important to previous generations as there are records of the gamekeepers back in the late 1800s taking time to plant it. The word Etnach derives from the Gaelic for juniper and that area of the upper Tanar remains for me a magical wilderness. Juniper also reminds me of our scout camps, when in the evenings the dreaded midges could make life unbearable. Burning juniper in our tents at night not only produced a memorable aroma, but did seem to keep those persistent insects at bay.

Still out in the hills, I recall the cranberry and the blaeberry. Cranberry jelly never enticed me, but the blaeberries were much sought after. They were in abundance on the lower slopes of the Strone opposite the Black Ship, making picking them for jam and blaeberry pie really worthwhile. It was always easy to tell when the blaeberries were in season, as the children had fingers, mouths and tongues stained blue.

My final thoughts on vegetation relate to another plant that is not welcome on an estate. Bracken, once it becomes established, can stifle all other growth and intrude on pasture and hill alike, as well as harbouring the dreaded tick so blamed for grouse infestations. At times as children we were employed on the thankless task of cutting it back from fields and heather, but without much success. Another frustrating exercise was cutting down thistles in the fields, only to see them having multiplied the following year. There were no chemical methods of eradication back in those days, but at those two jobs I felt we were no better than King Canute.

In retrospect, I am not sure whether my great interest in birds originated from collecting their eggs or from a genuine wish to know more about them. Certainly my eventual ornithological library was so extensive that I have no excuse for failing to identify them, being aware of their habits, or recognising their eggs. Each spring we had a routine of searching bush, tree or building to identify every nest in the vicinity. We became experts in this, but whereas in the early years we raided the nests for our collections, latterly we simply delighted in finding them. We continued to collect the rare specimens, but usually took only the odd egg and left the rest to hatch.

Blackbirds, thrushes and sparrows provided the bulk of our discoveries; seventy years later this is interesting, as the common sparrow and even the thrush has decreased markedly in numbers. Hundreds of sparrows used to haunt the stackyard and the silo up at the home farm, yet recently I saw none. Through the summer months the house martin and swallow were much in evidence and today their numbers appear much the same, with the martins nesting under the eaves of the old smiddy, now a riding stable, just above head height and flying in and out almost oblivious of humans. The screaming flight of swifts which circled the old mansion house in the evenings are no longer in residence; the ballroom is all that is left of that stately mansion with its nesting sites under the eaves.

The tree creeper nesting year after year above the sliding doors of an outdoor store and the redstart in the sawmill shed were easy to find. The dipper behind the waterfall below the lake could also be counted on to return, but finding the wheatear down some narrow burrow out on the moor was a time-consuming exercise. Some nests we were destined never to find despite hours out on the hills with our binoculars. The curlew defied us, while the golden plover with its mournful cry drove us frantic with frustration.

The great spotted woodpecker did its best to elude us with its nest high in a hole in an old rotten tree, but perseverance won the day. Using climbing irons to reach the entrance, we chiselled away for three days before we finally reached those precious eggs. Those climbing irons also saw us augment our collections with a sparrowhawk's nest. The keeper having shot the female, we heard from his son where we might find it in Belrorie wood and, sure enough, an intact clutch was shared out amongst us. A heron's nest on the top of a tall tree in Aboyne Castle grounds still remains the epic capture and I salute my medical friend Alan Simpson for his audacity in achieving what the rest of us believed impossible.

One bird we never laid eyes on was the magpie, which had in those days not reached our domain; along with the grey squirrel it only arrived many years later, much to the dismay of many. The red squirrel was common, while the rabbit population, despite the constant attention of the keepers through the years, has a tremendous ability to survive. Our fear that the capercaillie is heading towards extinction raises many memories of that impressive bird. The cock is a wonderful specimen and I recall with wonder being an eight-year-old, standing behind my father as many cock capers were driven across the Fairy Lake to our standing guns.

As a child I felt they were blotting out the sky and simply committing suicide to fly over practised shots. Their speed of flight, however, was deceptive, so my father was delighted to have downed a couple, making it a memorable day for us both.

The Lapwing, Peeweet or Peesie as we were wont to call it, is yet another wonderful memory. Immediately I can see the high ground beside

Cattle grid and the Fairy Lake only partially clear of weed
PHOTO: ALAN FINDLAY

Greystone Cottage with the birds diving, wheeling and calling as we cycled home from school. Then dragging a wing, they would scuttle in front of us, trying desperately to entice us away from their nest or the young crouching among the grasses.

Our greatest effort was reserved for that master of the skies, the peregrine falcon. Such an egg was next only to that of the golden eagle, but all our efforts were to be in vain, despite two attempts. Trekking miles up to the quartz cliff west of Mount Keen we were greeted early on by the warning screech of the mate. Carrying heavy ropes, quite unsuitable for such a venture, we tried to lower ourselves over the three hundred foot cliff to the nest. Common sense prevailed and we admitted defeat, not that the peregrine was placated, harassing us all the way back to Coirevrauch. This venture has left me with a huge appreciation of the peregrines as the masters of flight and a feeling of gratitude to have been able to see them in their secluded domain, still totally unspoilt by man.

Thoughts of securing the egg of a golden eagle were always truly fanciful. But fate can at times deal you a hand which defies all imagination. Having trekked out through the Allachy one September day towards St Colm's Well, I happened to see what appeared to be an eyrie quite close to the path and in a very climbable tree. Ascending it only to say I had done such a thing, I was astounded to find an egg lying there in full view. Surmising that so late in the season the nest had been deserted or the eagle had been harmed, I happily added it to my horde.

The greatest change nowadays is the almost complete absence of grouse and the blue mountain hare from large tracts of our mountains and moors. Our scientists are baffled as to the cause and much speculation abounds among the locals. It is certainly disheartening to walk through line after line of butts without a single grouse bursting from the heather, or hearing the familiar *kek kek* that made the hills such a place of pleasure.

The hen harrier can still be seen on occasions, but the kite is no longer around. McConnachie in 1895 recorded that "above the junction of the Allachy with the Tanar is the east end of Craig Daw, a long low crag close to the left bank of the water which was the breeding place of the Hen Harrier and the Kite, the latter better known locally as the Glentaner Gled." It is heartening that the golden eagle and now the osprey still form part of the attraction of the Glen. The prevalence of the buzzard, however, has got out of hand and along with crows and the lack of keepers make the running of a sporting estate very difficult.

For those of us who walked or cycled to school there was no more

Norval Smith

eerie sound in the autumn gloaming that the roar of a rutting stag. When I was travelling alone I found the experience nerve-wracking and hastened my flight home to the cosy reassurance of a parent. At the Tower of Ess, Cunliffe Brooks had his stone mason Norval Smith erect a handsome stone with the inscribed words, *Beware of the Stags*, a warning that one night we could be chased by a mighty monarch of the glen.

Fishing filled my junior years as no other hobby, apart perhaps from kicking a football in front of the Glen Tanar recreation hall or on the Aboyne Green. From an early age we boys roamed the length of the Tanar and its tributaries worming for brown trout and the odd sea-trout; very occasionally we were lucky enough to come by a salmon. It is to be noted that "to come by" does not necessarily mean by rod and line, but then boys will be boys, they say. This interest has been well covered in *Glen Tanar Exile*, save to say that we took so many trout out of that stream that I can only hope that future generations were less destructive than we had been, so allowing stocks to recover.

My image of past centuries is of a hardy race of youngsters having so little, but managing to survive, some to prosper. My generation was privileged to live on a sporting estate at a time when it was a millionaire's hobby. This was a halcyon age in my upbringing, never to be forgotten.

The estate before World War II boasted a very pleasant nine-hole golf course that employees could use, and fishing was allowed by rota on the Tanar, although as boys we largely ignored such tedious regulations. The laird had squash and tennis facilities, greatly underused in my time, but horse riding was popular with him and his family. The Norwegian sheltie or Fjord Horse, brought to Glen Tanar by Lord Glentanar in 1929, remains the bedrock of the present day riding stables.

The recreation hall with its lending library and full-size billiard table was the venue for whist drives and dances throughout the season. During World War II the dances were inundated with Canadian soldiers who brought a new dimension to estate living.

The summer sports and picnic on the golf course between the wars was another highlight for the children as was the annual ballroom Christmas tree. Over the years the various jubilees and coronations were celebrated with bonfires and parties with plenty of good things to eat and drink.

On 6th May 1935 King George V's Jubilee was celebrated at Glen Tanar with a large party at which each child released a balloon. The winner was Alan Mann of the Tower of Ess whose balloon was retrieved on 7th May some 800 miles away at Alt Klucken in Germany by Herrn Fritz Wilke. Alan was awarded a fine medal and has been kind enough to let me photograph it for posterity. On the obverse of the medal are the words *Stet Fortuna Domus* which appear on all the medallions for that jubilee. This translates into *May fortune attend who live here,* the motto of Harrow – Byron's old school and rival of the laird's school Eton, and coincidentally the motto on the Red House in Bournemouth, residence of Lillie Langtry where she met with the Prince of Wales. Somehow history knits together in these pages, culminating in these touchingly modest balloon flights from our quiet wee backwater in Deeside. Second prize went to Annie Hepburn of Hillhead, whose balloon was found at

Kassel in Germany, 650 miles away, while third prize went to Ean McLean, his being found at Bremen in Germany 550 miles away. Five years later we found ourselves sending, not balloons to Bremen, but Wellington bombers, such is the uncertainty of life.

Silver Jubilee Medal

A fitting postscript to this chapter came out of the blue. Calling to see Ian Hepburn in Golf Road, Ballater, to check some forgotten names, he took me through his impressive house to view his airy extension at the rear. Standing back, he pointed with no little pride to the massive object in the middle of the room. The full size billiard table that I had spent hours playing on as a teenager in the Recreation Hall was here in pristine condition. Ian bought it back in 1977 when the hall committee decided it was really too big and that they needed more room.

Viewing Ian's achievements in life from joinery, business, undertaking and antiques made me ponder why so many of those millionaires' employees' children have made such a success of their lives. Eight young Hepburns came from the tiny gamekeeper's cottage at Hillhead and five Strangs from the head keeper's home, all to do well in their different spheres. There seems little doubt that the background of a skilled work force, coupled to a good education and an atmosphere of betterment provided the launching pad that has led so many of us to thank our good fortune to have been brought up on the Glen Tanar estate.

24

ROADS, FORDS AND BRIDGES

R oads in the past were primitive affairs, often little more than cart tracks, but essential for trade and communication, and for warring armies to gain access to territory.

Glen Tanar boasted two major routes; the route from Glen Muick to Coirevrauch then out over the shoulder of Mount Keen to Glen Mark and the south. The other crossing was the ford below Dinnet bridge by Cobbleheugh, up the Firmounth road to cross the Tanar by ford and later by bridge around Braeloine; then making off across the face of the Knockie, the road meandered out over the hills to Tarfside and the south.

All along these lines of communication were small communities depending on passing trade to eke out their meagre livelihoods. Apart from supplying food and drink, travellers might require the assistance of a shoemaker, a blacksmith and some sort of general merchant. The community at Braeloine had such suppliers, without doubt. These communities themselves needed support so ensuring that agriculture, including meal milling, thrived, so spreading out dependency like ripples across a pool.

Following the 1715 rebellion General Wade was commissioned in 1724 to embark on a road-building exercise through the Highlands to allow army garrisons greater ease of access in case of future conflicts. Wade continued enthusiastically to penetrate

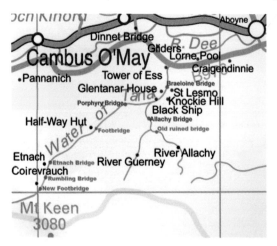

Map of the valley. Some of the bridges to be mentioned here are highlighted in blue.

Highland glens with roads and bridges until 1740 when he was promoted to greater things. His successor continued the programme after the '45 Rebellion. During my childhood we always called the Braeloine bridge the Wade bridge, although it appears that it was constructed rather later by an Aberdeen contractor. It is, however, a fine example from that period and an exciting entrance point for visitors to Glen Tanar.

Prior to bridges, fords were the means of travel; bridges under construction failed so often, swept away in winter torrents. The Tanar being a relatively small river, there were historical crossing points all along its banks. In 1725 there was an excellent timber bridge in the form of an arch at the Bordland which also boasted a fine inn where the forester lived. There was also a ford, but in due course the bridge was swept away and later the Bordland farm itself ceased to exist. Other records show well established fords allowing people to cross easily, for work and pleasure, at Knockieside, Bellastreen, Bridge-end, Greystone and Gartland.

Typical ford across the Tanar above Braeloine Visitor Centre

PHOTO BY ALAN FINDLAY

The Glen in the past had been accessed from the east by the south road, or as known by the locals, the Bordland road. It continued up to Knockieside where it crossed to the north bank and then continued on to Etnach. At Etnach the road crossed by a ford and thence to Coirevrauch. This road was said by the old folk to have been built with public money, which perhaps explains why years later the Dowager Lady Glentanar had to fight a court case to stop people driving up there. At first there was a ford at Knockieside, then a footbridge, followed by a wooden bridge for wheeled traffic. The existing stone bridge was erected by John Burgess, an Aboyne builder, at a cost of £70. The date of this bridge is not given but it is far plainer than those built for Cunliffe Brooks in the 1870s so may have been earlier.

Knockie Bridge: no sign of Brooks' quality mason's work

The north road came into existence with the Glen Tanar clearances, when the Earl of Huntly turned the estate into a hunting and shooting project. The crucial

233

This sign in one form or another has persisted since the Brooks' era

change for Glen Tanar, however, came with Cunliffe Brooks in the latter part of the nineteenth century. Set on converting this little back water into a prestigious estate, he built bridges, eliminated some roads and constructed others, changing the face of the countryside so that old people could hardly recognise the valley of their youth.

When Brooks built his prestigious Tower of Ess, he rebuilt the bridge to align it with his image of a Highland entrance. As the road bends over the bridge, you cannot admire the view unless you stop and walk around it. Even then it is dangerous with traffic coming at you from three directions.

The north road thus became the established road of access to the estate, but how Brooks allowed it to be accepted as a public road is not clear after all these years. Perhaps public money was again involved, but he certainly gave the impression that beyond his fine granite pillars was private property. The road also ran past Woodend where Brooks was to build his new mansion house, but here he does manage to divert it. Building the core of his establishment in this area with a large walled garden, stableyard and other essential buildings, he brought the public road up the Ca Canny Brae, so allowing him to keep his privacy behind closed gates.

The south road was supposed to be closed, but this never came about until much later when the Coats family became involved. There were farms and many houses up this south road in days gone by, but the clearances totally finished them off. One of Brooks priorities was to

The Rumblin Brig looking upstream. Inset: Inscription on upper side keystone – WCB 1873 and a mason's mark

rationalise all the established roads and paths. This was most noticeable in the area south of the river Dee where he rebuilt many farm houses and steadings, redirecting their entrances and creating proper roads around them. Older locals were said to be quite befuddled with the changes in the scenery. The road up the valley of the Tanar and also up the Allachy came in for upgrading when Brooks built a number of substantial bridges which still stand, as secure as the day they were constructed.

There are several smaller bridges which we pass over without much thought, but there are some which we cannot ignore. At the head of the valley there is the new Coirevrauch footbridge, just across from the ruins of the old drover's inn, from where the track leads on up Mount Keen. Coming back down the valley we come to the Rumblin Brig which crosses a deep rocky channel called the Rumblin Pot – a name that existed long before a bridge was ever contemplated. The river running through this small canyon is an impressive sight, especially in very high water. Built in the year 1873 the Rumblin Brig displays on its upstream keystone the initials WCB, year of construction and the mason's mark.

Further down the valley we come to the Etnach bridge with the stalker's cottage nestling into the hillside over on the north bank. This

Etnach Bridge, with (inset) WCB 1873 on the downstream side

bridge displays the same date of construction as its brother, along with the WCB on the downstream aspect but with a bold inscribed 'H' on its upstream outer aspect. Remembering that Brooks was still a tenant at the time, this mark must relate to the Huntly estates; was Brooks simply paying lip service to his son-in-law?

Pausing here we see the road branching off to the stalker's cottage of Etnach on the left and peeking over the bridge parapet you may be lucky enough to see an odd salmon lying there – well, they were certainly there in my youth. Remember that Etnach is where the Mackie boys walked from to get to Glentanar School in 1902 and 1916 as recorded earlier. Up the braes behind Etnach and out across the hills to Greystone, then down on to the South Deeside Road to reach the school. Nine miles in the morning and nine miles back again in the evening in all weathers, except in deep mid-winter for the youngest. This is the place, too, from which my bonny clever classmate of childhood days, Marigold McHardy, cycled to and from Aboyne School with never a complaint – and never late, unlike the rest of us.

Allan Brodie, author of *Adventure in My Veins* was brought up here, was a kennel boy in 1926 by the age of fourteen. He tells of becoming a fully fledged under-keeper on his fifteenth birthday, paid £1.10/- a week, and

The Half Way Hut Bridge PHOTO: ALAN FINDLAY

on the first day of February 1928 casting his first salmon fly at Waterside under the tuition of head keeper Peter Strang. In the early 1930s the estate became infested by a plague of ticks and sheep were reduced to skin and bone. A huge deer cull ensued, many deer carcases being sent to the worst hit of the mining areas during the Great Depression. Allan left to join New Scotland Yard in 1933 and thence followed a life of adventure from which he did not return for twenty-four years, to open a fishing tackle shop in Aboyne and spend the rest of his life in pursuit of salmon. He died in 1996, but was looked upon as a real trail-blazer for us as boys.

Coming back down the valley we reach the Half Way Hut and here it is worth stopping to view the footbridge over the Tanar, just opposite the hut. Retracing our steps even further we come to the Porphyry Bridge, known to us from childhood as the Forfary bridge.

This mispronunciation must have been handed down through decades of ignorance; Brooks obviously gave it this name as it was built amongst porphyry rock – a reddish igneous rock composed of large, conspicuous crystals. It is built on the same lines as the Etnach bridges but there are no inscriptions except for the mason's mark on the keystone. Crossing over the road to the Allachy side we find yet another identical bridge, again with only a mason's mark, but this one has attractive stone seating on the

Porphyry Bridge looking downstream, with mason's mark on keystone

up-side of the bridge, on its northern aspect.

Presumably all these bridges were built around the same time. The fact that the Etnach bridges are dated 1873 – when Brooks was still a tenant – did not stop him from improving the facilities for ease of access to his stalking and grouse shooting. If from here we proceed up the Allachy we soon come to the log stables, a ford and, within another three hundred yards, an unusable wood and iron bridge on the right. It likely also dates back to the Brooks' era, giving access to the hills beyond in order to bring deer carcases down to the larder.

Stone seating at Allachy Bridge

Back down the valley, we see where the bridges over the Black Ship succumbed to the raging torrent. The Knockie Bridge is next, then we come to the little footbridge which led from the mansion and estate houses to the chapel and golf course in days gone by. The original bridge had been built for Brooks by the same company he employed to fence in his estate.

Harper & Co., whose works were originally in Mealmarket Street, Aberdeen, built suspension bridges and patented a method of tightening the cables and wires used for both bridges and fencing. My colleague, retired surgeon Douglas Harper, has given me details of this method as used in his great-grandfather's business. The present bridge is not of this construction, suggesting that it was replaced in the Coat's era, but I remember no other bridge.

Black Ship Bridge in 1991, but no more PHOTO: COLIN SMITH

Age is now telling on the little footbridge, used only now for wedding guests attending the chapel. At the time of writing it is in the process of being replaced.

Next we come to the Braeloine Bridge which appears to me typical of a Wade construction, but details are scanty and dates vague. Documents seen by Dave Harding suggest it may never have been fully paid for.

New footbridge to the Chapel 2009

From this point to the Bridge of Ess there are no bridges and no foundations of the old Bordland bridge. The Bridge of Ash, renamed by Brooks as the Bridge of Ess (Gaelic *eas,* a waterfall or rapid) was redesigned and realigned. This was one of Brooks' most ambitious projects in Glen Tanar. From the chapter on his life we learn of his being ever present at its construction, and probably changing plans in a manner infuriating for his engineers. That the bridge has lasted unchanged since those days is a tremendous compliment to his builders, considering it is on a main road. The date 1894 is inscribed on the inner side of the west parapet mid-bridge. On the centre of the outer west side is the usual WCB and below it IP 1772, which is unexplained. Could this stone have

Braeloine Bridge

been from the original bridge and preserved lovingly by Brooks?

One more bridge to mention before we proceed westwards up the Dee is the one at Tanar mouth. A pedestrian suspension bridge, it was erected by Brooks just above where the Tanar runs into the Dee, presumably to allow fishers access the pools above the Lorne without

Tower of Ess Bridge. Inset (bottom), the plaque at centre of the arch – WCB and IP 1772. Inset,(top) 1894, when the bridge was rebuilt

A Harper's Patented Bridge Tensioner

Remnants of Tanar Mouth Bridge with tensioner still attached

having to go round by the Tower of Ess. Ean Mann remembers it from the time he lived in the Tower of Ess and passed this way from Aboyne School, from the mid-1930s. Even then it was dilapidated, the platform subsiding and treads missing, so making crossing hazardous. Now all that remains is some rotting wood with a Harper tensioner attached to mark the crossing point, so there is no doubt who constructed it. The tensioner is of an early type, suggesting that the bridge was built shortly after Brooks took over the tenancy of the Glen in 1871.

We are now back out on the South Deeside Road and moving out west to the last bridge of note from the past. The main road skirts along the

The Crofts' Pool Suspension Bridge
KIND PERMISSION ABERDEEN ART GALLERY & MUSEUM COLLECTION. ABDMS 004840.

Waterside Pool just short of Burnroot and there is a pleasant fishing hut on the bank overlooking the water. In this vicinity is another surprise that I never expected to uncover. Again my colleague Douglas Harper supplies the information and evidence.

Brooks through the years acquired Aboyne Castle and also Ferrar. It lies just beyond the Aboyne Glider Club, which is directly opposite Waterside. Whether Brooks felt a need to reach Ferrar more easily or gain readier access to fish the opposite bank is now conjecture. Whatever his reason, he commissioned Harper & Co. to erect a suspension bridge 400 yards below Waterside at the top of the Crofts' Pool. There is no memory locally of this bridge or when it was washed away, although it was still marked on maps in 1902 with a road or pathway shown leading directly to Ferrar. No sign remains of either foundations or a track to define exactly where it was, except for an ancient photo.

This appears to be a view from the top of the pool taken from the north bank. It is just possible to make out the South Deeside Road running east and, with magnification, a horse and cart just to the side of the south bank uprights. There appears to be a workman at either end of the bridge. There is also someone at the midpoint of the bridge dressed like a gaffer. Could it be Brooks, one wonders? It does not look as if the approach roadway has yet been completed at the south end, so was this a photograph taken by the builders? This must be a footbridge as the span appears huge for the slender supports, while the clearance above the summer water level looks ominously low to survive a winter spate. Under very strong magnification two houses are just visible on the south bank of the river. These were two ancient crofts, now just rubble, but giving the name to the pool – the Crofts.

Parapet of Corntulloch Bridge and Year 1874

The other bridge of importance to Glen Tanar estate in the past has been Dinnet Bridge, a public structure. Brooks had a well on either side of the north end of the bridge, so he was active in this vicinity. Having built the Dinnet church it is presumed he must have had a say in the kirk manse by the bridge.

Leaving Dinnet Bridge behind, go west out to the small bridge over the Corntulloch burn. It is just short of the turn down on the right to Corntulloch Farm and can be easily missed as only small parapets on either side of the road mark its position. Each keystone pillar has the date 1874 inscribed on its roadway face.

As with all Brooks' estate bridges, boundary walls and many of his roads, there is ample evidence of true solid craftsmanship; the fact that most stand today without the need for repair is testament to an age of real quality construction.

Cambus o' May Bridge from south bank

At the Pol Slachd pool beyond Deecastle there is a well, described in a subsequent chapter. Here again local knowledge and observation comes to our rescue. Colin Espie noticed that on both sides of the river at the top of the pool there were signs of a suspension bridge from days gone by. Locals recall fishers using it to reach both sides of the water without a detour. It was also used by school children from the Haugh and Cambus o' May to reach Inchmarnoch school. Again a date in the 1870s seems reasonable, and doubtless yet another Harper suspension bridge, but no record of it exists, nor memory of its being swept away.

The final bridge on the Dee valley associated with Glen Tanar is the Cambus o' May Bridge. Although one side of it sits on the estate bank, the bridge itself was a gift to the district from a Mr Alexander Gordon in 1905. Not only is it built in a lovely setting, but it is in itself hugely attractive. Visitors flock to the region and the young take delight in jumping off it into the dark pool beneath.

The modern day Coirevrauch bridge, so solidly constructed, will hopefully still be in place a hundred years from now, a challenge to the durability of Sir William Cunliffe Brooks' structures of old.

The new Coirevrauch Bridge and Mount Keen in 2008

25

THE TANAR VALLEY ARTEFACTS

Sir William Cunliffe Brooks left behind a vast array of inscribed objects on Glen Tanar estate, objects which appear at first sight the products of an eccentric hobby. Wells, horse troughs, memorial stones, road signs and buildings all leave the impression of a man lost in admiration of his handiwork. Many stones would have required yearly attention to keep vegetation at bay and to renew the lettering; and he probably barely considered how they would fare after his death, as we collectors ignore such trifling matters.

One characteristic type of stone reappears again and again throughout this discourse. This oddly-shaped stone (shown here at Fasnadarach House)

The stone at Fasnadarach

appears to be made up of pure limestone set into a harder rock, and eroded by weather or water. Over the years we have looked everywhere for its source, but without success. A geologist has expressed the opinion that Brooks may have imported them, as the only place known for this type of limestone is way up the Pollagach burn at the back of Mill of Bellamore. To date we have uncovered none of these stones, either in the rivers or local quarries, but the search goes on.

1. Queen's Well

Brooks was very enamoured of his close neighbour, Queen Victoria, who visited the estate in his time. He named the Queen's Well in her honour – just across the Knockie Bridge and 100 yards along the south road going west – as Victoria may have passed this way. This well, dated 1874, is on the left side of the road on a raised platform with stone steps at either end.

1. Queen's Well at Knockie Bridge, with crown above a V and dated 1874

2. The Jubilee Stone

On the north side of the Knockie bridge is an inscribed stone, the Jubilee Stone. It sits at the west end of a fenced copse of trees in the middle of the road.

2. The Jubilee Stone

3. The Glentana Stone

Staying in this area we walk round to the top of the lake where the feeder stream comes out of its conduit. Here on the wall an intricate inscription is set into the face of the outlet, the initial letters from top to bottom spelling *Glentana*.

> *Gelida, Limpida, Effluens, Nitida, Tremula, Ampla, Nivalis Aqua.*
> *Cool, Clear, Flowing, Glittering, Quaking, Copious, Snowy, Water.*

Nothing was more certain to anger Brooks than people in his employ daring to use that one letter too many, that 'r' at the end of the name.

3. The Glentana Stone

4. Home Farm well

Along the base of a well at the junction of the Home Farm road where it meets the

4. Home Farm inscribed stone. The lettering had originally been applied in gold paint.

5. *Glad from the Heart of the Mountain*. Note typical eroded stone above inscription slab

side road into the farm manager's house at Bellastreen is this inscription worked in finely-cut letters, the script is small and not easy to read, despite traces of gold paint.

> *We plough the fields and scatter,*
> *The good seed on the land*
> *But it is fed and watered*
> *by God's almighty hand.*

5. Home Farm steading well

> *Glad from the heart of the mountain*
> *Leap I to flash in the sun*
> *Eager with rill stream and fountain*
> *Nimbly to run*
> *Take me and guard of my treasure*
> *Ample the sum of my store*
> *Needful am I to true pleasure*
> *All the world o'er.*

This inscription is also at the Home Farm, at what had been a well in Brooks' time. It is in the heart of the steading, set into the junction of what had been the mill and stables, under the eaves. The dung heap and pig sty are nearby.

6. The Home Farm duck pond

The dried-out old duck pond at the Home Farm may hide an interesting relic. It is said that Brooks had the floor of the pond set in granite blocks, inlaid with an outline of the Prince of Wales feathers. Certainly in my youth the pond was picturesque and well kept, with a fountain playing. I do not remember the feathers, but Jimmy Oswald said an old keeper Charlie Milne saw it in his youth. Jimmy was hell bent on proving this and a few years ago we went to dig out the pond and find the inscription. By this time, however, the pond was grown over with grass and an irate lady who was renting the area for her ponies sent us off with a flea in our ear so the feathers remain undiscovered.

6. Duck pond. Pedestal for the fountain is still obvious.

7. Below Home Farm

A roundish large stone – amateurishly inscribed *PE 1747* – used to be set on top of the garden wall of Bellastreen, the house of the Home Farm manager. The wall is now demolished and the stone lies alongside the main road, just below the house. The fact that Brooks rescued this stone and set it into his wall suggests that it did date from 1747, but no one in my time has ever known for sure.

7. PE 1747 stone preserved by Brooks, origin unknown

8. Opposite Bellastreen

This inscription is set into the lintel stone above the conduit that brings the stream all the way down from the kennels. It is on the lower side of the road opposite Bellastreen and across the road from the PE *1747* stone, an example either of Brooks' sense of humour or of his own sense of importance. Why did he put it here, out of sight of all apart from small boys playing up the conduit? There had been a path down from Bellastreen in the old days, across the main road and over the conduit, down an iron ladder, now rusted, into the round field. One of Brooks' tall eroded stones is still in place on top of the wall, to allow people to steady themselves descending the ladder.

8. *Welling Springs make Grateful Brooks*

9. Braeloine Horse Trough

10. Facing East towards the Trough

11. Brooks Stone to his Stalker

9. Braeloine Bridge Horse Trough

Now let us walk down to the Visitor Centre car park at Braeloine. On the side of the road facing the path across the bridge there is a well marked horse trough with a heading stone inscribed, *Cead Mille Failte.* Hundred thousand greetings.

10. Chapel of St Lesmo area

Crossing the Braeloine bridge let us wend our way round to the Chapel of St Lesmo. Before going into the graveyard let us walk on about a hundred yards. On the left of the path is an inscribed stone facing a D-shaped stone platform with stone seating, and a drinking trough on the SW side.

> *Drink weary Pilgrim*
> *Drink and Pray*

Prior to the completion of the chapel of St Lesmo it is said that Brooks conducted his own church service from the top of this mound. When you remember that he harangued the villagers in Aboyne at the bonfire just before his death, he was obviously not averse to public speaking from his experience as an MP.

11. Chapel of St Lesmo

At the entrance to the church the two graves with the tall Celtic stone at the head are those of Sir Cunliffe and Lady Brooks. The main graveyard is set out to the east of the church and here lie Lord and Lady Glentanar, alongside their daughter Jean and one of her sons Robert. Others interred there are mostly employees. The tall stone in front of the gravestone to Brooks' stalker Donald Mackintosh and his wife is the one brought down from the hill in 1877, after Brooks had killed the haunted stag (Chapter 9).

12. Mansion House

At the northern end of the round field, below the old mansion house and ballroom, there is a small fenced copse containing a large upright inscribed stone from the Coats' era.

> *Here lies Captain, hunter of George Baron Glentanar. Charger in France during the Great War of Thomas Baron Glentanar. A noble fearless and faithful animal. Died 1926 aged 20 years.*

Out in front of the ballroom of Glentanar House there is a high bank enveloped in rhododendrons. A path runs along the length of these rhoddies and at the south end there is a little alcove containing many headstones. In front of them all is a little metal image of a Scottie. This was the graveyard through the 1920s and 30s of Lord and Lady Glentanar's many dogs. Among the well-remembered names is Slenta, the golden retriever immortalised in the portrait of Lady Glentanar and daughter Jean; painted by Cowan Dobson in 1938, it still hangs in the ballroom.

13. The 1861 Victoria mystery

One of Queen Victoria's famous big trips took her in 1861 over the hills from Glen

12. Captain's Resting Place

12. The little Scottie in front of the gravestones.

14. *Beware of the Stags:* as children this warning made us very anxious in the rutting season.

15. Pillar and tower behind

15. Close up of quality and inlaid flower

Muick to Etnach, over the shoulder of Mount Keen, down into Glen Mark and on to Fettercairn. Returning by the Cairn o Mount, the Queen is said to have lunched in the vicinity of the present Glentanar House and a stone with the date 1861 was said to have been placed there. Alex Inkson McConnochie in the *Royal Dee* talks of this, but I have found no evidence that this stone still exists.

14. Tower of Ess

The district between Braeloine and the Tower of Ess appears devoid of relics, but as we approach the Tower gates from the Glen Tanar side there is a very fine granite wall along the northern aspect of the road. At the near end the topping off stone has a graceful carving by the mason Norval Smith. *Beware of the Stags* is a consummate example of the fine workmanship that made so many of these inscriptions a delight.

15. Tower of Ess gate pillars

These two beautiful pillars exuded the atmosphere of a very private property beyond, built to deter the inquisitive. On each aspect of the pillars there are inlaid central motifs at the base of the pyramids. On the pillar nearest the Tower there is a shamrock facing east, a thistle facing north, the word TANA on the south aspect, while on the west, what would we expect but WCB. The north pillar has a rose facing east, the date 1895 facing north, what appears like a clover on facing south, and a distinctive open hand on the west.

16. Well o' Welcome

The Tower of Ess is an imposing structure modelled on an ancient keep and set on a curve over a deep pool in a pine-clad ravine. The rebuilding of the Bridge of Ess in 1894 was also designed to capture the atmosphere of the setting. Brooks spent an inordinate amount of time getting it to suit his perception of a Highland glen. It is in the garden facing out onto the main road that we find the next inscribed stone – the Well o' Welcome.

16. *Well o' Welcome* **in Tower front garden**

17. Tower of Ess garden

In the front garden climb up the impressive stone steps to sit atop the wall. Now notice at your feet three little fishes to keep you company.

Direct your glance to the front door of the Tower. There on the wall to the right of the doorway is yet another inscription in Gaelic: *Fasgadh*, or shelter in English

Before leaving the area there is one more stone to be viewed. Coming out on to the main South Deeside Road turn left, walk for a dozen yards and you will see an inscribed stone set into the granite wall on your left. Finely inscribed, it indicates the miles to the bridges of Aboyne, Dinnet and Ballater.

17. Three little Fishes Figure

18. Drink Weary Traveller.

Leave the Tower of Ess behind, cross the bridge and turn into the road on the right. This is the old south road up the Glen, still referred to by some of the ancients as the Bordland road which leads to the ruined farm of that name. Hopefully the gate is

17. *Bridge O' Ess.* **Distance in miles to the bridges of Aboyne (1½), Dinnet (3¼) and Ballater (9¾)**

18. Drink Weary Traveller in the Land, And on thy Journey Fare, Tis sent by God's all Giving Hand, And stored by Human Care

19. Inspection Pipe

20. Drink- Speed- Fare- Well

open, so carry on for about 400 yards until you find an inscribed horse trough on your left.

19. Inspection Pipe

Go west to the fork in the road and proceed over 200 yards up the track to your left, along the east side of the Allt Roy burn. A little below and to the west of that track is a wooden railed compound where there is a sunken area paved with concrete slabs. On the uphill side is a large boulder, on the lower side of which is an upright stone slab with the words *Inspection Pipe* inscribed diagonally.

20. Drink- Speed- Fare- Well

Continuing up the road you come to a junction. Take the right branch and 100 yards ahead, just down the bank on the right there is a small fenced-off area enclosing a well.

21. Honest Water

Returning to the South Deeside Road, turn right towards Aboyne and after half a mile see a well on the right hand side of the road, opposite a white quartz cairn atop the wall.

Again we find signs that Brooks had his doubts about alcohol. Beside the *WCB* at the end of the trough there is the inscription of Brooks' favourite stone mason, Norval Smith, who scoured the valley for suitable stones to inscribe. Smith lived in Aboyne and after Brooks' death there is no record of where he was employed. He died in 1922, aged 71, in a collision with a car when he was riding his bicycle near St Thomas' Church. His granddaughter visited the district until a couple of years ago, and made a point of looking at her ancestor's carving. She died in her nineties, but her daughter and granddaughter still come to Aboyne to maintain the tradition.

*21. **Honest Water Never Left Man in the Mire***

22. Craigendinnie Gates

Continue towards Aboyne and, at end of long straight, the Craigendinnie House gates are on the right. On the left hand side of the road facing the gates there is a distinctive well using Brooks' typical eroded stones, but he thought fit not to inscribe them on this occasion.

21. End of trough: WCB and Norval Smith

23. Lorne Pool

Our starting point is here at this Craigendinnie well above the Lorne pool. Take the path down to the Dee from behind the well and proceed west a few hundred yards until you reach a gate and an attractive walled-off rest area. There you find the stone inscribed, *Dry Lines No Fish*.

The story related to this stone has a number of variations, but Neil Williams, late of Dalwhing Farm and now at Ballaterach, tells it thus. Cunliffe Brooks paid an unheralded visit to find his ghillie asleep on the bank. Sending him home, he told him he would call him back in due course. Brooks then got his workers to construct the path and walled area and finished it all off with the stone. Inviting his ghillie, to come and see his handywork, he sacked him on the spot – a story that

22. Unnamed well with River Dee over back wall

23. *Dry Lines No Fish* – Is this Cunliffe Brooks being a Despot?

24. *The Fear of the Lord Is a Fountain of Life*, in 1911. The man holds a copper cup in his right hand.

25. The Rest and Be Thankful Stone

leaves a sour taste locally. Another version since told is that there were two ghillies involved and both were similarly made to suffer.

---

24. The Fungle Stones

Coming from the Craigendinnie gates towards Aboyne the popular walk up the Fungle is approached most often by the track up from the main road on the right, a short distance before the junction with the Aboyne bridge. Walk in to the foot of the Fungle. The Altdinnie burn forms the boundary here between Glen Tanar and Birse, so when you cross the wooden bridge over the burn you are back on the Glen Tanar side. Walking on to the bottom of the hill you come to pillars where once had been a gate. Just beyond this is a hillock on the left of the path and on its east side is a well. *The Fear of the Lord is a Fountain of Life* confirms Brooks' strong religious convictions.

This photograph is courtesy of Denis Yule, from his extensive collection around the Queen's Loch of an era long past.

---

25. The Fungle

Walking on up towards the top of the valley we come to the *Rest and Be Thankful* on the left of the track. Two inscribed stones guard the entrance to a flat area with stone seats set in a rough triangle. Of all Brooks' stones this is the one best known to ramblers through the ages. The Fungle was hugely popular, especially in the early 1900s, and this was a regular resting place for tired legs and bursting lungs. The stone seating and the vista are very appealing, but the trees now intrude and lacking attention, it is only a shadow of its former attractiveness.

The stone to the left shows two dates: 1869 was when Brooks came to the district on the occasion of his daughter's marriage to the Marquis of Huntly, while 1900 was the year he died. The great man had made sure that his passing would be recorded somewhere on his beloved estate.

In addition to the initials of Brooks and his years associated with the district, this stone also has an inscription across the top.

25. WCB 1869 to 1900

O Ye Mountains O Ye Waters
Praise Ye the Lord

The Fungle was of great importance as the principal drove road linking Aboyne over the hills to Tarfside and the south, so Brooks' memorial is well placed.

Yet another Brooks' house greets us at the top of the Fungle where a lonely keeper watched over this outlying aspect of the estate and did indeed keep guard over his employer's interests.

25. Looking back down the Fungle Brae from the Rest and Be Thankful

25. The Guard at top of the Fungle

26

ARTEFACTS BY THE DEE

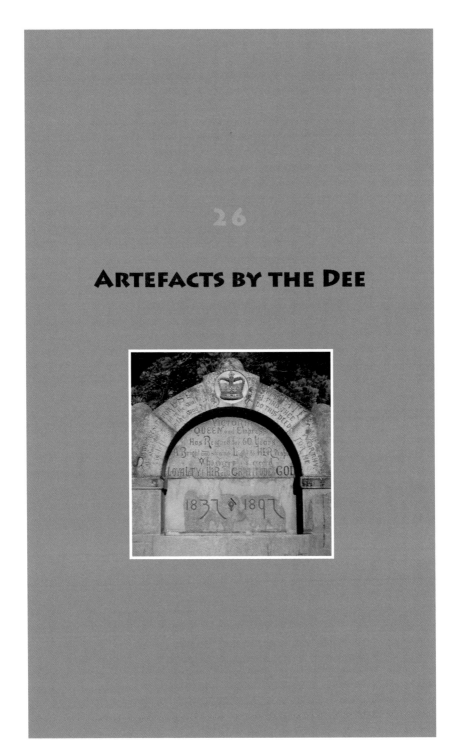

L eaving Aboyne by the South Deeside Road we pass the Tower of Ess and come to the Jones' sawmill on our right, then Burnroot Farm on the left. Stop just short of the farm steading and in a layby is our first well.

1. Horse trough buttressed by carved granite blocks

Where is a Will C.B. ... there is a Way U.C.

1. Burnroot Farm

In some old photographs there are large round balls on top of the two inscribed granite blocks, but like the copper cup, they have been removed. But who can blame the culprits, as no one seems to care if the trough disappears below the undergrowth.

These inscriptions symbolise Brooks' attitude to life. It is interesting that he feels it necessary to record it in granite, again playing on his own name

Where is a Will (Cunliffe Brooks)
– There is a Way (You See)

In the past this well was an impressive stopping point, with its stone seating in a semicircle on each side. This is the type of project I hope the Deeside Heritage Society might restore as a salute to our past.

2. Jones's Sawmill

On the opposite side of the road from the well and down a steep bank there is another well, surrounded by a protective wooden fence. This well held very cold water and in the past was used in the summer by the farmer's wife, Mrs Greenlaw, to keep her butter cool – until the cows came along and ate the butter! To approach this well you must now report to the Jones's sawmill office to comply with their Health & Safety regulations.

2. A Thousand Years in THY Sight are but as Yesterday

3. Glen Tanar School Wall

Along the road we soon come to Glentanar School with its imposing fountain, set facing south-west and situated at the south-west end of the school grounds.

This is Brooks' most important memorial of this type on the estate, but it does not suit all tastes. It is fussy in the extreme, with too many inscriptions set around it. It is impressive, but continuing neglect makes it less of a tourist attraction than it should be.

The inscription on the left of the crown reads: *Shape thyself for* USE. *The stone that may fit in the wall is left not in the way.* On the right of the crown it reads: *Then may* FATE *thy measure take and say – I find thee worthy do this deed for me.*

Then below the crown it reads: *Victoria* QUEEN *and Empress has Reigned for 60 years. Bright and shining Light to Her people Who everywhere record* LOYALTY *to* HER *and* GRATITUDE *to* GOD.

1837–1897

3. Glentanar School, Schoolhouse and Fountain

3. Imposing or inelegant?

4. *To Farm Only*

5. *Well Begun is Half Done*

4. Cobbleheugh Farm Road

Take the farm road along the side of the school; almost opposite the school entrance you spot this stone on the left side of the roadway.

This stone has had an eventful life. It started life in Brooks' time around Craigendinnie House. It migrated to the Home Farm at Glen Tanar, probably in the late 1940s, where it spent a miserable time – sometimes propped up, sometimes fallen over – near a steading.

Last year it disappeared then reappeared just up the Cobbleheugh road in all its glory, perfectly whitened with the letters picked out in black. There are obviously still folk in the Glen looking after our heritage.

5. Cobbleheugh Farm

Leaving the fountain, take the farm road past the side of the school until you come to Cobbleheugh Farm. Here at the side of the house there is a well-tended inscribed stone

This stone originally stood outside Candycraig farmhouse up the hill facing the school. When the house was converted into a holiday home the workmen, making a car park, discarded the stone in a ditch.

Sandy Murray, the farmer of both rented farms, had his wife to thank for rescuing the stone and taking it to Cobbleheugh for safe keeping.

No doubt others stones have disappeared forever. The adage on this stone is also recorded on a panel in the school.

6. Fir Munth Stone

This stone can be accessed from the Braeloine Centre up the hill over Belrorie, or from the road up from the Glentanar School, up what we called the Firmy Brae. At the top of this brae stands an imposing block of granite supposedly telling of historical facts from our warring past. That these 'facts' – both the reference to Edward I and the Duke of Montrose having come this way – are fallacies is unfortunate, but Brooks was obviously mislead by some local historian. It is now a rather romantic folly as we know that the passes further east were used by these armies. The wording on the stone is difficult to make out, but is as follows: *Fir Munth Ancient Pass over The Grampians. Here crossed the invading armies of Edward 1 of England AD1296 and 1303*. Across the foot of the slab was added: *Also the Army of Montrose 1645*

6. The Fir Munth Stone

PHOTO: ANNE BURGESS

7. The Worm of the Still is the Deadliest Snake on the Hill.
To us as children the deadliest snake on the hill was the dreaded adder.

7. Belrorie Road – Snake's Well

This stone is but sixty yards from the above stone further down the road from Belrorie. Reaching the road at a V-junction, on your right is a recessed area with stone seating and although now very boggy, it had been a proper well in earlier times. A long flat stone with a distinctive message sits at right angles to the road. Here again Brooks is voicing his dislike of alcohol, but no one seemed to realise the significance of the message in my childhood. In fact the ordinary employee seemed totally uninterested in either the buildings or the artefacts.

8. *Wilcebe Road*

9. *Aulton Road*

10. The Flush Stone

11. *Well to Know When You are Well Off*
Well close by Newton Farm

8. Wilcebe Road

At this V-junction the road to the left takes you on to Newton farm, while the road straight ahead lands out on the South Deeside Road at Fasnadarach House. On the wall at this left branch is the Brooks' name for this road – Wilcebe Road. Yet another derivation of Brooks' initials.

9. Aulton Road

Continue along Wilcebe Road leading to Newton farm for three-quarters of a mile until you come to an inverted V-junction. The road doubling back on your right leads down to Tillycairn Farm, but on the wall on your right as you turn to go down this route you find the name Aulton Road.

Is this Brooks preserving a name from the past, as in 'old toon' referring to an old farm, or is he just being his eccentric self?

10. Flush Stone

Twenty yards past the above junction going towards Newton there is a large roundish stone on the left grass verge with the word *Flush* inscribed. It was originally some fifty yards back where there was a spring and also some sort of waterworks in Brooks' time. The significance of the inscription is not apparent and its relevance to our study is uncertain, but it is recorded nevertheless.

11. Well to Know

Almost half a mile along this road you come to a horse trough on your left. This one is unusual, as apart from its fine carving, it has still the original copper cup – a rare occurrence nowadays.

12. Wilcebe Road

Pass Newton farm on your right and the road turns downhill, now running north. Half way down, a bay leads into a field, at the entrance to which is another fine well.

13. Wilcebe Road

At the foot of the hill lies Netherton Farm, another of Brooks masterpieces. On the left side of the road before you turn the corner, there is a huge Wellingtonia on the other side of the granite wall. On the wall itself is yet another inscription telling us where we are.

Brooks planted many Wellingtonias that still stand tall and strong today.

14. Dinnet Bridge

Walk down Wilcebe Road until it meets the South Deeside Road just before the Dinnet Bridge. We retrace our steps here to take in three further stones before going on to Deecastle.

Turn right towards the bridge and cross to the north bank. The well on the west side of the bridge is in the private grounds of the Old Manse and the owners are due our respect.

It is easiest to reach it by descending the east side of the bridge and crossing the gate to the other side; the well is close to the bridge.

This is another fine example of the mason Norval Smith's inscriptions.

15. Dinnet Bridge

Under the bridge on the north wall is a record of the height of the Dee in 1884.

**12. *Drink, Thank, Think.*
Characteristic headstone**

13. The huge Wellingtonia

**14. Inscribing a well so close
to the river seems rather odd.**

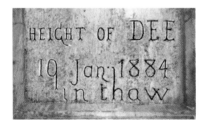

15. Spate height of Dee in 1884

265

16. Well of Healing

17. *The Well of Grace*

18. Corntulloch Well: Large number of eroded stones used here

16. Dinnet Bridge

Returning to the east side of the bridge, walk down the bank of the river for about thirty yards to a small stone by a boggy sort of well. Again the position and purpose seem peculiar, but it is so often difficult to get inside the Brooks' mind.

17. South Deeside Road

Return to the South Deeside Road and turn left across the bridge. A quarter of a mile on, just before the road leads off towards the Snake's Well, there is a small well let into the boundary wall of Fasnadarach House. Brooks' daughter Lady Cecil lived here and her father probably supplied the house – another quirky touch.

18. South Deeside Road

We are now going out west and our first stop is just over a mile away, twenty yards beyond the Corntulloch farm road end, where there is a well on the left side of the road. We see a pile of eroded stones above an inscribed stone and horse trough. The number of stones used here in such a haphazard manner raises the question as to whether their source is relatively close at hand.

19. The Shilling Stone

Before leaving Corntulloch it is worth going down to the farm and having a look at what has been called a Shilling Stone.

This is yet another of Jimmy Oswald's finds and I personally have some doubts about this particular one. He said that in times past travellers could by law expect food from farmers if they were far from home and that the farmers had a special stone in which they would grind just enough meal for the visitor. Let us go and see this stone. Having crossed the fields from the farmhouse to the river, we turn left along the river bank for 240 yards. We come to a broken wicker gate with a path leading down a steep bank. At the foot of the bank is a round stone with a small, hollowed out centre. It doesn't fill one with enthusiasm, but there may be just enough in our history to make the case for this being such a stone.

Sheelin, shillen and shilling are old names relating to grain being removed from the husk and the blowing away of the chaff. Shilling stone, however, brings blank stares from our experts and the literature seems devoid of such a reference. A quern or quern-stone as a hand-mill for grinding is well documented so was shilling stone simply a local name? With the establishment of the meal mills in the district, farmers who had ground their own grain using querns and shilling stones were ordered by the Superior to have them broken up, with his factor going round the farms to see that this was carried out. Whether this stone is one that escaped the eagle-eyed factor or is nothing more than a base stone for a gate post, I leave the experts to fathom.

20. Little Tullich

Let us turn to the more definite works of Cunliffe Brooks. Back on the main road turn right and make for Deecastle. Turn in

18. Corntulloch Well: *Men May Come and Men May Go But I Go on for Ever.*

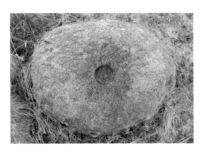

19. The Shilling Stone – an interesting thought but is it credible?

20. *He Sendeth the Springs among the Hills*

267

21. My Lord's House

21. Initialled *AR* stone in My Lord's House

22. Stone at entrance to Deecastle – not ancient but attractive

to the farm on the left, but stop at the bottom of the hill before reaching the farmhouse. We are going up to the cottage Little Tullich, so be prepared for a stiff walk. Reaching the house at the top keep straight out along the right side and across two fields in a southerly direction to reach a boggy piece of ground where we find yet another inscribed stone.

21. My Lord's House

Descending from Little Tullich a short distance it is worth making a detour, branching off the path after the gate and walking through the trees on the right to come to a huge pile of stones on top of one of the banks. Today they look a jumble, but at one time there had been a small chamber on the south side with stone seating and perhaps other chambers.

This structure is recorded from way back, but no one now is sure what it was made for. The fact that it has always been known as My Lord's House suggests that, as the Huntlys were the landowners, it has some relevance to their time there when Deecastle was one of their homes.

Some thought it a lookout for deer hunting, but it is not in a position to make this a possibility. Others think it has its roots in pre-Pictish times. It is quite conceivable that someone simply built it as a folly. However Dave Harding's team found a stone in the central chamber inscribed with interlocking letters 'AR' which tends to indicate it was built with some purpose in mind.

22. Deecastle

Going back down to the South Deeside Road, walk round to the west entrance to Deecastle where you will see not only a horse trough with two separate inscribed stones, but a neatly painted stone sign of welcome.

22. *Work as tho you might live for Ever; Live as tho you might die to day* **Water trough with two inscribed stones on either side**

23. South Deeside Road

Continuing along the main road for a few hundred yards come to the left turn-off for Tombae and Greystone. It is a short walk up hill to the cottage of Tombae; on the ground along the wall to the garage is another stone, said to have been moved here some years ago, but its original site is unknown.

23. *As Heaven Gives Me So I Give Thee*

24. The Pol Slachd Pool

Coming back down to the main road from Tombae, proceed west to the bottom of the hill just before Inchmarnoch. Cut back across the fields to the top of the pool with the Needle Stone in the shallow stream above it. There is a fishing hut here at the salmon pool called Pol Slachd – Gaelic for the pool in the hollow.

The Needle Stone in the stream above this pool is unique, as is the mythology associated with it. It was believed that if an infertile girl could squirm her way through the hole in the stone from the top side she would readily become pregnant. One woman doing it the other way round failed to conceive for a couple of years, but once she returned and did it the correct way round she became pregnant the next month.

24. The Needle Stone

24. *Drink of this Spring and think of the River*

25. Well overgrown and almost invisible

26. Trough cleaned and inscription highlighted

26. Inscriptions on both sides of trough

Now walk a short distance – 75 yards – down the bank from the fishing hut and find a well situated 10 yards up from the bank.

Drink of this Spring, And think of the river, Where the thirst of the soul, Shall be quenched for ever.

25. Inchmarnoch Well

Coming back on to the main road it is a short walk downhill to Inchmarnoch. Cross the bridge and continue out the main road past the last house, called Tassachd Cottage. Twenty-five yards on the left bank there is a small well, rather overgrown with no inscription, but it looks typically Brooks.

26. Pannanich

We are out at the boundary now between Glen Tanar and Glen Muick. Just before Pannanich Hotel there are two cottages below the road on your right, shown as Glascorrie on the map. Opposite them and eight yards into the trees on the left there is a Queen Victoria Jubilee water trough with inscriptions on both sides and at the foot.

On the east side: *Drink weary traveller in the land And on thy journey fare Tis sent by God's all giving hand And stored by human care.* On the west side: *From earth I flow seaward I go Refreshing the world on my way My duty done my guerdon won I rise on celestial ray.*

Let us now retrace our steps and look for those stones further up in the hills.

27

DISTANT RELICS

The remainder of Brooks artefacts lie in more remote areas of the estate. Their position often to us defies common sense, but then had we spoken to Brooks he would probably have given us rational reasons. Let us start along a well known walker's route, traversing the side of the Knockie hill and out along the Firmounth, eventually towards Tarfside.

1. *Let Well Alone:* **No sign of a well**

1. The Firmounth

Ascending up on to the Firmounth road from the Knockie bridge we pass the viewing point on our left and set out south-west. Twelve yards beyond the track turning off to our left we come upon a stone with a real Brooks' fairy tale.

The story goes that after having wined and dined well at Brooks' table one evening, a guest decided a walk would help his digestion. Having come along this path he had slaked his thirst at the well and spent the next week in bed with acute gastro enteritis. In typical fashion, Brooks responded with an inscribed stone to warn off his future guests.

2. The Monks' Well

Walking on out along this road for a quarter of a mile we come to a lonely pine, surrounded by a wire fence, on the left of the path. On the opposite bank is an inscribed stone indicating we are near the Monk's Well. This reference is now difficult to ascertain as no records appear to exist to back up Brooks' comment about monks. The number 813.9 appears to refer to height above sea level

This inscribed stone appears to indicate a well further down the hill and sure enough, we find a flat slab on a grassy terrace. This covers a small square stone-lined well still containing water Further down the hill is a modern cistern relating to the water supply to the estate.

2. Note the arrow on the left and the number 813.9

---

3. Firmount – Marker Stone 1

A further quarter of a mile on between the Monk's Well and the burn of Counciltree there is a marker stone on the left bank of the road inscribed with the figure 803, which appears again to indicate altitude.

3. Marker Stone 1

---

4. Firmount – Marker Stone 2

A similar stone, but with an indication that we are perhaps two miles from the mansion house, is just a few hundred yards further on. It stands proudly on the left bank, at the junction where a road branches off to the left up the east bank of the East Burn of Drum to Baudy Meg.

---

5. The Menawee Stones

Now that we are out here on the Firmount road we should take this left branch. The road is quite substantial so we progress quite easily up behind Baudy Meg for about a mile-and-a-half. Keep looking to the right and between Baudy Meg and Duchery Beg two pyramid-

4. Marker Stone 2 and mile indicator

5. The Haunted Stag

5. WCB lay here to take deadly aim

5. The Haunted Stag meets his fate

shaped statues topped off with large round stones become obvious out across the heather. This area of ground between these hills is known as the Menawee. The pillar nearer the path is where Sir William lay to take aim at the stag standing further uphill near the second stone marker. Both balls are suitably inscribed, but the weather has wrought havoc and now only the rudiments can be read. Also both pyramids are suffering some settlement and may well eventually topple over if they are not repaired.

Inscriptions on either pillar:

LEFT: *267 yards availed not his power of flight*
Nor keenest sense of fear and sight
Sure bullet to its fatal mark has sped
Death pang scarce felt the Haunted Stag is dead
WCB
9 Oct 1877.

LEFT, BELOW: *On Menawee 267 Yards*
9 Oct 1877
THE HAUNTED STAG KILLED BY
W. Cunliffe Brooks MP.

6. St Colm's Well

Back at the Firmounth road junction, we think of the long walk out to the St Colm's Well, three-and-a-half miles out along this roadway. Passing high above the Allachy river on our right, we come out on to open ground with the Forest of Birse over on our left. The road can be rough and boggy at times and never ending to our young children. Passing Hill of St Colm on our right we come to

Gannoch. Here beside the well is a large flat stone with a smaller inscribed boulder on top. The inscription takes the form of a Celtic cross and the words *Well Beloved*. A rather disappointing stone, perhaps, for all that hard trek?

7. Allachy Valley

Back in the Allachy, instead of proceeding out along the high ground towards St Colms we branch right down a side road, which takes us down to the floor of the valley to link in to the estate road. Now turn left into this road and walk the short distance to the established ford. Over the ford and up the bank on the other side we come to a fairly recent stone.

Glen Tanar National Nature Reserve
Declared on 21st September 1979
To the Memory of Lord Glentanar
Who protected this fine remains
Of Caledonian Pine Forest
And his Grandson Robert Bruce
Who helped so much towards
The formation of the Reserve
Unveiled on 21st September 1979
By Dr Jean Balfour

8. Upper Allachy

On past the Nature Reserve stone for about 250 yards, ignore a side road going right and just beyond that scramble down the river bank. You should find a ruined foot bridge close by; cross the river as best you can. On the opposite bank, turn downstream for about 20 yards and eight yards in from the river come upon a large recumbent stone.

6. Celtic cross and *Well Beloved*
PHOTO: HANS KRUUK

7. To the Memory of Lord Thomas Glentanar and his grandson Robert Bruce 1979

8. *John Milne, Deer Stalker,*
1847–1882

8. Alfie Dawson at the old
footbridge just above the John
Milne Stone

9. Not up to Norval Smith
standards but this does capture
the atmosphere of our glen

Reported in the local Aberdeen press dated 6th February 1882 under the heading, Fatal Gun Accident at Ballater: *"A melancholy gun accident occurred at Glentanar on Monday afternoon whereby John Milne, a gamekeeper in the service of Mr Brooks MP lost his life. A party of about 30 guns were out at a hare hunt between Glentanar and Ballaterach when one of the guns went off and the contents were lodged about Milne's side and neck. He being not more than 10 yards distant, death resulted almost immediately. This sad accident has cast a gloom over the whole district where the deceased was so well known and so highly respected. For upwards of 30 years he had been a gamekeeper in Glentanar; and as a deer stalker he had few equals."*

That we are in the Allachy and nowhere near Ballater or Ballaterach shows that reporters even then had little idea of the district they were covering. The '111 Miles' on the stone is presumably again the distance from the Mansion House.

Retracing our steps down the valley we get an excellent view of the linden tree at the Black Ship and marvel at its stature.

9. North Road up Tanar

This stone is about 300 yards before you reach the Black Ship if you come up the north bank of the river from Glentanar House. It sits on the bank on your right hand side and can be tricky to find as so many of these heathery banks look the same.

I feel this is one of Brooks most nostalgic stones and oozes the atmosphere of the Glen Tanar forest. Although it is not large, and the inscription would not be considered of great merit, nevertheless it is certainly my favourite:

> *The Pine is King of Scottish Woods,*
> *And the Queen ah who is She?*
> *The fairest form the Forest kens*
> *The bonnie Birken tree*

10. *From Earth I Flow, Seaward I Go, Refreshing The World On My Way, My Duty Done, My Guerdon Won, I Rise On Celestial Ray.*

10. Road to Etnach

Now that we are on this north road up the valley with the Tanar on our left let us go and look at these outlying stones. A few hundred yards short of the Half-Way Hut on a bank on the right of the road is this example. Many of these banks look alike so take your time, as this stone tends to get covered with vegetation and discoloured by water dripping down from above.

11. The Half-Way Hut

Stop at the Half-Way Hut and have a snack. This cosy hut has sheltered not only shooters and beaters, but many weary travellers over the years. Now let us move on past the Admiral's tree, 300 yards beyond the hut on the right. Not a very inspiring tree, surrounded as it is by seedlings, but important to the late Lord Glentanar.

11. Half-Way Hut

12. Fair Fare Well

At the junction where the road to the Shepherd's Hut branches off up hill and we turn in here.

Reaching the locked gate you are almost there, for just beyond the gate and before reaching the hut on the right there is a muddy messy spring, the cattle having

12. *Fair- Fare- Well.* **Another Brooks conundrum.**

13. *In Vino Veritas, In Acqua Sanitas*

churned up the earth around it.

---

13. In Vino Veritas

Leaving the Shepherd's Hut behind re-cross the locked gate and take the hill road to the left which goes over to Deecastle. It climbs steeply uphill for about one-and-a-quarter miles and then descends towards a small lochan on the Black Moss. There is a line of butts on your left as you start the descent; at the level of the seventh butt, walk due east for about 400 yards into the rough terrain and you should stumble across a significant Brooks' stone.

In Vino Veritas, In Acqua★ Sanitas

This adage goes back to Greek times and says that in wine there is truth, in water there is health.

Despite three years of searching we had been unable to find this stone. Jimmy Oswald had e-mailed me in July 2006 to say, "This stone is easy to find and if you are up some afternoon we could drive to it". Jimmy, however, was to desert me before I could get there.

In July 2009 my son and two grandchildren joined me in one last attempt to discover this Oswald stone. Breasting the hill up from the Shepherd's Hut, with Cairn Nairvie on our right, I gazed across the wide morass of deep heather and reeds stretching away towards the Burn of Glendui. We set off heading east for 400 yards. Further out than we had ever been before, my son turned up hill along the same line and his shout of success was almost unbelievable. Situated facing north-east on a green patch of ground, barely thirty yards below a recently-burnt strip of heather and marked with an ancient wooden post, *In Vino Veritas, In Acqua Sanitas* had at last become a reality. Proudly we photographed it and took that important GPS reading [GPS at 1,567 feet – N. 57'01.675, W. 002'57.475] so that others might find it.

Colin Espie points out that the old road across the moss ran much further east than the present track, so that the well and stone could then have been close by the roadside.

★ *The spelling is normally 'aqua', but Brooks deviates with 'acqua' I leave it to the Latin scholars to adjudicate.*

14. Even with a copper cup

14. Son Peter with a most satisfying discovery

14. Mount Keen

Walk down from the Shepherd's Hut to the main road then to the ruins of the old hostelry at the foot of Mount Keen. Cross the fine new bridge and ascend well over the shoulder of the mountain towards Glen Mark, then strike off west across the peat hags into the next valley. Here you come upon the East Grain burn. A short way down from the top of the ridge, perhaps ten yards on the eastern aspect of the burn, you come upon an inscribed stone and a well.

Again a Jimmy Oswald discovery back in the 1970s but Jimmy and I could not find it again until Colin Espie, out stalking, came upon it by pure chance. *Quae Amissa Salva* – What is Lost is Found [GPS at 2,145 feet – N. 56'58.503, W. 003'00.429].

Eoin Smith, late head keeper on Glen

Tanar has come up with a possible explanation. The East Grain was a favourite area for stalkers to use and perhaps someone left a telescope behind one day. Brooks was a stickler about such things and would have sent his stalkers out to find his lost property.

To mark the success of the mission why not put a marker down for future generations? That it had become covered over through the years wouldn't have bothered Brooks.

15. Road from Etnach

On our way down the valley from Mount Keen it is worth recording another lost stone. At the junction with the road coming down from the Shepherd's Hut there is a line of grouse butts up on your left on Cairn Nairvie.

In the vicinity of the third butt from the bottom there is yet another Oswald discovery. Found by a beater probably in the 1960s it was recorded by Jimmy Oswald as a slab of stone inscribed as a chequer board. So far it has defied discovery but hopefully, like *In Vino Veritas,* it may yet be found again.

16. Lord Frederick's Walk

There is one more stone to visit, so we come down the Glen from the Half-Way Hut to the Porphyry Bridge. Go right over the bridge and a couple of hundred yards before you reach the Allachy bridge turn right up the well-marked track called Lord Frederick's Walk.

It is a stiff pull to the top, but once up

you descend towards the ford over the Burn of Allnaharvy. Fifty yards short of the burn there is a stone set into the bank on your right with the inscribed words – *Purity, Freedom, Life*

16. *Purity Freedom Life*
Is there a sense here of Brooks the Puritan

17. Level with the Monk's Well

A final lost stone. Back across the Porphyry bridge and on to the north road down the valley we come to West Lodge just above the estate sawmill. Continue round this road and out the Queen's Drive until you see the large farm dam down on your right. Now directions become obscure, as this particular stone has not been seen since the end of World War II.

From beyond this dam, outwith the tree line, climb up the hillside. Mid-way to the top of Creag na Slice, among fairly dense undergrowth, is a stone inscribed *Level with the Monk's Well*. What this signifies and why it was put here has long been forgotten and even Jimmy Oswald was never able to find it. I hope that by alerting walkers to its presence it may one day be uncovered.

Let us look at the somewhat less interesting boundary stones to be found around the estate. I am greatly indebted to the archaeologists Sheila Duthie, David Harding and Hazel MacFarlane for most of the following references.

18. In the area of St Colm's Well

Boundary stone has been located on Gannoch at the side of the summit cairn. Four other boundary stones are noted in this area, all inscribed with a B on one surface.

20. Black Burn Boundary Stone B – with Mount Keen behind

Gannoch North – 170 metres NW of Gannoch summit, cairn adjacent to the boundary ditch.

Gannoch Firmounth South – at the east side of Firmounth, adjacent to boundary ditch across Gannoch, opposite corner of iron fence running up to Hill of Cat.

Gannoch South – 290 metres SSW of Gannoch summit cairn, adjacent to boundary ditch.

Gannoch Firmounth North – near east side of the Firmounth, adjacent to boundary ditch on NW slopes of Gannoch."

19. Davidson's Stripe

Situated some distance to the SW of Duchery Beg and the upper pillar of the Haunted Stag but quite near the Fungle Road there are two rough boundary stones inscribed with the letter B on the march with Birse. A stripe is the green area often seen at the top of a hill where the area is gathering into a stream, but who was Davidson? Open for suggestions.

20. Boundary Stone Mount Keen

To the west of the path over the shoulder of Mount Keen there are two iron boundary posts and at the head of the Black Burn a distinctive cairn marker inscribed with a bold letter B.

21. Pannanich Hill

Finally trekking over to the north side of the estate on the boundary with Glen Muick the team of Duthie, Harding and

MacFarlane has described further boundary stones. A direct quote from their report reads: "The summit cairn of Pannanich Hill lies on rocky slabs some 10m NE of the triangulation point. About 1m E of this cairn, there is incised sharply on level rock the letter 'B' with a fainter letter 'H' on the SW side. The 'H' probably denotes Huntly lands at the time of these boundaries being drawn up."

This completes all known references to the outlying inscribed stones, except for the odd boundary stone that may have been missed.

28

Estate Buildings and Schools

Brooks added greatly to our built heritage during his years on Glen Tanar. Many of his buildings are of a design essentially more English than Scottish, which has led some to disdain his work. In the context of appreciating imaginative concepts as well as fine quality work, this seems a very parochial attitude. I feel his buildings were a pleasant innovation, but accept that on a larger scale across the country they would demean our Scottish tradition. The Tower of Ess is the entry point to all this alien architecture, but at least Brooks used Scottish architects to build his mansion house on the site of the old Woodend Farm. The house, seen in Chapter 16, dates back to the 1890s and exhibits a fussy design of turrets and high chimneys.

Lord Glentanar in the 1930s upgraded the bedrooms on the southern aspect to give the house a more modern appearance

As the march of time caused deterioration and upkeep costs escalated the Hon. Mrs Jean Bruce decided to demolish the house in 1972, leaving only the ballroom standing. A regrettable and difficult decision, but understandable.

Up the hill from the mansion house Brooks designed his core working platform to control and run the estate. The three-

1934 – Major reconstruction of the southern aspect of Glentanar House

The finished mansion after modernisation of the southern aspect

The Ballroom – all that now remains of the Mansion House

minute walk to his estate office was ideal for him, so that he could see that all his orders were being adhered to. With this command post so placed at the top of the Stableyard, he could view all that transpired. The game larder just across the road would be next for his attention.

Estate Office at top of Stableyard

The Stableyard was an important piece of the infrastructure, comprising worker's houses and bothies for gardeners, stable-boys and odd job men. A large coach house and very commodious stables at the end of the yard led through to a back area where the blacksmith at his forge was ready to shoe horses at a moment's notice. At the top of the yard, in what is now termed the Butler's Lodge, I was to spend some of the happiest days of my life.

Hugely important building to Brooks – his game larder

It is worth stopping to admire one building not belonging to the Brooks' era. The Recreation Hall overlooking the Stableyard was presented to the workers by Lord Glentanar on 31st December 1926. It still exists, but is in urgent need of some tender loving care.

Old electric battery storage station – now Woodend, a delightful holiday house

Up the hill, behind this recreation hall, Brooks set out a squash court and tennis courts with an extensive kennel area directly behind them, enough it was said for fifty dogs. The gamekeepers' bothy and the head keeper's house were further on, with various other workers' houses, all set around a pleasant open area. Not satisfied with building ordinary houses for his workers, Brooks introduced a small tower here to add character to his planning.

Stableyard with the Butler's Lodge on the near corner

As children we were enthralled by the lake, the boat-house and Miss Jean's doll's

The shingle-roofed Recreation Hall

Tower and Gamekeeper's House to the right.

The Lake and Boathouse

Miss Jean's Doll's House

Lower end of Stableyard with siren on top of high building

Greystone Cottage

house, hidden away in the Wander Walks. Whether the doll's house existed as such in Brook's time is doubtful.

Leaving the public car park above the Stableyard you descend the Ca Canny Brae, a steep brae where as children we sledged, achieving tremendous speeds that took us around the corner at the bottom and on for another two hundred yards to the steps at the bottom of the farm manager's house at Bellastreen.

Now we pass on the left the rather quaint little cottage of Greystone. This is a departure from our stuffy buildings of the past and Truefit the architect and Brooks would have chuckled to themselves at their originality.

The Tower of Ess has already been described in chapter 25, so let us examine some of Brooks' farm building along the banks of the Dee. In conversation recently with Sandy Murray, who has farmed Candycraig and Cobbleheugh over the decades, he proudly pointed out to me that Candycraig boasts the earliest date of rebuilding on the estate. Recording as many dates as I could find seemed to bear out Sandy's contention, as 1890 was the earliest I could unearth on a building. This is the year that Brooks bought the estate from the Huntly trustees and his first opportunity to take things into his own hands. Prior to this he appears to have concentrated on more mundane things like building bridges and improving roads.

Candycraig is now converted into a holiday home and its outhouses are gradually falling to pieces. Even out here

Brooks has recorded his presence on the gable end of an old steading which, unusually, looks to be of inferior quality.

The next farm to be revamped was Ballaterach, of Byron fame, although it seems that the new farm buildings were not erected on the original site.

1894 is the year when Brooks really gets his large work force to building in earnest. This year appears on various farm buildings and his very elegantly inscribed WCB block is now being produced regularly.

Tillycairn farm has also been blessed with the Brooks insignia and stands out impressively. A Greystone barn also boasts the WCB crest and date 1894.

Burnroot is another with the outbuilding closest to the road resplendent with the WCB crest. It is as if he is showing off his prowess to all and sundry, as the buildings he puts his crest on are the ones most evident to the passing public. At Burnroot, however, another outhouse has the date 1899 above the windows, while below is a stone obviously preserved from a building dated 1803. Some of these buildings from the past must have been reasonably well constructed, as at Cobbleheugh there is an old stone recording the date 1818.

Newton farm does not boast any dates, but its construction represents Brooks' farm buildings at their best. Some of the buildings are now in an advanced stage of dilapidation, but it is still worth studying the masonry work and the roof design and slating. The farm house and adjoining house are still habitable. The photograph shows

Candycraig: WCB 1890 on the lintel

Ballaterach Farm: WCB – 1893

Tillycairn – 1894

Greystone Farmhouse

Newton Farm – fine quality horse and dog trough

Little Tullich, another Brooks innovation

Typical Brooks crest on his renovated farms

mason work and a horse and dog trough just next to the steading. What would justify this level of quality in an area unseen but by the farmer and his workers? Is this a sign of Brooks' eccentricity at work?

Fasnadarach House was said to have been built by Brooks for his daughter who was married to Lord Cecil, but we have no date of its completion. There is a degree of asymmetry to this house which suggests it may have pre-dated Brooks and been enlarged or, conversely, it may have been added to after Brooks. The house stands in ample grounds overlooking the Dee and has some lovely views. The surrounding layout carries Brooks' imprint, with one of his signature eroded stones prominent in the garden.

The other large house of real quality that Brooks built on the estate was Craigendinnie House, which bears the date 1894 above a side entrance. It is the concensus of opinion that all the outstanding qualities of Brooks' design and construction came together in this project. Sadly, the ravages of death duties and the economic problems of running a large estate have resulted in its being sold, its grounds no longer forming part of the traditional Glen.

The other buildings of note are the schools, the first of which pre-dates Brooks, although he was involved in its upkeep prior to his building the new school in 1897. The old school, now called Geanbrae, lies up the Candycraig road directly south of the new school and is privately occupied. Inchmarnoch School is tucked in behind other houses at Inchmarnoch and is used as a photographic studio at present.

Glentanar School must have ranked high in Brooks' assessment of his own achievements. It surprises me that scarcely a person appears to recognise the building as of startling design for this part of the world and worth preserving, not only for its unusual outward appearance, but the genuine atmosphere of Victoriana of its interior.

Inside there are two rooms, the infants' and the dominie's, separated by two sets of panelled doors, Both have fireplaces with inscribed stone surrounds. In the infant's room the adages read, *Order is HEAVENS First law"*and below, *A stitch in time saves nine.* The surround in the headmaster's room says, *Spare the rod and spoil the child,* and below, *As the twig is bent so is the tree inclined.*

Other adages festoon the dividing doors either side of the fireplaces. On the infant classroom side, on the partition nearest the windows the inscriptions read, from the top:

Sloth makes all things difficult. Industry makes all things easy.
Drive the business, don't let that drive thee.
Work TODAY you may BE hindered TOMORROW.

On the other partition is written:

Evil is wrought by want of thought as much as by evil intent.
A place for everything and everything in its place.
What is WORTH DOING at all is WORTH DOING well.

In the headmaster's room, panels read:

Fasnadarach House

Craigendinnie House and cottage

Bellastreen House, home of farm managers and a factor

Glentanar Old School

Inchmarnoch School

Coming down the Firmy Brae this is the prospect ahead

The fireplace adages

The separating doors

Plaque on east frontage of school

Forgive for all the souls on earth that
live to be forgiven must forgive.
Forgive then seventy times seven.
For all the blessed souls in HEAVEN,
Are both Forgivers and Forgiven.
On the other partition is written:
In the street of the by and bye you arrive
at the house of never.
Procrastination is the thief of time.
DRIVE the business, DON'T let that
DRIVE thee

That this school should take up so much space shows my measure of its importance.

Brooks took great delight, too, in some buildings outwith the estate. In Aboyne, apart from the Castle, there are houses built by him and carrying his motif. Although these are outwith the remit of this book, I will give you a flavour of what is out there to be appreciated. In the Square next to the George Strachan's grocer's shop is a building boasting a tower and with the words Charleston Cottages above the lintel of the doorway. On the corner is an example of Brooks' fanciful masonry with a curved inset for the window and his usual, but on this occasion, a modest WCB. This building was used to house a coach and horses for Cunliffe Brooks' frequent use.

A further building of note designed by George Truefitt, as part of the Aboyne Castle estates, is the Coo Cathedral, which was part of the model farm built for Brooks and completed in 1889. It is described on the Scottish Civic Trust website as, "Romanesque arcades of dressed stone forming nave and aisles with a Basilican interior". Originally designed as a cowshed, it has been transformed to house concerts, fancy parties and other social events.

Brooks' imagination and enthusiasm are now largely forgotten in the village, but my friend and expert informant on local history Jim Cheyne is doing his best to ensure that this part of the heritage of the village is never overlooked.

Aboyne Square – next to Strachan's shop, a 'modest' WCB building

Charleston Cottage – Brooks' fanciful masonry with a curved inset for the window, and a restrained WCB

The Coo Cathedral

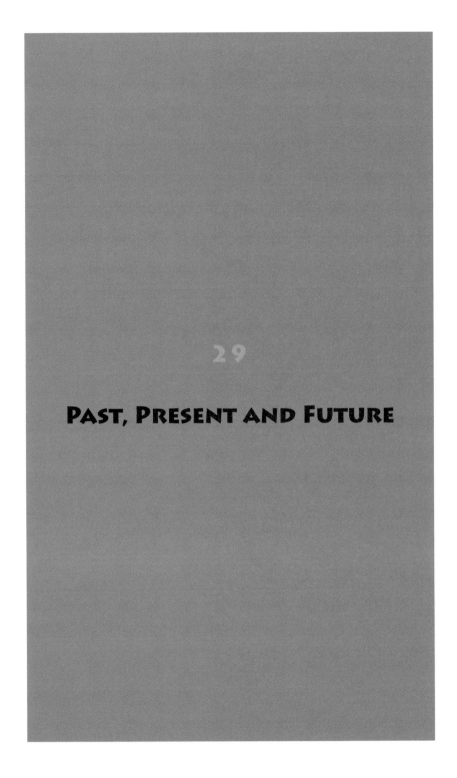

29

PAST, PRESENT AND FUTURE

Cunliffe Brooks and the remnants of the Caledonian forest are the two dominant factors which have put Glen Tanar on the modern map. The Coats' family also added their own distinctive style over the last hundred years. Not that Brooks was the first to pioneer a vision of a Scottish utopia. The feudal system almost bankrupted many Highland lairds who, having used up most of their resources, were delighted to find wealthy city dwellers taking over many of their liabilities and modernising their properties. Brooks was the ultimate example of this Victorian breed, with his inexhaustible drive to build roads, bridges, water and sewage plants, model farms and homesteads.

The first written evidence of replanting the woods is into the Coats' era in the 1920s to 1930s, although no detailed records were kept. It seems that much of the timber felled during and after World War II, as well as some in World War I, had been planted. Forestry records only started with the appointment of Duncan Ross as head forester on the estate in 1947. Under his management a determined effort was made to repair the wartime damage, including the gradual thinning of areas of old forest in preparation for seeding.

The reversal of Brooks policy of deer fencing in 1937, along with culling, allowed the forest to regenerate as well as helping control the tick population and assist grouse numbers. My old Glen Tanar friend Douglas Young, as son of the factor, remembers his father's comments on life with the laird. He recalls particularly the fantastic cost of the 1936–37 fence; in a child's mind £1 per yard for seven miles seemed an extortionate amount of money to spend on a fence. He also remembers every second post being topped off with heather to warn the grouse of its presence.

When the war intervened in 1939 the focus of the estate returned to maximising food production, which included grazing livestock in the forest. Lord Glentanar went to great lengths to prevent the felling of native pinewood by sacrificing the commercial woodland first. It is said that these financial sacrifices saved the parent trees that have seeded in subsequent surges. Good husbandry has preserved the forest in good condition and it has nearly doubled in size since 1935.

The period 1945 to 1974 was dominated by agricultural objectives. By 1967 as many as 2,000 sheep and 400 cattle were making use of forest pasture. Part of the deer fence was re-sited in 1968 to a lower alignment to allow deer access to the upper margins of the forest to reduce incursions and pressure on the fence. Deer were again shot and driven out of the woodland areas, but despite all these measures a woodland population persisted.

When Lord Glentanar died in 1971 his daughter the Hon. Mrs Jean Bruce inherited the property. The sheep were sold, and the cattle herd was reduced to bring it into balance with available winter feed. The demolition of the mansion house in 1972, leaving only the ballroom standing, was a major decision. A substantial, but more modest dwelling was erected by the Hon. Jean behind the ballroom.

The Allachy was recognised in 1969 as a site of special scientific interest (SSSI) and during the period from 1977 to 1979 the estate, represented by Robert Bruce, Lord Glentanar's grandson, made an agreement with the National Conservancy Council (NCC), now Scottish Natural Heritage (SNH), to extend the area of SSSI to include the Nature Reserve, the estate receiving £116,000 in settlement. NCC purchased 185 hectares of land and the settlement involved a variety of assets and compensation for income foregone.

Recognising the increased public interest in the site, The Glen Tanar Charitable Trust was set up. The Hon. Jean's eldest son Robert Bruce was killed on 14th July 1979 at the tender age of 26 while climbing at Chamonix in the French Alps. This was a severe setback for the estate, which continued in the Hon. Mrs Bruce's name up until 1986; she remained a trustee until her death.

Her son John Bruce inherited Balmanno estate in Perthshire, along with the Mill of Bellamore; her daughter, Mrs Clare Carson, the western end of the estate down to Inchmarnoch, and her son Michael Bruce inherited the remainder, apart from what was held by the Charitable Trust.

The financial climate no longer benefits the estate. Now its ability to continue comes at the expense of the infrastructure of the past. Tourism and recreation hold the key to the future, and revenue comes from sources such as property – commercial and residential – forestry and conservation.

The development of holiday homes and the ballroom as a venue remains high on the estate's priorities, along with the partnership with SNH. The salmon fishing has shown a welcome recovery in stocks over the past years, but there is a continuing dearth of grouse. Grouse shooting can now be enjoyed only by a millionaire class of shooter, resulting in a severe loss of revenue. The stalking remains popular, especially with the Europeans, and so long as the recession does not bite too deeply should give a positive return.

In 2003 a survey of Glen Tanar estate was set up by archaeologists Sheila Duthie, David Harding and Hazel MacFarlane to assess the 142 sites of interest that had been recorded. Of this number the team had already looked at 110 in the field. Another 100 possible new sites had been reported during 2005, including roundhouses, clearance cairns, sheiling huts and pens, farmsteads, whisky stills and inscribed stones dating from the late 19th century.

Their assessment concluded: "Over the next 12 months it is intended to continue with a prospective survey in the field, to pursue historical research, to plan township and sheiling sites and to commence recording of standing buildings initially photographically". The team are still involved in this study and a report will be published in due course.

Calling on the owner Michael Bruce in his estate office I asked him about the future. There was a pause, followed by a slow grin and the one word, "Survival". But he feels that with public attitudes changing, our rural heritage will gain support from society and the Government. "With Tom Glentanar's establishment of a set of family natural land-use values, Glen Tanar is well placed to thrive in this environment."

There have been disposals along the way. Michael Bruce has sold Tanarside and the Lorne pool on the Dee to a friend, and Dalwhing farm and its steading for private development. The old pre-Brooks school of Geanbrae and the adjacent cottage were sold to a long-standing tenant farmer. It must be a temptation to cover any shortfall in finances by selling off more properties, but I sense that Mr Bruce wishes to resist this as far as possible, "only selling properties for which I could see no direct future in the estate's hands. Releasing surplus properties has allowed others to invest in their refurbishment".

The estate is now fragmented, and who knows what this younger generation will think of sentimental old people worrying about a few decrepit ancient houses and granite inscriptions.

Michael Bruce robustly challenges my views, seeing me as taking the 'glass half empty' approach as opposed to the 'half full' attitude of himself and his wife Claire. I find this heartening as there is no place for pessimism among our young. His parting words were to the effect that the estate now employs more workers than when he took over.

I genuinely wish him continuing success.

SEE FOR YOURSELF

For those who have yet to savour our glen, the road through the Tower of Ess gates leads to the Braeloine car park where for a small fee you can leave your car. The Braeloine Centre just over the bridge is worth a visit, with information and photographs to whet the appetite. The rangers are often on hand to give advice and walks from this spot are very popular. Cars can go a mile beyond Braeloine, up the Ca Canny Brae to the parking place overlooking the stable yard and recreation hall. This is the end of the public road for motor vehicles, but it is a useful place for mountain bikers to saddle up. The south road up the Tanar from the Tower of Ess remains a private estate road for motor vehicles, but is a Right of Way for walkers and cyclists.

If you are interested in holiday accommodation I can thoroughly recommend the cottages, both for their attractive settings and for their furnishings and fittings. Animal and bird life are abundant and the lake is well stocked with some really fine trout, while the riding stables in the old smiddy provide lovely picturesque treks on Glen Tanar's traditional Norwegian Fjord ponies.

Information on salmon fishing and stalking is available from the estate office or the website. So, too, are details for hiring the ballroom and private chapel for functions and weddings.

The Glen Tanar Ranger Service is situated at the Braeloine Centre, Glen Tanar, Aboyne, AB34 5EU and can be found on-line at www.glentanar.co.uk or htpp://rangerglentanar.blogspot.com

Plea for the Future

I am conscious that when I pass on there will be very few left who have lived through this era, so time is short for we chroniclers. This book is driven by nostalgia and also by the fear that much in Glen Tanar is approaching the point of no return. Lovely farm buildings are beginning to collapse and the iconic Glentanar School is standing there, proudly demanding that we should rescue it for posterity. That a thriving modern community like Aboyne has such gems within its district and yet shows no interest in helping to preserve our exciting heritage is so disappointing.

Is this a sign of the times when close-knit communities have been so fragmented that the present generation feels little attachment to their surroundings. It is not yet too late for those with Glen Tanar's future at heart to heed one of Brooks' old adages from the walls of his school: *A stitch in time saves nine.*

Involving the local Heritage Society in maintaining Glentanar School is a project close to my heart. The funding implications are daunting, and there appears no local leadership in sight to meet the challenge. Michael Bruce is pragmatic, though, saying: "Find a use for the building that can afford the refurbishment cost".

Any profits from this book will be willingly given. Can we stir ourselves and preserve at least this one memorable building for posterity?

EPILOGUE

I n writing this book I am conscious of encroaching on a world peopled by distinguished men of letters who by dint of a clever phrase can paint imaginative pictures. Over the years I have often found bare history so boring that often it is the small aside, or the author's personalised comment that revives my attention. I trust that my own comments may in some small way interest my readers.

I am a living part of this continuing story of Glen Tanar – many authors are not – and my feelings and prejudices are close to the surface, so 'saga' better describes my intention than 'history'.

Looking into the past of just this one small valley and its northern border along the Dee has often sorely tried my patience. As I unearth one fact so another appears and so it goes on until you wonder if you can ever finish the exercise. I had seven attempts at the Byron chapter before I called a halt and if anyone knows anything more about my friend Lord Byron, don't call me!

Many authors have written articles and books around my subject. Now they all feel like long lost friends, except that each and every one of them is dead. Often lost among the pages of their books I would have loved to have picked up the phone to chat over our mutual interest. The Rev. J. G. Michie at the Dinnet kirk would be first on my list, with his close links to my old school. Then Francis C. Diack would have kept me spellbound with his intricate knowledge with statistics on every farm on the estate. Amy Stewart Fraser, while really a quine of Glen Gairn, had such a detailed memory that I could have sat at her feet for hours. That her son was Dr Mark Fraser, a paediatrician at Aberdeen Sick Childrens Hospital in my early days, makes me regret that these contacts slipped past me in my years of ignorance.

In my student days, for six years from 1948, I spent holidays grouse-beating in Upper Strathdon – some of the most memorable and enjoyable times in a long life. The experience has left a lasting and sombre effect on me, however, as I have viewed the desolation of the ruins dotted around the valleys and hillsides. Sitting quietly on a broken-down dyke beside some ruin, waiting for the line of beaters to appear, allowed me to peer into the past. That solitary, twisted rowan by the front door added to the melancholy and made me wonder just how much good fortune it had ever brought the family. In my youthful mind I could hear children's laughter, or see some bent old widow at the door in the twilight, wondering how she would get through another harsh winter in that barren place.

Glen Tanar never had that effect on me and in retrospect I begin to understand the reason. Whereas out in the Corgarff area of Strathdon the area had run down gently leaving obvious ruins behind, the clearances of the Glen had come swiftly and swept away what might have been seen as eyesores. Many old homesteads were removed or covered up, so the sense of a populated valley with its own history was eliminated. Below the surface, though, the remnants of that old life still exist.

Tarrying in the stillness of a summer's evening it takes little imagination to hear that indistinct cacophony of past tongues from our Bronze Age ancestors to Picts, Gaels, Norwegians and English. Those memorable Canadian and French-Canadian voices also join in the mix from World War II as the lumberjacks felled thousands of trees from their Burnroot camp and brought a different way of life to the locals. Now, our modern valley has Polish accents ringing around the hills, making one wonder what else will be added in the years ahead.

Yes indeed, Glen Tanar is truly a valley of wonderful echoes and enthralling hidden treasures.

SOURCES

1. **Aberdeen and North-East Scotland Family History Society,** (2001) *The People of Glen Tanar, Aboyne and Birse 1696*
2. Aberdeen Central Library, Rosemount Viaduct, Aberdeen AB25 1GW.
3. *British Civil Wars.* Gordon, G., 2nd Marquis of Huntly (1590-1649). www.british-civil-wars.co.uk
4. **Brodie, A.** (1989). *Adventure in My Veins.* Triple Cat Publishing
5. **Callander, R.** (2000) *History in Birse,* Birse Community Trust, Pole Star (AUP) Ltd. Scotland
6. **Chalmers, M.** (2006). *The Deeside Vision of a Merchant Banker.* Leopard magazine
7. **Coats, G.** *Collection of Watercolours and Sketches.* Glen Tanar Private Collection
8. **Darwin, T.** (1980) *Glen Tanar National Reserve.* Notes on the land-use history of the Reserve Area. (Unpublished manuscript, NCC.)
9. **Diack F.C.** (circa 1930) *The Glen Tanar Estate Papers.* (unpublished)
10. **De-la-Noy, M.** (1985) *The Honours System.* Alison & Busby, London
11. **Dinnie, R.** (1882) *Anecdotes;* (1865) *An Account of the Parish of Birse,* Lewis Smith, Aberdeen
12. **Duthie, S.; Harding, D.; MacFarlane, H.** *National Monuments Record of Scotland* (via Canmore website). Aberdeenshire Sites & Monuments Record (SMR)
13. **Farquharson, G.** (2005) *Clan Farquharson – a History.* Tempus Publishing
14. **Fouin, F.L.P.** (2005) *Glen Tanar Exile.* Librario, Elgin
15. **Fowle, F.** (2008) *Impressionism & Scotland,* National Galleries of Scotland
16. **Fraser, A.M.** (1973) *The Hills of Home.* (1977) *In Memory Long,* Routledge & Kegan Paul
17. **Fraser G.M.** (1924) *Glen Tanar,* The Deeside Field
18. **Fraser, G.M.** (limited 1983 edition) *The Old Deeside Road.* Robin Callander, Finzean
19. *Glentanar and Inchmarnoch School Records from 1872 to closure.* School Records, Old Aberdeen House, Dunbar Street, Aberdeen AB10 1AQ
20. **Glentanar, M.L.** *The Dowager's Diaries, 1880-1935.* Glen Tanar Private Collection
21. **Graham, Cuthbert.** *The Glentanar Millionaire,* The Scots Magazine
22. **Grant, E.** (1898) *Memoirs of a Highland Lady.* Longmans
23. **Harper, D.** (2009) *Spanning Turra and the Far-Flung Empire,* Leopard magazine
24. **Harper & Co.,** Fencers and Bridge Builders from 1857. www.harperbridges.com

25. **Harper, P.** (circa 1930) *Population and Houses of Glen Tanar.* Private publication
26. **Huntly, C.,** Marquis of. *Milestones, Auld Acquaintances* and *Further Reminiscences.* Hutchison & Co. London
27. **Institute of Chartered Foresters** (1990) Silvicultural Systems
28. **Keir, D.** (1934) *The Coats' Story.* Private publication
29. **Langtry, L.** (1925) *Days I Knew – an Autobiography*
30. **McConnachie A.I.** (1895) *Deeside* and *The Royal Dee* (1898)
31. **Macgillivray, W.** (1855) *The Natural History of Deeside and Braemar.* Printed for Private Collection, London
32. **Mawson, T.H.** (1927) *The Life of an English Landscape Architect*
33. **Michie Rev. J.G.** (1896) *History of Loch Kinnord, The History of Logie Coldstone, The Braes of Cromar* and *Deeside Tales*
34. **Miller, H.G.** and **Ross I.** (1992) *Management and Silviculture of the Forests of Deeside*
35. **Mitchell, I.R.** (2000) *On the Trail of Queen Victoria in the Highlands.* Bell & Bain
36. **Moore, T.** (1835) *Notices of the Life of Lord Byron.* John Murray Publisher
37. **National Library of Scotland,** www.nls.uk
38. **Pearce, S.** (1971) *A late Bronze Age Hoard from Glentanar, Aberdeenshire.* Proc Soc Antiq Scot, 103 (1970-1), 57-64
39. **Pearce, S.** (1977) *Amber Beads from the late Bronze Age Hoard from Glentanar, Aberdeenshire.* Proc Soc Antiq Scot. (1976-77)
40. *Records of Invercauld* (1803). Private publication
41. **Scottish Civic Trust.** www.scottishcivictrust.org.uk
42. **Scottish History Online.** *Picts & Celts,* scotshistoryonline.co.uk
43. **Simpson, I.J.** (1947) *Education in Aberdeenshire Before 1872.* University of London Press Ltd
44. **Smith, R.** (1995) *25 Walks Deeside.* HMSO
45. **Smith, R.** (2001) *Land of the Lost,* John Donald Publishers, Edinburgh
46. **Spiers S.M.** (2002) *The Kirkyards of Glenmuick, Glentanar and Kirkton of Skene.* Aberdeen and North-East Scotland Family History Society
47. **Spiers, S.M.** *The Kirkyard of Aboyne.* Aberdeen and North-East Scotland Family History Society
48. *Statistical Account of Aberdeenshire, 1843 by Ministers of Respective Parishes.* Blackwood and Sons, Edinburgh
49. **Strang, A.** (2007) *The Distance Slabs of the Antonine Wall.* Self Published
50. *The Aboyne Papers.* Private records
51. **Wilson, I.** (1992) *Herrin Dinna Get Tae Heaven.* Private publication
52. **Wyness, F.** (1968) *Royal Valley: The Story of the Aberdeenshire Dee.* Alex. P. Reid & Son, Aberdeen.

INDEX